POLITEXT 186

The ISPS Code - 3
Solving emergencies on ships

POLITEXT

Ricard Marí Sagarra

The ISPS Code - 3
Solving emergencies on ships

EDICIONS UPC

Publication sponsored by the Ministry of Public Works (2009)

First edition: September 2009
Reprint: November 2009

©   Ricard Marí Sagarra, 2009

©   Edicions UPC, 2009
    Edicions de la Universitat Politècnica de Catalunya, SL
    Jordi Girona Salgado 1-3, 08034 Barcelona
    Tel.: 934 137 540   Fax: 934 137 541
    Edicions Virtuals: www.edicionsupc.es
    E-mail: edicions-upc@upc.edu

Production: LIGHTNING SOURCE

Legal deposit: B-36520-2009
ISBN: 978-84-9880-371-6

This work may only be reproduced, distributed, publicly disclosed or transformed with permission from its copyright holders, with the exception provided by the law. If you need to photocopy or scan a part of this work, please contact CEDRO (Spanish Centre for Reprographic Rights) at www.cedro.org.

Index

Introduction 11

1 On board organisation 15
    1.1 Regulatory sources 15
    1.2 Considerations on the ISM Code and quality standards 16
        1.2.1 Officers' responsibilities and authority 17
        1.2.2 Risks 19
        1.2.3 Inspections 19
        1.2.4 Implementation 20
        1.2.5 In relation to emergencies 20
        1.2.6 Identifying training needs 20
        1.2.7 Objectives 21
    1.3 Addressing emergencies 21
        1.3.1 Emergency analysis 21
        1.3.2 Emergency plans 21
        1.3.3 Responsibilities 23
        1.3.4 Regarding documentation 24
        1.3.5 First steps in the general response procedure 24
        1.3.6 Aspects related to ship chandlers 31
        1.3.7 Navigation and manoeuvring procedures 31
        1.3.8 Port watch checklist 32
        1.3.9 Other safety checks 32
        1.3.10 Bridge watch. Daily checks 33
        1.3.11 Bridge watch. High seas navigation 33
        1.3.12 In cases of boarding 35
        1.3.13 About grounding/stranding 36
        1.3.14 Flooding/structural failure 37
        1.3.15 Fire 38
        1.3.16 Helicopter assisted operation 39
        1.3.17 Unlawful actions — Stowaways 39
        1.3.18 Preparedness for security related aspects 39
    1.4 Partial conclusions 40

2 The port. Internal Emergency Plans 41
    2.1 Introduction and legal framework 41
    2.2 Objectives and goals of the Internal Emergency Plans (IEP's) 44
        2.2.1 Principles of the Internal Emergency Plans 44
        2.2.2 Basic data for preparing IEP's 45

  2.2.3 Actions for preparing an IEP 45
  2.2.4 IEP structure analysis 46
  2.2.5 Relationship between IEP's, External Emergency Plans (EEP's)
    and Mutual Assistance Plans 53
  2.2.6 Activating the EEP from the IEP 57
 2.3 Essential components with an operating character in a fictitious PFSP 58
  2.3.1 Risk evaluation 59
 2.4 Partial conclusions 60

3. Security team 61
 3.1 Current crews in national ships 61
 3.2 Influence of personnel and action plans 62
  3.2.1 E.R.I.C. method 63
  3.2.2 M. Gretener's method 63
  3.2.3 K.A.O. method 64
  3.2.4 Summary of the personnel and action plan parameter 64
 3.3 Influence of time and difficulty in acting 67
  3.3.1 ALPHA factors method 67
  3.3.2 K factor method 68
  3.3.3 G. Purt's method 68
  3.3.4 E.R.I.C: method 69
  3.3.5 M. Gretener's method 69
  3.3.6 Summary of the personnel and action plan parameter 69
 3.4 Crew level on security training 70
  3.4.1 Crew functions according to the ISPS Code 73
 3.5 Partial conclusions 73

4 Organisation of emergencies on board 75

 4.1 Organising an emergency 75
 4.2 Synthesis of emergency actions (bridge officers) 75
  4.2.1 General 76
  4.2.2 Stranding 76
  4.2.3 Boarding/collision 77
  4.2.4 Abandon ship 77
  4.2.5 Fire 81
  4.2.6 Actions in case of contact with the sea bottom 83
  4.2.7 Actions in case of hull failure 84
  4.2.8 Actions in case of excessive heel 84
  4.2.9 Engine room flooding 84
 4.3 Organising emergencies at the port 84
 4.4 Terrorism and piracy 85
  4.4.1 Other sources 85
 4.5 Stowaways 86

5 Principles and considerations towards a response 89
 5.1 Response 89
 5.2 Strategies (motives) 90
 5.3 Tactics (methods) 90
 5.4 Piracy 95
  5.4.1 Introduction 95

- 5.4.2 Strike methods 97
- 5.4.3 Purposes of piracy 98
- 5.4.4 Piracy acts and armed robbery 99
- 5.4.5 Illicit actions against passengers and the crew 101
- 5.4.6 Anti piracy contingency plan 104
- 5.4.7 Partial conclusions on piracy 106
- 5.5 Terrorism 106
  - 5.5.1 Introduction 106
  - 5.5.2 Terrorist methods and objectives 108
  - 5.5.3 Impact of terrorism in passenger ships 109
  - 5.5.4 The nature of terrorism 109
  - 5.5.5 Maritime terrorism 110
  - 5.5.6 Maritime terrorist strikes. Case history 110
  - 5.5.7 Parcel and letter bombs 111
  - 5.5.8 Check and bomb search plan 111
- 5.6 Drugs 112
  - 5.6.1 Assessment of vulnerability to drugs 113
  - 5.6.2 Involved persons 113
  - 5.6.3 Drug trafficking 114
  - 5.6.4 Protection measures against drug traffic and consumption 115
  - 5.6.5 Indicators of assistance for identifying drug abuse 117
  - 5.6.6 Physical symptoms 118
  - 5.6.7 Drug search plan 119
  - 5.6.8 Actions to be taken when drugs are found at sea 119
  - 5.6.9 Partial conclusions about drugs 120
- 5.7 Other forms of criminal violence at sea 121
  - 5.7.1 Extorting passenger ships 121
  - 5.7.2 Sabotage 121
  - 5.7.3 Protection measures against sabotage 122
  - 5.7.4 Assaulting 123
- 5.8 Hijacking yachts, and other violent acts against smaller vessels 126
- 5.9 Labour conflicts 128
- 5.10 Immigration related violence 129
- 5.11 Ecoterrorism 130
- 5.12 Conclusion 130

6 Ship security application case 131
- 6.1 Work scheme 131
- 6.2 Passenger ship security 131
- 6.3 Security 133
  - 6.3.1 Protecting the outside 133
  - 6.3.2 Identification 134
- 6.4 Means of division 134
- 6.5 Accreditation card 134
- 6.6 Structure of a control system 135
- 6.7 Security aboard the "Sedna" 137
  - 6.7.1 Information plan for the "Sedna" 137
  - 6.7.2 Protecting the outside of the "Sedna" 139
  - 6.7.3 External personnel control 141
  - 6.7.4 Antiterrorist/antipiracy security in passenger ships 141
  - 6.7.5 Antiterrorist/antipiracy security in the "Sedna" 147

6.7.6 Suspects aboard 153
6.8 Yet another application of the Ship Security Plan to the same ship 155
    6.8.1 Captain and crew 155
    6.8.2 Defining security levels 156
    6.8.3 Security related communications and information 157
    6.8.4 Applying security measures on the ship 159
    6.8.5 Signposting 162
    6.8.6 Keys 162
    6.8.7 Authorised personnel 162
    6.8.8 Controlling the cargo 163
    6.8.9 Controlling provisions and services to the ship 164
    6.8.10 Unattended baggage 165
    6.8.11 Controlling ship security surveillance 165
    6.8.12 Lighting 165
    6.8.13 Ship search 166
    6.8.14 Automatic intrusion detection devices 166
    6.8.15 Contingency plans 167
    6.8.16 Bomb threat 168
    6.8.17 Stowaways 171
    6.8.18 Ship occupation or hijacking by armed strikers 171
    6.8.19 Piracy 173
    6.8.20 Other emergency situations 176
    6.8.21 Ship evacuation and abandonment 176
    6.8.22 Security related equipment maintenance 176

7 Analysis of the interrelationships between plans 179
7.1 Analysis procedure 179
7.2 Impact of security on the "safety" concept 181
    7.2.1 Risk Classification 182
7.3 Addressing antisocial acts 195
    7.3.1 Relationship of antisocial acts with emergencies 195
7.4 Deriving from social activities 196
    7.4.1 Controlling multitudes in emergencies 196
7.5 Terrorist actions 197
    7.5.1 Related with explosives and fires 197
    7.5.2 Terrorist actions with weapons and NBC agents 198
    7.5.3 Terrorist actions with hostage holding 199
    7.5.4 Intended boarding in emergency preventative management 200
    7.5.5 Directed impact of an aeroplane against the ship 201
7.6 Emergency determinants in security aspects 201
    7.6.1 Action of possible anticipation, by typology 201
    7.6.2 Emergencies related with antisocial acts 203
    7.6.3 Emergencies as preceding terrorist acts 204
    7.6.4 Emergencies related to unlawful social acts 205

8 Conclusions 207

Bibliography 211

Introduction

Day by day, the implementation of new regulations related to maritime security and the need of a faithful compliance presents obvious difficulties, both interpretation related and functional (operative and practical).

Wide compliance with SOLAS is already complex in itself, when one considers the many checks and updates that should be constantly carried out in order to maintain the ship and her crew above the minimum required standards, which become a routine.

The routine condition may become interrupted when an emergency occurs, within the broad range of possibilities offered by maritime activities, with specific manifestations, evolutions in time and final consequences; these, while they have been considered individually and mostly isolated, may acquire in the ship wide spectrum magnitudes and interactions that are difficult to control, and it is not acceptable just to give up because an intervention procedure is not available for controlling a complex situation.

This study intends to analytically evaluate those obligations resulting from applying the IMO regulations on emergencies that, because considered independently one from another, may result in serious shortcomings when addressing a complex emergency situation, as they will contradict, or global consideration of interactions will be insufficient.

Implementation of the ISPS Code opens new perspectives; in this sense, the main analysis will be on existing relationships between Internal Emergency Plans, procedures prescribed in the ISM Code, Ship Security Plan, Port Facilities Security Plans, Ship Security Officer's functions, task forces external to the ship, etc.

This study pursues the following targets:

- ➢ Extracting from the aforementioned legal instruments, as well as from the particular ones usually accepted on board, those sections directly related to emergency plans, identifying the weak points present in their mutual relationships.
- ➢ Supporting the organisation and harmonisation of emergency plans, marking those aspects that should be modified in order to optimise the organisation of both human resources and equipment normally available on board, as well as reducing repetitions that produce overlaps, and therefore loss of effectiveness.

> Gaining a wide, detailed, specialised vision of the real situation on ships, in order to confront their risks, their vulnerability by ship type and activity, and finding the best ways for solving them.
> Identifying the system's weak points in order to use them in the National and International Inspection Processes (PSC).
> Supporting ship crew internal organisation, by simplifying procedures and harmonising the effort that should take place independently before receiving external assistance.

Influence of the ISPS Code

Within the Industrial Safety concept, practically the whole range of maritime accidents are, to a higher or lesser extent, a direct consequence of the human factor, of an unintentional human error, when one or more causes materialise unexpectedly at any given moment, therefore in an undesired way.

A strict and stringent execution of the security plans assists in attaining a dramatic reduction in accidents, because the mechanisms of occurrences are predictable and mostly quantifiable, as they depend, amongst others, on physical and chemical factors, on preventative procedures and on the organisation of the participating teams; therefore, the effectiveness of prevention is a direct function of the investment.

By introducing security as defined in the ISPS Code, the person-to-machine relationship, which until now could by highly controlled when considering safety, is replaced by a person-to-person relationship, which includes a wide spectrum of wills, intentions, purposes and targets, this favouring a noticeable decrease in the controlling effectiveness of the preventative levels, as they cannot be objectively measured or quantified; because of this, everything related to the "safety" concept shifts to a second level, since it depends on the causes encompassed in the "security" concept.

Looking at it schematically (Figure 1), full safety (red) was the sum of all particular actions (grey), *i.e.*, all efforts and intentions that made operational safety possible for a given activity, while *security* actions (yellow), while not completely forgotten, ran very independently from the former, with criteria and actions dedicated and based very particularly on external on-shore perturbations, were somehow partial, and no attention was paid to the lesser problems that might arise within port facilities, whether from the shore or from the sea.

As the ISPS Code comes in force, the *security* block locates itself at the upper vertex, casting its determining factors (different colours) in the opposite sense to the former. Partial aspects that, once analysed become effective, will not need to be changed, but new alternatives will have to be considered and implemented according to the threat level.

The end of its application comes, in turn, either when the threat disappears, or when the criminal or terrorist action materialises, in which case the Internal Emergency Plans (IEP's) become the primary object for immediate action, in order to minimise the derived consequences and damages.

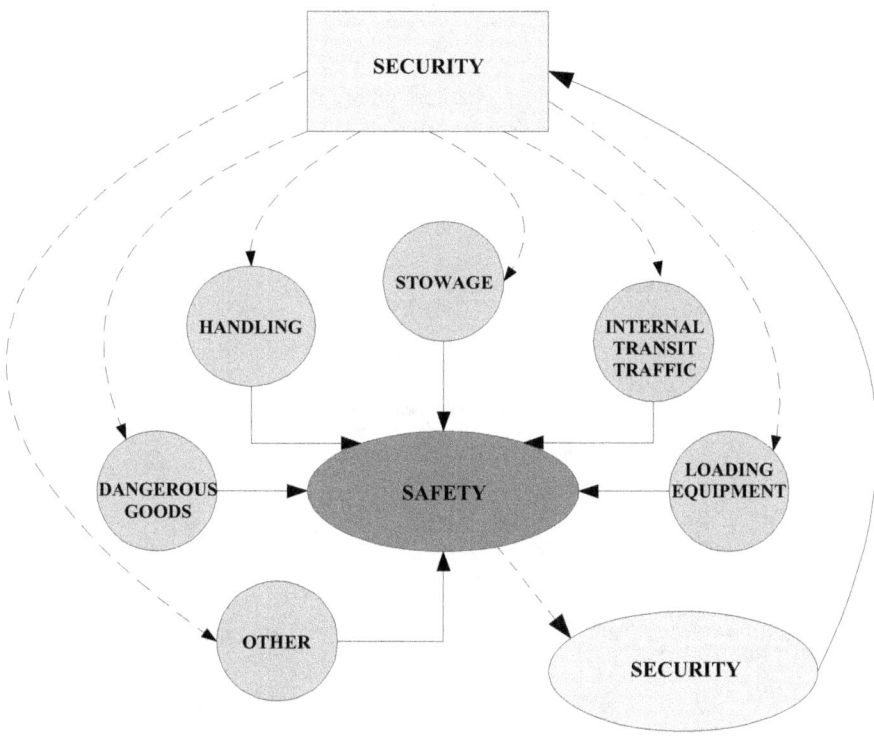

Figure 1.1

Schematic development of the study

Presentation and analysis of the various chapters in this work will be carried out according to the blocks detailed in Figure 2.

There are basically two parts, although closely related to each other within the common denominator that the ship represents, which finally converge into one line of conclusions.

As a whole, each of the blocks is a specific chapter for addressing, as necessary and as extensively as required, the considerations, the identification of limitations and particularities that condition any Emergency Plan in its application to a given ship, always pursuing harmonisation with the remainder of the Safety (Emergency) Plans, since, as shown in the aforementioned schematic, nothing should be left unattended or unrelated to the prevailing demands for guaranteeing the safety of persons and goods.

Program related study contents

Each block in Figure 1.2 will open up in those chapters where it may be required to cover the group of subjects related to emergencies, mainly those referring to:
- ✓ Organisation
- ✓ Functions of persons in charge
- ✓ Procedures
- ✓ Internal and external interactions
- ✓ Specific equipment and its maintenance
- ✓ Etc.

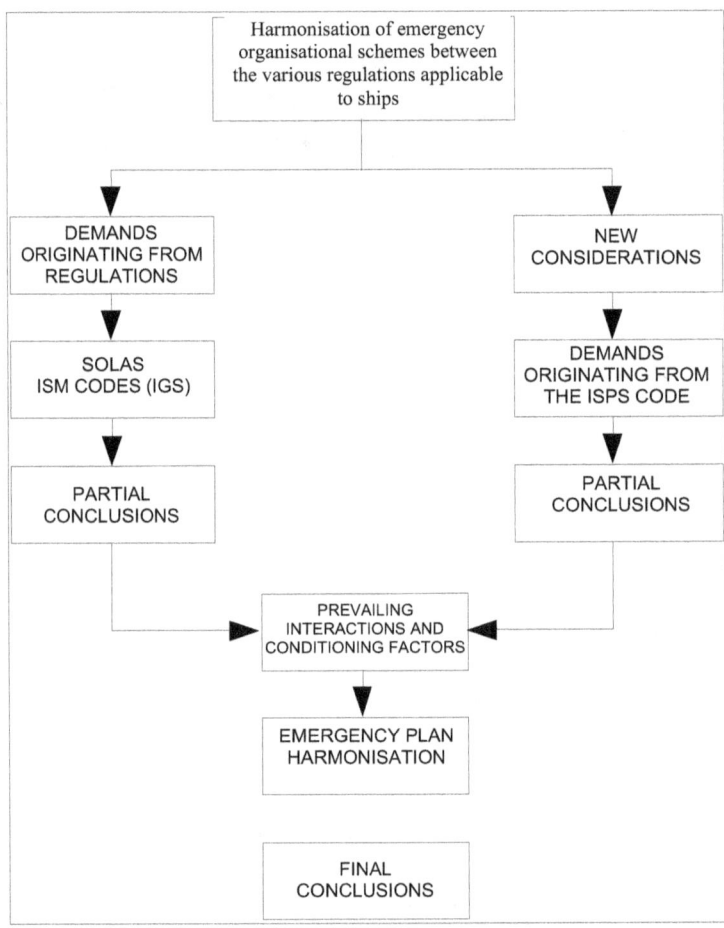

Figure 2

1 On board organisation

1.1 Regulatory sources

The crew's response in emergency situations related with maritime and port activities is a consequence of the application of the various regulations, basically comprised in conventions, codes and rules issued by the IMO and the EU, and consequently, in their adaption to the internal Spanish regulations.

For crew organisation, the following are relevant on board:

- SOLAS 1974 (application since May 25, 1980), SOLAS Protocol 1978 (May 1, 1981), Protocol 88, STCW 1978 (28.04.84), STCW 1995.

- FOM/2296/2002 Order of September 4, which regulates the Training Programmes for Professional Degrees for Merchant Marine Bridge and Engine Room Sailors and Port Masters, as well as the Specialist Certificates to confirm professional competence.

- The International Safety Management Code for the Safe Operation of Ships and for Pollution Prevention (ISM), adopted under Resolution A.741(18) in force since 1st July, 2002, and by virtue of Chapter IX, "Management for the Safe Operation of Ships", of the SOLAS 74 convention.

- Since July 1, 1996, certification according to the ISM Code is effective for all passenger ships and Ro-Ro freight ferries sailing between EU ports, by virtue of Council Regulation (EC) no. 3051/95 of 1995

- Application, when appropriate, of standards EN-ISO 9001:2000 and En-ISO 14004:1996, as they add to the basic safety rules that have to be applied to the crew's daily works, enhancing safety and procedures.

1.2 Considerations on the ISM Code and quality standards

The Integrated Management System (IMG) is a Manual comprising a set of standards (EN-ISO 9001:2000, EN-ISO 14001:1996) that are adequate and effective, capable of ensuring, amongst other objectives[1]:

- Sufficient training to respond to non intentional accidents, so that assistance may be offered when action is required in certain emergency cases, or on works that become tedious and therefore induce human errors that are hazardous for the crew's health or for the environmental conservation.

- That the normal loading, transportation and delivery activities of carried goods, and works on board, develop with the highest levels of quality.

- That the patterns that the crew should comply with reflect on their activities by not impacting or harming the environment.

The 14001 standards comply with all environmental regulations: MARPOL, SOLAS, ISM, and European directives; therefore, they prevent an increase in sanctions, and they enhance safety, quality and protection of the marine environment.

The 14001 standards set future environmental objectives. Shipping companies should apply them in order to reduce marine and environmental pollution.

The EN-ISO 9001:2000 and EN-ISO 14001:1996 standards oblige companies that hold the corresponding certificates to undergo yearly audits, while the ISM Code prescribes them every 5 years; furthermore, this inspection has not been implemented in all countries due to the lack of resources for carrying it out.

The Integrated Management System requires unavoidably the participation of every crew member in the ship, as well as of any person related with the ship and her cargo, whether directly or indirectly.

Optimisation of available resources should be attained by the crew by applying adequately those procedures developed in accordance with the EN-ISO 9001:2000 and EN-ISO 14001:1996 standards and with national and international safety regulations.

Objectives are based on continued training for the whole crew, since without permanent training, safety cannot be improved, neither environmental conservation, nor the setting of quantifiable targets for the various crew levels that should contribute to their satisfaction, resulting in providing the shipping company, and therefore the global maritime activity, with more competent personnel that makes work easier, increasing the crew's response and decision making capacity; and, lastly, that may allow regrouping standards.

---

[1] Only those directly related to safety and emergencies are selected, specifically excluding customer satisfaction quality management.

1.2.1 Officers' responsibilities and authority

Captain

The shipping company delegates its authority on the ship's Captain, who is responsible for, and holds the highest authority with respect to, quality, health and safety, and environmental protection (as well as for the remainder of navigation related aspects, etc.).

The Captain holds the highest responsibility on the ship, and he is to exert his authority over any crew member.

The first officer allocated to these functions possesses the necessary training and qualifications for applying his Quality and Environmental Policies, and to supply his on shore personnel and ship crew with the appropriate means to achieve his targets.

Resolution A.443 (XI), in considering that safety and marine environmental protection should become the Captain's main concern in any possible circumstance, and that no economical or any other kind of pressure should hinder the decisions that the Captain may have to make in this respect, deems that the Captain's decisions regarding safety and marine environmental protection must not be inappropriately influenced by instructions issued by Shipowners, Shippers or other stakeholders.

The Captain adopts any necessary decisions according to his professional judgement, which fall within the Captain's responsibilities and authority by virtue of Resolution A.741(18) in terms of:

- Implementing the Company's Safety and Environmental Protection principles;
- Promoting the application of these principles amongst the crew members;
- Issuing in a clear and plain way the appropriate commands and instructions;
- Verifying that prescribed measures are complied with;
- Reviewing the Integrated Quality-Safety-Environment System and reporting its deficiencies to the Management.

Each crew member has a responsibility and authority on board, depending on his task on the ship.

The Captain is the highest operating authority in all the activities of the Shipping Company, whether commercial, administrative, procurement related, service related, safety related, environmental or quality related.

The Captain is responsible for:

- Defining the general policies, in order to attain the set targets;
- Motivating the crew, in order to achieve the forecast quality objectives;
- Watching over the compliance with all standards relevant to quality, safety and health, and environmental continued progress;
- Ship organisation and safety;
- Emergency organisation and development;
- Inspections;
- Determining hazards for the ship;
- Smuggling and private commerce;
- Health and safety of everyone aboard.

First Bridge Officer

The First Bridge Officer has the following functions:

- Defining and following the Annual Strategic Plan;
- Following the EN-ISO 9001:2000 Quality Objectives;
- Following the EN-ISO 14001 Environmental Objectives;
- The First Bridge Officer has the highest responsibility for: personnel, internal health and safety, and pollution prevention;
- Taking charge of crew training (abandon ship drills, usage of antipollution devices, spillages...);
- Maintaining fire fighting equipment and safety of human life at sea;
- Taking charge of emergency equipment;
- Crew training;
- Navigation safety and preparation of arrival at port.

Second Bridge Officer

- Participates in the ship inspection,
- Communications.

Third Bridge Officer

- Assists in the ship inspection,
- Equipment inspection,
- Survival and fire fighting equipment inspection,
- Ship's Medicine Chest,
- Ship's Infirmary.

Command staff

The Captain, together with the First Officer, sets the appropriate communication procedures for the ship and her crew, and ensures that communication takes place, considering the Quality Management System effectiveness.

These processes will be carried out by means of crew meetings, internal circular letters, informative notes posted at the Crew Purser's Office and at work places.

For this purpose, schematics and representative drawings should be posted visibly, in order to help their comprehension and memorisation.

Information sessions should be held, in order to keep all crew members up to date on eventual changes.

1.2.2 Risks

The maritime world entails a number of risks. Both the environment and the conditions in which tasks are developed in the maritime industry make it necessary to prevent eventual risks that may result in maritime accidents.

Every mariner is to keep at all times an "emergency" attitude. Every crew member is subject to a number of hazards:

- Risks related to accessing the ship: ship berthed, anchored or stationary at sea, ship dry docked (graving dock, floating drydock or slipway);
- Risks related to being on board: derived from the ship's construction, the sea or the crew;
- Maintenance or operative risks: manual vertical movements (lifting/delivering), manual horizontal movements (carrying by hand), mechanical vertical movements (hoisting, etc.), mechanical horizontal movements, stowage.

1.2.3 Inspections

Inspections constitute a pre-accident analytical technique, the object of which is to detect risks before they may become accidents.

Safety inspections have two objectives:

- Locating and identifying risks,
- Studying and fostering corrective measures.

Preparation of inspection: an appropriate method for the facilities to be inspected; should clearly state where and what to observe, and should be available as a reference for future inspections.

Parts to be inspected include:

- General facilities: deck, crew cabins, engine and boiler room, command bridge, galleys and pantries, holds and storerooms, ship access ways, gangways, hatches and scuttles, doors, ports and portholes;
- Ambient conditions: vapours and gases, smoke, noise, lighting, vibrations, temperature and humidity;
- Utilities: electrical, compressed air, water and inertisation;
- Internal safety facilities: firefighting (extinguishers, hydrants, automatic systems, emergency exits, firefighting pumps), salvage (visual signals, acoustic signals, lifeboats and liferafts, life rings, life jackets);
- Operative: hoisting equipment, cables, chains, etc., stowage;
- Machinery: main and auxiliary;
- Tools: manual, mechanical and electrical;
- Pressurised vessels: boilers, steam generators, water and gas containers;
- Special hazard works: works at height, handling hazardous goods;
- Personal protection equipment: working and waterproof clothing, gloves, safety footwear, masks and breathing equipment.

1.2.4 Implementation

To make the Integrated Management System feasible, there must be no difficulties in implementing it. For this purpose, the following is established:

- Prior to the definitive implementation, duly qualified personnel should be sent to the ship in order to train the crew and make them aware of the new methodology; alternatively, training may be provided in adequate premises off ship, in order to attain better results.
- It should be implemented progressively, beginning with the Captain, who should show a positive attitude and full involvement.
- Subsequently, it will be introduced in the bridge, machine room, and to the remainder of the crew.
- Often, the crew feels insecure regarding certain matters, and this influences directly on manoeuvres and other operations carried out on board.

1.2.5 In relation to emergencies

Independently of what Emergency Plans and Emergency Procedures prescribe, the Captain should:

- Identify, describe and set the procedures to face any eventual emergency situation on his ship;
- Program and manage the identified emergency drills;
- The application of emergency response procedures may be modified by the Captain when an emergency occurs.

Regarding non compliances, the Captain should:

- Report non compliances, accidents or potentially hazardous circumstances, and initiate the analysis and assessment actions for the originating circumstances;
- See that corrective and preventative measures are applied, towards solving them.

1.2.6 Identifying training needs

- The Captain or the organisational unit head identifies, through the identification sources determined in the program, the existing training needs.

- The Captain or the organisational unit head assesses the possibilities for satisfactorily providing the identified necessary training with the own resources available on the ship or organisational unit. If the outcome is positive, he will define the training program.

- The Human Resources Manager decides whether training activities have to be immediate or should be included in the Annual Training Plan.

- The Human Resources Manager defines and allocates resources for initiating the immediate training activities, and notifies the applicant about the decision adopted.

- Once training has been given, the Human Resources Manager assesses whether the need has been satisfactorily met. In this assessment, the Training Records should always be filed together with the Evaluation Record.

1.2.7 Objectives

To define management principles for organising and ensuring an effective Company response in front of emergency situations that may affect the safety of the crew, the ship or the marine environment.

Emergency preparedness requires response identification, analysis, planning and definition, as well as scheduling drills that may allow the crew to face these situations with confidence.

1.3 Addressing emergencies

The Company identifies emergency situations that may affect ships as a function of their characteristics and operating conditions.

In each ship, the Captain identifies and defines the specific emergency situations in which his ship may become involved, depending on the type of cargo, transits and the specific operating conditions.

The following sources are considered, among others, when identifying a new emergency situation:

- Direct identification
- Non compliance study and analysis
- Experience from other ships and companies
- Technical publications review, new regulations

1.3.1 Emergency analysis

Identifying a new emergency situation requires an analysis, so that the need for preparing a plan or procedure for facing the situation is assessed.

The possibility of carrying out drills or planning the appropriate training for the particular situation is one of the aspects that should be analysed more in detail.

1.3.2 Emergency plans

An effective response from the Company in front of an emergency situation requires the appropriate programming of a set of activities, which are comprised in:

- The Ship's Emergency Plan
- The Onshore Emergency Plan

Ship's emergency plan

A procedure should be in place for every possible identified emergency situation, describing the ship's organised response, including as a minimum:

- Crew roles, according to Minimum Safety Manning Roster;
- External Communication Methods;
- Methods for notifying the Company and the Authorities;
- Instructions and procedures for the response of safety teams and equipment;
- Specific circumstances in which the emergency may occur;
- Others.

IMO (MSC) recommendations may be followed to organise the emergency response under a modular structure.

The Organisational Chart describes the emergency situation response as identified according to the requirements of SOLAS and MARPOL for hydrocarbon spillage contingencies, even though different specific emergencies may be envisaged for each ship type, depending on the significance and approach to consider.

Onshore emergency plan

The Company onshore organisation in front of an emergency situation is documented in the so-called Emergency Plan, which includes:

- Defining the Emergency Organisational Structure, including the definition of those responsible for carrying out various executive, informative and coordination functions;
- Communication methods between organisations that participate in the emergency, such as authorities and the ship;
- Information collection methods regarding ship, cargo and crew;
- Allocation of resources and relief teams to address and eventual emergency extension.

Emergency Plans set by the competent authorities for the ports in which ships usually operate should be considered.

Table 1.1 Emergency Situations

Emergency situations
Dangerous goods mishap
Steering system failure
Electrical system failure
Collision - boarding
Grounding - stranding
Flooding
Fire
Man overboard
Medical emergency
Search and rescue
Assistance at sea request
Helicopter operations
Abandoning
Spillage or pollution

1.3.3 Responsibilities

Independently of what may be set in each of the documents defining the various plans and in general, the following responsibilities are established:

- The Safety Manager is responsible for fostering and analysing the identification of eventual emergency situations, and for assessing the degree of effectiveness of the Emergency Plans;
- The Captain is responsible for the onboard implementation and scheduling of the emergency preparedness drills.

Emergency situation identification

The procedure in Figure 1.1 may be followed, which includes the following functions:

- The Captain and/or the Safety Manager identifies the Emergency Situation;
- If the situation has not been described, it should be described by defining: identified potential causes, aggravating conditions, consequences and affected equipment or systems, potentially affected persons, and others;

- The Captain or the Safety Manager is to plan the response, defining the tasks to be carried out and the response team, the necessary means, the actions to organise, the communication channels (internal and external), and the criteria for requesting external assistance;
- If from the response planning it is concluded that no resources are available on board to face the emergency, the necessary additional means should be requested from the Company;
- The procedure and checklist should be prepared.
- The necessary periodic drills should be programmed, for acquiring the appropriate skills to face the emergency situation;
- Safety meetings should be held with the whole crew, in order to address all emergencies.

Assessing the external communication system

- Any event, incident or emergency may have impacted the media; it is therefore necessary to follow up and check that what is being told conforms to reality.
- Event impact on the media should be analysed.
- This procedure should be checked.
- After some days, a visit should be made to the affected audiences.

1.3.4 Regarding documentation

Both the Code Documentation and the Technical and Safety Documentation should be:

- Maintained and updated, completing or seeing to the completion of records and applicable documents;
- Duly handled, particularly Ship Logs, Official Documents, Navigation Charts, Sailing Directions, Ship Drawings Sets, Certifications, etc.

Every person requiring it may access the documentation, with prior authorisation from the Captain.

Unless otherwise specified, all documents are to be filed and kept in an appropriate environment during three years.

1.3.5 First steps in the general response procedure

- Gathering information
- Notifying the Fleet Manager and the Press Secretary
- Summoning the Crisis Committee
- Initiating the Information and Follow Up System
- Assessing available data

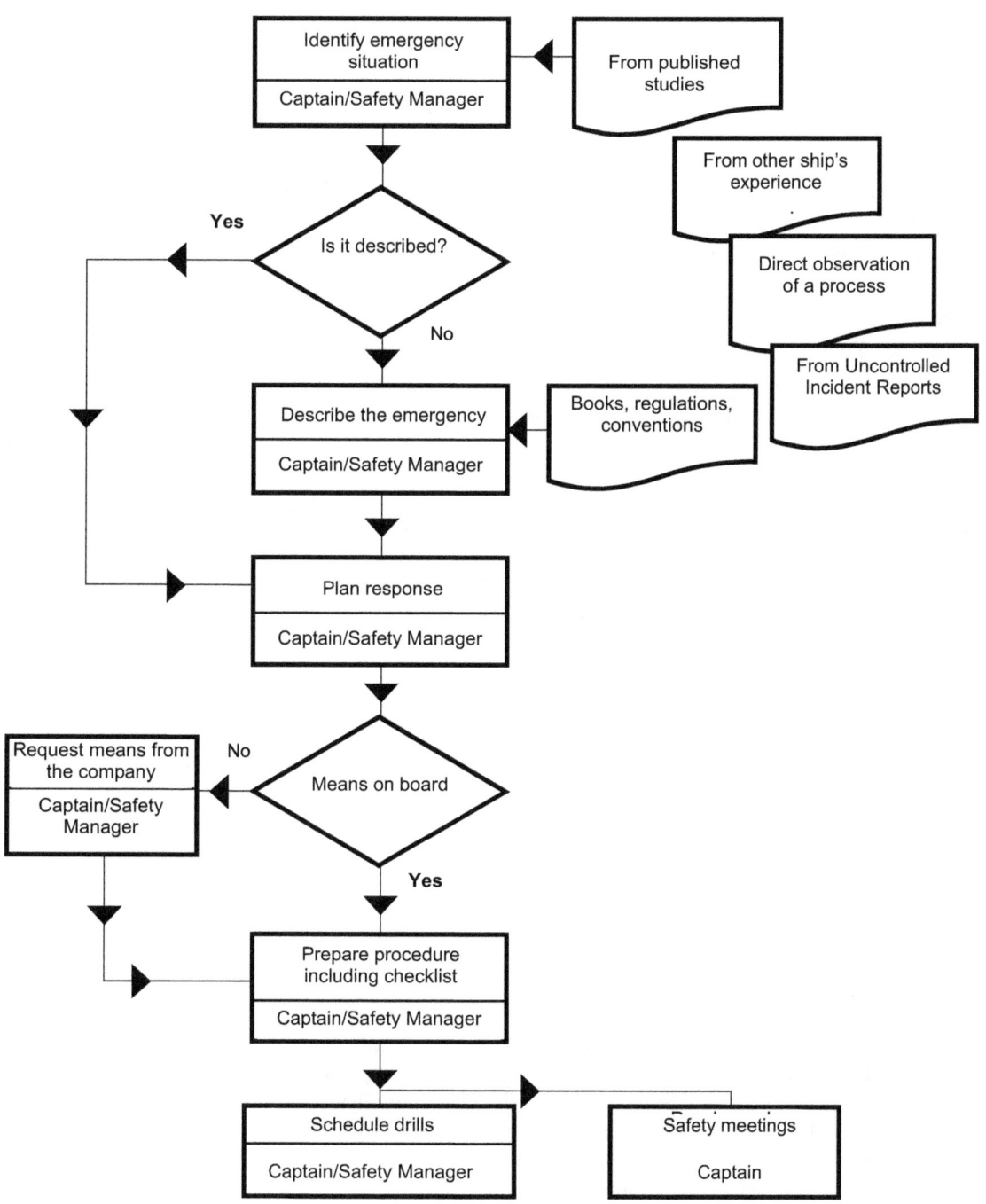

Figure 1.1

Activating the internal and external warnings plan

Internal level

Notify:	Responsible part:
• Fleet Safety Manager	Captain
• Fleet Manager	Captain / Fleet Safety Manager
• Patrimonial Safety	Safety Manager / Fleet Manager
• Legal Counselling Manager	
• Environment, Safety and Quality Manager	
• Press Secretary	
• Insurance Companies	
• Personnel of the closest facilities	
• Company's Top Management	Fleet Manager / Press Secretary

External level

Notify:	Responsible part:
• Marine Terminal Manager	Captain / Fleet Safety Manager
• D.G.M.M.1 (Maritime Accident Coordination Centre)	
• Civil Maritime Authority	
• Port Authority	
• Agent - Consignee	
• Insurance Companies / P&I	
• Charterer / Consignor / Consignee	
• Town Council	
• Facility Manager / Press Secretary	
• Local Authorities. Fishermen Guild, relatives	
• Media, local Environmental Associations.	

Onshore emergency (Figure 1.2)

An Onshore Emergency triggers when there is awareness of any anomalous circumstances that may occur in port facilities, both those affecting directly the berthing area where the ship is, and those that might affect the ship's safety when considering the effects originating in that distant area, whether to consider eventual problems during evacuation, or the possibility of blocking the manoeuvring water areas to allow the ship to go out to sea, if it had been thus planned for these typified conditions; communications will be directed on the following principles.

---

[1] *Dirección General de la Marina Mercante* — The Spanish Directorate General of Merchant Marine

The following are selected, from amongst others, for the study's purpose:

- The Safety Manager will be made aware of the emergency situation through the channels defined in the Communications Manual for crisis situations. He should collect as many data as possible in order to gain as accurate a picture as possible of the real situation.

- The Safety Manager should pass on to the Fleet Manager all the information and data gathered.

- The Fleet Manager is to assess the situation and decide whether it is a crisis situation; if not, further data and information are to be gathered.

- If the Fleet Manager deems it is a crisis situation, he should summon the Crisis Committee; Phase I is declared (any accident with a local impact, managed at the local level).

- The Fleet Manager should coordinate the crisis situation response, supported by the necessary assistance from the various organisations within the Fleet Area, following the guidelines of the Communications Manual for crisis situations and the Contingency Plan for communications.

- If the crisis situation is in Phase II (any accident with a national and/or international impact, managed at local, national and international level), the Fleet Manager should summon the President and the M.D., who will join the Crisis Committee.

- Once the emergency is solved, the Safety Manager should prepare a report on its solution and on the uncontrolled incidents that occurred, which originated the emergency.

Ship maintenance and inspection management

Ship safety depends both on the crew capability of facing emergencies with sufficient skills, and on the state of the equipment used to support actions; therefore, a preventative procedure should be considered.

From amongst others, the following are selected for the study's purpose:

1. The Inspections and Maintenance Manager should set up management principles for handling preventative maintenance; these are reflected in the Preventative Maintenance Manual general approach.

2. The Safety Manager should define the safety checks periodicity, in accordance with the Company's own requirements and the requirements set by the various Authorities.

3. The Inspection Manager should plan the activities that are to be developed under the periodicities defined in the Preventative Maintenance Manual for the five year cycle.

4. Inspections and tests to be carried out during the ship immobilisation for repairs should be supervised by the Ship Inspector.

5. The Department Manager should schedule operations, taking into account the frequencies set in the Preventative Maintenance Manual, the equipment with problems, and experience as revealed by the historic analysis of every ship component. The Department Manager should schedule checks with the defined frequencies.

6. If the operations schedule is compatible with the ship operating conditions, the Captain should authorise its execution. Otherwise, the schedule should be modified.

7. Inspections and testing on which maintenance activities are based should be carried out according to the requirements in the Preventative Maintenance Manual; they should be supervised by the Department Manager. Safety equipment checks and testing should be carried out in accordance to the applicable regulations.

8. After maintenance activities have been carried out, reports should be issued according to the Preventative Maintenance Manual forms. After safety checks have been carried out, periodic reports should be issued as required.

1 On board organisation

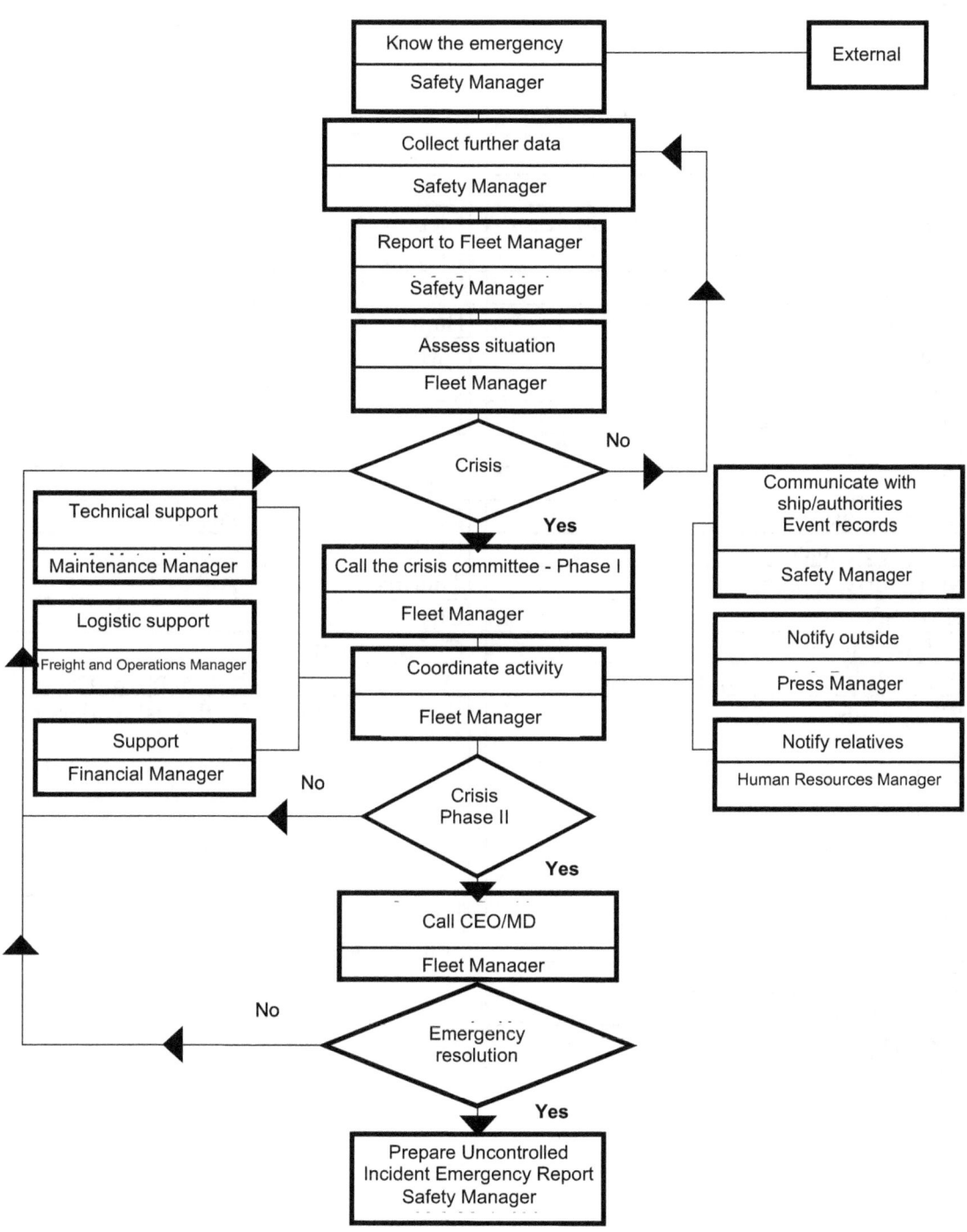

Figure 1.2

Checks

Table 1.2 Checks

Weekly	Monthly
Firefighting Team Equipment Cabinets	Electric Actuators
Firefighting Cabinets	Lifeboats
Firefighting Hydrants	Barbed Wire
Foam Generators	Ballast Monitor
Fire Extinguishers	GMDSS
Lifeboats	Portable VHF Sets
Emergency Lighting	Chain
Life Rings	Fire Detectors
Liferafts	Portable Gas Detectors
Escape Masks	Portable Oxygen Analysers
Electric Actuators	Diving Suits
Motor driven pump	Thermal Protective Aids
GMDSS	Life Jackets
Ballast Tanks	General Vents
Pump Room Ventilation Windscoops	Discharge Pumps Emergency Stops
P/V Valves	Watertight Doors, Portholes, Rollers, etc.
Tank Probes	Inert Gas
High Level Alarms	Cargo and Ballast Tanks
Pump Room Alarms	Pump Room
Inert Gas	Antipollution Equipment
Aldis Lamps	
CO_2 System	
Ventilation Windscoops	
Galley	

Documentation and data control

From amongst others, the following are selected for the study's objectives:

- In front of a document to be issued, distributed or prepared, the Safety or Quality Manager should decide whether the document should be a controlled document or not. If control is not required, it may be distributed.
- If the document is ready, or if it is an external document for distribution, it will be distributed to the addressees, using the "Document Distribution" form, which identifies the document type, its name and the addressees.
- If the document needs to be prepared, since it is a procedure, the issuer should set it according to what has been established.
- Prior to document approval, it should be reviewed in order to ensure conformance and consistency with the Management System.

1.3.6 Aspects related to ship chandlers

As ship chandlers are considered to be strangers to the ship, and since there is a large variety in each of the visited ports, a control follow up must be in place.

The following are selected, from amongst others, for the study's objectives:

- The organisation manager should propose a new supplier for evaluation.
- The organisation manager should document the satisfactory supplier relationship history; in view of the satisfactory results on the last purchase orders, the supplier may be included in the Selected Suppliers List, which is handled by Inspection and Maintenance.
- If the supplier holds an ISO 9000 certificate that covers the services or products to be supplied, the organisation manager should request a certificate copy and include the supplier in the Selected Suppliers List.
- If the product is approved by a Body that is recognised within the maritime industry, the organisation manager should request a copy of the approval certificate, and include the supplier in the Selected Suppliers List.
- If none of the above conditions are met, the Inspection and Maintenance Manager should send the supplier a questionnaire for evaluation; if satisfactory, he should include the supplier in the Selected Suppliers List.
- If evaluation proves negative, the supplier should be rejected, unless supply is urgent and no other supplier is available.

1.3.7 Navigation and manoeuvring procedures

One of the main objectives of Maritime Transport is achieved by the ship sailing from one port to the other, beginning the marine adventure with control on its own specific risks and on those that may arise from particular cases related to public safety aspects. Therefore, control procedures are established.

The following are selected, from amongst others, for the study's objectives:

- The Captain should issue the appropriate instructions on the voyage to the Deck Officer before sailing.
- The Second Deck Officer should gather the necessary information in order to prepare the Voyage Plan; for this purpose, he should complete the data check, collection and evaluation list.
- With the collected information and the completed checklist, the Second Deck Officer should: document the Voyage Plan, prepare the Voyage Plan Sheet filling in the remarks section of each Way Point with any remarkable data from the Way Point close by area.
- The Captain should review the Voyage Plan; if nonconforming, he should return it to the Second Deck Officer.
- If conforming, the Captain should decide to begin the voyage, and issue a copy to the Chief Engineer.
- The Captain and the Officer of the Watch should control throughout the voyage its development as planned.
- The Officer of the Watch should report to the Captain any circumstance that might involve altering the Voyage Plan.
- The Captain should decide on the required modification to adapt the Voyage Plan to the current demands.

1.3.8 Port watch checklist

The following are selected, from amongst others, for the study's objectives:

- Time and height for high tide and low tide.
- Are the Fire Plan and the "No Entry", "No Smoking", and "International Connection" signs at the access door?
- Anchor state and chain length.
- State of towlines and cables, prow and stern emergency towing systems.
- Pilot ladder stowed on deck.
- State of platform, gangway, net and lighting.
- Weather conditions.
- Engine availability in case of emergency.
- Is supervision present when bunkering, loading potable water, discharging oily residues and/or waste?

1.3.9 Other safety checks

- Compliance with MARPOL, Annex V on waste containers.
- Smoking restrictions.
- Signs and lighting.
- Composition of the watch.
- Periodic inspection rounds covering all the ship, and compliance with the checklist sections.
- Restrictions on mobile phones.
- Surveillance of close by areas to the ship.

- Reinforced surveillance on areas susceptible to entry of stowaways.
- Signs for works and special orders.
- Special port rules.
- Observance of safety and firefighting measures.
- No external condition endangers the ship, neither does it create any danger for others.
- Port and Terminal emergency telephones are ready and permanently attended.
- Procedures for reporting to the competent authorities in case of pollution, according to SOPEP.
- Entries in the Log Book / Navigation Log.
- Lighting on deck and close by areas to the ship.
- Flags.
- Reception of supplies and equipment.
- Surveillance of pressure values and leakages on manifold and tray, and checks on Sea Chest Valves.

1.3.10 Bridge watch. Daily checks.

The following are selected, from amongst others, for the study's objectives:

SHIP: **DATE:**   **LOCATION: l=**   **L=**

Has the following equipment been checked?

- Bridge and Engine Room Telegraphs, Tachometer
- Bridge Telephones
- Deck Clock
- Clocks and Chronometers
- I.G. Pressure Recorder
- Alarms in general
- Radars
- Auto Alarm
- Whistle Signal
- Instructions on change over from automatic pilot to hand steering and vice versa

1.3.11 Bridge watch. High seas navigation

The following are selected, from amongst others, for the study's objectives:

SHIP: **DATE:**   **SITUATION:**

- Is the maintenance of the lookout given the right priority?
- Are the NAVAREA, HYDROLANT and HYDROPAC navigation warnings checked regularly, as well as any other long range weather report?

- Are local weather changes checked, and is the barometer read regularly?
- Are reports issued in areas where it is mandatory to do so?
- Is the ship position fixed at regular intervals, at least hourly?
- Have preparations for landfall been made?
- Are all charts and nautical publications corrected and up to date?
- Are all the electronic ship position systems operative?
- Have the GMDSS Log Book checks been made?

In relation to the anchoring manoeuvre

Once it is known that the ship will be anchoring, the Officer of the Watch should carry out appropriately in advance the checklist verifications, and record the results in the Log Book.

The Officer of the Watch should report to the Captain the bridge's readiness for initiating the anchoring manoeuvre.

The Officer of the Watch should check and maintains watch conditions during anchoring, as indicated in the checklist.

Anchoring checklist

SHIP: DATE: PORT:

- Is an Anchoring Plan in place, which includes?:
    - Wide margin speed reduction,
    - Wind and current directions and forces,
    - Tidal stream when manoeuvring at low speed,
    - Space requirements for anchoring or leaving the anchorage,
    - Engine test.
- Have the following been duly notified of the ready for anchoring time?:
    - Captain,
    - Engine Room,
    - Personnel involved in anchoring.
- Is the following equipment ready for use?:
    - Anchor and windlass,
    - Lights and marks,
    - Sounders,
    - GPS
    - Internal and external communication systems,
    - Radar,
    - Port map or large scale chart,
    - Nautical publications relevant to the area,
    - Navtex.

- Is the cover of the compartment where the anchor shackle is located open?
- Is an emergency hammer available?
- Has a watch during anchoring been set?
- Have communications with Port Authorities or Control Tower been established, in order to know the anchorage location and any other instructions?
- After anchoring, has position been reported to the Port Authorities?

1.3.12 In cases of boarding

The Officer of the Watch should act according to the checklist for collision/boarding cases. The crew, on hearing the emergency alarm signal, should gather at the muster point (emergency centre) and place themselves under the command of the person assigning them the list of duties for emergency cases.

The Captain should act according to the checklist. The Captain, having all the information available, should assess the situation.

If, as a consequence of the accident, there is flooding or structural failure, the Captain should apply the appropriate procedure to the situation.

If both ships are stuck together and it is not dangerous to separate them, the Captain should provide, within his capabilities, any assistance the other ship may require.

The Captain should manoeuvre in order to separate the ship. If the Captain deems dangerous the separation of the ships, he should request assistance.

If while waiting for assistance, or while assistance is given, the Captain considers that conditions have worsened, he should decide to abandon ship, and apply the corresponding emergency procedure.

Once the ships have been taken apart, the Captain should apply the procedures required by the new situation of the ship.

The Captain should report the accident using the Uncontrolled Incident procedure.

Contents of this procedure should be developed at the theoretical level in meetings held with the crew, in which the Captain or the Safety Officer should present in detail the operations to be developed and how to complete checklists.

Checklist. Collision/boarding case

SHIP: DATE: VOYAGE No.:

- Issue emergency alarm signal.
- Manoeuvre in order to minimise effects of collision/boarding.
- Stop engines.
- Close watertight doors and fire doors.

- If after dark, light deck.
- Report to the Captain.
- Establish communications with Engine Room.
- Confirm bailing pumps are ready.
- Change VHF set to channel 16 o, if necessary, to channel 13.
- Establish communications with the other ship.
- Position correctly the ship on the chart.
- Have the ship's position available in the radio/GMDSS station room, satellite station, and in any other automatic hazard transmitter.
- Confirm emergency through internal communication channels.
- Confirm that all engine room equipment is ready for use.

1.3.13 About grounding/stranding

When grounding/stranding occurs, the Officer of the Watch should act according to the checklist.

The crew, on hearing the emergency signal, should gather at the muster point (emergency centre) and place themselves under the command of the person assigning them the emergency roles.

- The Captain should participate and verify the items according to the checklist.
- The Captain should assess the situation with all the available information.
- The Captain should apply the corresponding procedure if flooding or structural failure has occurred.
- The Captain should request the necessary assistance if he deems that refloating the ship is dangerous.
- The Captain should manoeuvre in order to refloat the ship, if the operation entails no danger.
- The Captain should apply the abandon ship procedure if conditions worsen and make this decision advisable.
- Once the ship is refloated, the Captain should apply the appropriate procedures to the ship's situation.
- The Captain reports the accident following the method stated in the Uncontrolled Incident procedure.

Checklist. Grounding/stranding case

SHIP: DATE: VOYAGE No.:

- Stop engines immediately.
- Issue General Emergency Alarm.
- Report to the Captain.
- Close watertight doors.
- Keep the VHF set on channel 16 or, if possible, on channel 13.
- Establish contact with emergency teams.
- Show lights/marks and issue the appropriate acoustic signals.
- Light deck if after dark.

1 On board organisation 37

- Confirm switch over to high intakes.
- Confirm bailing pumps are ready.
- Verify communications systems.
- Have the ship's position available in the radio/GMDSS station room, satellite station, and in any other automatic hazard transmitter.
- Confirm that all engine room equipment is ready for use.
- Data recording:
    - Course and speed of ship at the time of grounding.
    - Sounder trace.
    - Large scale chart.
    - Corrected navigational warnings.
    - Nautical publications.
    - Lighthouse books
    - Tide tables

1.3.14 Flooding/structural failure

Upon knowledge of flooding, the Officer of the Watch should act according to the checklist.

The crew, on hearing the emergency signal, should gather at the muster point (emergency centre) and place themselves under the command of the Officer leading the team they belong to.

- The Captain should act according to the checklist, verifying its items. The Captain should assess the situation, based on the available information.
- If other circumstances come in, the Captain should apply de appropriate procedure.
- If the Captain cannot control the flooding, he should request assistance.
- Once flooding is under control, the Captain should adopt surveillance measures.
- The Captain should assess damages and consequences.
- The Captain should apply the abandon ship procedure when circumstances make it advisable.
- The Captain should use the Uncontrolled Incident procedure to report the accident.

Checklist. Flooding/structural failure case

SHIP: **DATE:**   **VOYAGE No.:**

- Issue General Emergency Alarm.
- Report to the Captain.
- Close watertight doors.
- Identify and locate water ingress, as well as its magnitude.
- Interrupt electrical supply through flooded area.
- Communications with emergency teams.
- Confirm bailing pumps are ready.
- Heel and trim effects.
- Verify communications system.

- Have the ship's position available in the radio/GMDSS station room, satellite station, and in any other automatic hazard transmitter.
- Manoeuvre to the best course and speed in order to minimise ship movements.
- Confirm that all engine room equipment is ready for use.
- Prepare drawings for breakdown control.

1.3.15 Fire

- Upon knowledge of the fire, the Officer of the Watch should act according to the checklist.
- The crew should gather at the muster point (emergency centre) and place themselves under the command of the Team Leaders.
- The Captain should act according to the checklist, verifying its items.
- The Captain should assess the situation, based on the available information.
- The Captain should apply other appropriate procedures, if other circumstances appear that require it.
- The Captain should request assistance for controlling the fire.
- Once the fire is under control, the Captain should adopt the necessary measures to prevent reignition.
- The Captain should assess damages.
- The Captain should apply the abandon ship procedure, if circumstances concerning the accident should make it advisable.
- The Captain should report the accident according to the Uncontrolled Incident procedure.

Checklist

SHIP: **DATE:**   **VOYAGE No.:**

- Issue Emergency Alarm.
- Report to the Captain, if absent from the bridge, and to the Engine Room.
- Crew ready.
- Communication with the Team Leaders.
- Confirm that firefighting services and pump are ready.
- Switch on deck lights if after dark.
- Inform the crew about the fire.
- If fire is in the Engine Rooms, get prepared for an engine failure.
- Close ramps/screens/fire and watertight doors/skylight
- Stop ventilation and air conditioning.
- Have firefighting drawings ready.
- Have the ship's position available at all times in the radio/GMDSS station room, satellite station, and in any other automatic hazard transmitter.
- Have information ready for communications (onshore emergency plan).

1.3.16 Helicopter assisted operation

- The Captain should request a helicopter for the necessary evacuation, agreeing on the meeting point.
- The Captain should issue the necessary instructions to prepare the manoeuvre, completing the checklist.
- The First Officer should verify the checklist items, overseeing for a safe, uneventful operation.
- The Captain should check the helicopter departure, to declare the manoeuvre completed.
- The Officer of the Watch should update the voyage plan.
- The Captain should report the accident according to the Uncontrolled Incident procedure.

1.3.17 Unlawful actions — Stowaways

- The Captain should adopt the cautions stated as examples in the checklist, in order to keep the ship under extreme surveillance.
- If strangers have boarded the ship and are not located, the Captain should create security patrols that will patrol the ship until they are located.
- Once the stranger is located, the Captain should obtain all possible information, following the checklist.
- The Captain should report the mishap to the agent, the competent authorities and the designated person.
- The Captain should adopt due measures to prevent the stranger from moving about freely in the ship.
- The Captain should prepare information to send to the P&I representative.
- When the stowaway leaves the ship, the Captain should require him/her to sign a statement; if he/she refuses to sign, the Captain should make a note of it on the Navigation Log with the signatures of two witnesses, thereby certifying the truthfulness of the statement.
- The Captain should report the mishap following the Uncontrolled Incident procedure.

1.3.18 Preparedness for security related aspects

The Security Level established for the ship is Level 1.

The main activities carried out towards the ship's security are:

- Once moored in any of the ports for loading or delivering, all outside doors of the bridge deck and "B" and "A" decks should be locked. Watertight doors in lower and aft decks should also be locked, except those on the mooring side, in order to allow passage for the crew to carry out their tasks.
- Tight doors for the air conditioning system, emergency generator, hydraulic crane and winches, doors for inert gas, galley, outside mess room door, doors for pump room and prow storeroom, should be padlocked. This is done in order to control people accessing and exiting the ship.
- Once moored, and having completed all tasks for setting down the gangway or platform, placing the "No Smoking" and "No Mobile Phones", as well as the emergency plan next to

- the gangway, a sailor should keep watch, never leaving the ship access unattended; this sailor will be relieved by the next watch sailor.
- If any person not belonging to the crew intends to access the ship for whatever reason, prior to getting on the gangway the sailor must identify him/her and the reason for boarding, requesting some type of identity document. He should then call the Officer of the Watch, who will decide whether to allow the visitor on or not. If so, the visitor should be met on the deck by the Officer of the Watch or by a cadet sent by the Officer. If the visitor carries any bag, parcel or briefcase, it must be inspected by the Officer of the Watch. If for any reason either the visitor or what he/she is carrying is suspicious, the Officer should warn the Captain, who will in turn warn the Port Authorities.
- All visitors, whatever their reasons for accessing the ship, whether port agents, ship chandlers, inspectors, etc., must be registered in the visitors log, with name, identity card or passport, reason for accessing, and entry and exit time.
- The sailor on watch, apart from keeping watch at the access door, should make rounds on the deck, inspecting the state of ropes and reporting any findings, as well as reporting the approach of any alien vessel, to the Officer of the Watch.
- During sailing and stay at port, safety rounds should also be made, two on every night watch, to check that everything is in order and that there is no hazard that may affect the ship or her crew.
- The Ship Security Officer should supervise all activities focused on enhancing the ship's security. The Security Officer is an Officer belonging to the ship, in this case the First Deck Officer.
- Regarding port facilities, in order to enter the port, identification and destination must be requested.
- Furthermore, when arriving at the mooring, the person on watch there will only allow passage of people who are listed in the crew list that has been sent from the ship to the port facility prior to arrival. Even then, at some port facilities, signing on the log is required prior to leaving; in other facilities, in order to access or leave, a pass card plus, mandatorily, an identity card or passport, are required.

1.4 Partial conclusions

For the present study, the following items are significant:

- Documentation is available to the whole crew, whatever their rank and position on the ship;
- The Captain is the main responsible person, and he holds the highest authority;
- The First Officer is responsible for the crew and its training;
- The Second Officer is in charge of communications;
- The Third Officer is in charge of the Infirmary and the Medicine Chest;
- The majority of risks are identified within the Safety at Work and Operating Safety concepts, with only some references to Security;
- Both Emergency Plans are considered: on the ship and onshore;
- Checklists are used as organising, follow up and control tools for the relevant variables.

2 The port. Internal Emergency Plans.

2.1 Introduction and legal framework

The "Planning", "Emergency" and "Civil Protection" concepts are strongly related; furthermore, none of them have a unique, univocal interpretation; to a large extent they are subject to ambiguity and confusion, both in their theoretical elaboration and in their practical application.

A clarification of concepts is sought; the preliminary base is reached, from where to start in order to determine fields of action and individual, corporate and public organisation responsibilities regarding emergency plans. Firstly, a clear distinction must be established between what is known as the "Civil Protection Concept" and "Civil Protection Service".

The "Civil Protection Concept" has its doctrinaire basis on Decree of 29th February, 1968, as a set of actions aimed at preventing, reducing or remediating damages to persons and goods, caused in peace time by any aggressive agents or by natural elements or extraordinary causes, when they become a public calamity due to the magnitude and seriousness of their effects.

From the moment this type of activities received their legal configuration, the existence became evident of obligations and services of which individuals and territorial corporations within the State were in charge of.

The former is mentioned in the Spanish Constitution, when stating that citizen duties may be regulated by law in the event of great risks, catastrophes or public calamities[1].

Regarding the latter, the Decree of 29th February, 1968, already stated that, depending on the magnitude of the hazards, damages and disasters, the collaboration of all affected parties was deemed necessary in order to prevent or mitigate them, by applying all possible means and resources; for this purpose, it accepts a typically municipal or provincial condition of the protective function of people and goods, which in certain cases could attain a national character. The "Civil Protection Concept" becomes assigned, in the measure of its own resources and possibilities, to all components of society, both to its individuals and to corporations, whether public or private.

---

[1] Spanish Constitution (SC), Article 30.4

Then, the "Civil Protection Service" has its legal bases on the Constitution, as the obligation of the public authorities to guarantee the right to life and physical integrity, as the first and most important of all fundamental rights[2], within the national unity and territorial solidarity[3] principles, and within the essential demands for effectiveness and administrative coordination[4].

Currently, the supporting legal framework is Law 2/1985 of 21st January, on Civil Protection.

Its first article already defines Civil Protection as a public service, as the expression of a permanent action of the public authorities aimed at studying and preventing serious risk, catastrophe or public calamity situations, and at protecting and succouring persons and goods, should these situations happen. Competence for providing this public service is assigned to the State Civil Administration and, within the provisions of the law, to the other public administrations. Law 2/1985 recognises the diversity and amplitude of emergency situations, as well as the needs they generate, in terms of human and material resources. The law continues by defining that Civil Protection is to act through procedures for ordering, planning, coordinating and managing the various public services related to the emergency being faced.

It stipulates that *"centres, establishments and dependencies where catalogued activities take place"*, i.e., which may originate an emergency situation, *"should have a self protection system in place, with its own resources, as well as the corresponding Emergency Plan for risk prevention, alarm, evacuation and succour actions"*[5]. In this way, the preparation of emergency plans, already in place in a large number of facilities with hazardous activities, becomes mandatory.

As a consequence of what is discussed above, planning is configured as the essential technique in Civil Protection. Its importance is shown by Law 2/1985 dedicating the whole Chapter 3 to emergency case actions and Civil Protection Plans.

Civil Protection Basic Rules, provided in Article 8 of Law 2/1985 and approved by Royal Decree (RD) 407/92[6], includes the essential guidelines for the preparation of autonomic, provincial, supra provincial, insular and municipal territorial plans, and of special plans by activity sector, emergency type or specific activities.

RD 407/1992 stipulates in Article 5 that *"Special Plans should be prepared to face specific risks, the nature of which requires an appropriate technical-scientific methodology for each one of them"*. Article 6 also lists risks that should be addressed with special plans in territories requiring it, amongst which chemical risks and those related to the carriage of dangerous goods are found.

Special plans should be prepared according to the relevant basic guidelines for each risk. These basic guidelines should establish the minimum requirements about basis, structure, organisation, operating criteria, action measures and coordination instruments that have to fulfil the special plans they refer to.

---

[2] Art. 15 SC
[3] Art. 2 SC
[4] Art. 101 SC
[5] Art. 6 Law 2/1985 of 21st January, Civil Protection
[6] Royal Decree 407/92, of 24th April, Civil Protection Basic Rules (BOE [Boletín Oficial del Estado — *Spanish Official State Bulletin*] — 1st May, 1992).

In Spain, prior to the enactment of RD 407/1992, there was legislation in place addressing, within wider contexts, the preparation of external emergency plans by the corresponding organisations in the State, autonomic or local administrations, and the preparation of internal emergency plans by certain industries. This legislation is RD 886/1988 of 15th July[7], on prevention of major accidents in certain industrial activities, which was developed in compliance with Directive 82/501/CEE of 24th June, 1982, of the European Community Council[8].

The legal framework to be applied to the emergency plan field in the industrial area is primarily determined by its national or international origin. However, Spain has implemented within its legal framework, by means of ratification, virtually all regulations coming from international organisations with forums representing countries with an outstanding interest and renowned background in the evolution and enhancement of technology applied to prevention and safety in the industrial world.

Rules related to internal emergency plans that industries should develop may present an inductive aspect and/or a complementary aspect:

- Inductive, when the text prescribes the preparation of emergency plans within various sectors of the industrial field;
- Complementary, when it sets patterns for structuring the plans and/or assists their complete development.

Some significant examples would be:

- RD 952/1990, of 29th June, modifying annexes and completing stipulations of RD 886/88 of 15th July, on prevention of major accidents in certain activities[9].
- Directive 80/1107/CEE, of 27th November, on protection of workers against risks related to exposure to chemical, physical and biological agents at work.
- Directives 87/216/CEE, of 19th March, 1987, and 88/610/CEE of 24th November, 1988, modifying Directive 82/501/CEE.
- Resolution of the Council of 30th January, 1991, approving the Basic Guideline for the preparation and approval of emergency plans in the chemical industry.
- R.I.D. (Standards). European agreement on international carriage of dangerous goods by rail (R.1986,2710 and R.1988,2652). The equivalent standard in Spain is known as T.P.F.
- A.D.R. (Standards). European agreement on international carriage of dangerous goods by road (R.1986.3463 and R.1987.561). The equivalent standard in Spain is known as T.P.C.
- Convention No. 134 of the International Labour Organisation (ILO), "Prevention of Accidents (Seafarers)".

---

[7] Royal Decree 886/86, of 15th July, "Prevention of Major Accidents in Certain Industrial Activities". BOE of 5th August, 1988 (Issue No. 187).
[8] Known as the "Post Seveso Directive", related to major accident risks in certain industrial activities.
[9] BOE of 21st July, 1990 (Issue No. 174).

2.2 Objectives and goals of the Internal Emergency Plans (IEP's)

Traditional objectives of an internal emergency plan may be summarised in the following items:

- Preparing measures and action and security means in order to minimise emergency damages;
- Having informed, trained and organised personnel available for the necessary actions aimed at preventing or minimising damage in eventual emergencies;
- Maintaining operativity and effectiveness of measures and action and security means for emergencies;
- Maintaining all permanent and temporary "occupants" informed at all times on how to act in case of emergency.

When intending to fulfil these initial objectives, the following goals are sought:

- Rescuing and treating injured persons;
- Protecting other persons;
- Minimising damage to goods and the environment;
- Initial containment of the incident/accident and, finally, controlling it;
- Identifying casualties;
- Tending to the medical needs of injured persons;
- Providing authorised information to the media;
- Ensuring remediation in the affected areas;
- Preservation of reports and necessary equipment for subsequent investigation of emergency causes and circumstances.

2.2.1 Principles of the Internal Emergency Plans

IEP's include the necessary information for handling an emergency.

The IEP should be ready and set up under the responsibility of the facility manager, and generally under the coordination of a person in charge of safety, who oversees its updating based on the evolution of:

- Risks
- General structure and production organisation
- Resources for acting

The IEP must be known to those who take part or make decisions in case of accident, particularly commanders and technicians.

Furthermore, it may be said that, although the Internal Emergency Plan is primarily aimed at allowing control over serious situations (explosions, fires, toxic releases, spillages, etc.), it would seem convenient not to exclude from its application scope lower level accidents or incidents, if they require assistance, succour or similar information, even though they may not be so significant.

2.2.2 Basic data for preparing IEP's

Internal Emergency Plan requirements will vary depending on features, size, risks and needs at each facility.

In preparing a specific IEP, at least some of the following starting bases should be considered:

- Facility size and complexity
- Products handled: raw materials, intermediate materials, end products, etc.
- Number of workers and/or persons not in the facility's payroll
- Type of processes taking place
- Potentially hazardous facility areas
- Technical response capability towards the accident
- Available means to face the emergency
- Density of people in potentially hazardous areas

2.2.3 Actions for preparing an IEP

Generally, the IEP preparation process may be drafted by completing the following five fundamental stages:

1) **Risk study**, carried out either under a regulatory obligation and/or by the own decision of the company, which will justify the need or the convenience of preparing an IEP. For this purpose, causes and possible consequences, both internal and external, of the accidents must be considered beforehand.

2) **Defining resources for acting**, which should be used under a reasonable expectation that consequences of an eventual accident shall be controlled. These resources for acting may be:

   a) Human
   b) Organisational
   c) Material.

Furthermore, from their origin's standpoint, they may be internal and/or external.

3) **Preparing the action procedures**, depending on the possible accident types and according to their phases. Usually there are three procedure types:

- Action procedures: alert and succour actions;
- Information procedures: both internal and external, adequate to the corresponding levels of the accident nature;
- Normalisation procedures: subsequent to the accident, to remediate the affected areas, bearing in mind also the need for investigation.

These procedures should translate into instructions adapted to each situation, and must be known to the persons who have to use them. Hence the need for personnel training, emergency drills and simulations, for launching the IEP.

4) **Writing the IEP**, enacted by Management, should be distributed to persons, organisations, etc. that might become involved.

5) **Implementing, reviewing, and updating**: by mandate (Art. 6-4) of RD 886/88, on accident prevention at sea in certain industrial activities, it must be done every four years. In modern chemical industries it is often reviewed yearly; however, it would seem logical that the review should be done also when modifications are made to the scope and inventory of dangerous substances, and when changes or improvements are introduced in the risk assessment methods and new safety techniques are developed and implemented.

2.2.4 IEP structure analysis

Ports and port facilities may or may not have a larger size than an industrial company, but, to a greater or lesser extent, both should consider the same principles for designing and implementing the Internal Emergency Plans.

Site characteristics, dimensions, risk level, available personnel, security means and many other factors make it impossible to establish an internal emergency plan model that should be valid for all industrial companies or facilities. If a method can be developed for creating and maintaining internal emergency plans operative in industrial companies, it follows a structure with three fundamental phases:

 A.- Assessing the plant/facility risk
 B.- Writing the emergency plan
 C.- Implementation and maintenance

  A.- Risk Assessment
  A.1.- Studying plant/facility design, project, implementation and operation standards
  A.2.- Studying the operating organisation
  A.3.- Studying the environment
  A.4.- Risk inventory
  A.5.- Risk quantification
  A.6.- Self protection means inventory
  A.7.- Borne risk assessment

  B.- Writing the Emergency Plan
  B.1.- Emergency procedures
  B.2.- Action plan
  B.2.1.- Emergency level
  B.2.2.- Chain of command
  B.2.3.- Emergency organisation
  B.2.4.- Alarm signals
  B.2.5.- Emergency communications
  B.2.6.- Evacuation and transportation
  B.2.7.- Summary chart
  B.2.8.- Annexes

  C.- Implementing and maintaining the emergency plan

A. Risk assessment

A.1.- Studying plant/facility design, project, implementation and operation standards.

Subjects relevant to the activity in the Health and Safety at Work General Ordinance, the High and Low Voltage Electrical Technical Regulations, the Pressure Vessel Regulations, and in other special regulations, such as those on chemical product storage, lifting devices, T.P.C., etc., should be studied.

Once the applicable regulations are known, design standards and codes used for the plant/facility projects should be reviewed, i.e., DIN, ASME, UNE standards, etc.

Finally, internal standards (company know-how), based on experience, on company's own developments or on company's own approvals of existing standards, should be studied.

A.2.- Studying the operating organisation.

Plant/facility work places should be systematically analysed, particularly those directly related with facility operations and maintenance, be it on the field or related with management and supervision; surveillance level, supervision quality and information availability level should be checked.

The appropriate balance between the preparation of information and the comprehension capabilities of all participants in the production process will allow making an inventory and quantifying the actual risks borne by the plant/facility in relation to this item.

A.3.- Studying the environment.

The environment around the plant/facility is composed of many factors. Urbanisation is one of the most important factors, and amongst the various urban aspects some are outstanding, such as access to the plant/facility, existence of inhabited centres and public places, and site topography.

Weather conditions for an area are very important. Temperatures, rainfall and wind are often the major risks present in our country, both as initiators of emergency situations and as possible influences on the development of the various emergency actions.

Finally, social environment may impact risks, emergency responses and public opinion pressure. This factor is present in every society, either as an emergency initiator or determining the necessary response to face it.

A.4.- Risk inventory

All the information gathered should be reflected on a list or inventory of risks borne by the plant/facility:

- Non compliance with legal regulations
- Construction with no specified code
- Non standardised construction

- Deficient facility surveillance
- Deficient information on production process
- Incorrectly focused supervision
- Random plant/facility access
- Population in risk areas
- No forecast of catastrophic weather situations
- Uncontrollable leaks (gases) and spillages (liquids)
- Lack of foresight of sabotages
- Disconnection with public assistance organisations
- Lack of foresight of relations with mass media
- Others, depending basically on the type of plant/facility being dealt with

A.5.- Risk quantification

The whole risk inventory is valueless unless each borne risk is accompanied by quantification.

There are several methods and techniques for assigning risks relative values, which lead to a ranking of higher to lower risks.

Analytical methods (*e.g.*, Fault Tree Analysis, FTA) are well focused and mathematically covered, as long as error probability values are available, which is not the case for much of the equipment, and even less for persons. Empirical methods (*e.g.*, HAZOP) are basically aimed at identifying fire, explosion and chemical risks when designing a plant/facility; they are applicable to the first stages of a project, when process and detail engineering modifications are easy to introduce.

They can also be used as development instruments for safety audits on existing plants/facilities, as guides for process unacquainted auditors.

In the more usual cases of operating facilities, using the FINE method is recommendable, which summarises comprehensibly the evaluation of the risk materialisation probability and the frequency of materialisation, and leaves to the expert the estimation of consequences. At this working stage, the projected emergency and firefighting systems are not considered. Once probability, frequency and consequences of risk materialisation are known, relative values are assigned (as recommended in the FINE method, or as discussed and created within the organisation) and multiplied; a risk classification is then available.

A.6.- Self protection means inventory

Generally, information should be collected on:

- Fixed firefighting systems;
- Alarm and detection systems;
- Mobile firefighting and emergency means;
- Available personnel;
- Personnel organisation and training on firefighting and emergencies.

A.7.- Borne risks assessment

Sorted from greater to lower risk, the self protection means available at the plant/facility should be listed on a table. Reaction capability and time of availability, *i.e.*, the power of the self protection means, should be assessed.

Non neutralised risks will be known as black spots.

B. - Composing the emergency plan

B.1.- Emergency procedures

An Emergency Procedure is a collection of instructions that an operating group in the plant/facility (emergency group) should follow in order to address any uncontrolled situation that might occur at the facilities under their competence. They should consist of a specific section, defined by the nature of work and equipment, and a common section, defined by the plant/facility general organisation. The specific section should include:

- Emergency operating instructions (actions on electric systems, flooding systems, etc.);
- Instructions on the use of special fire protection and emergency equipment available in the area (deluge, screens, etc.);
- Instructions on the use of common emergency items at the plant/facility (fire extinguishers, masks, etc.);
- Instructions on calling alarm and reporting an anomalous situation (telephones, alarms, etc.);
- Instructions on adopting an organisation for emergencies at the plant/facility;
- Instructions on evacuation.

The common section should reflect instructions for assisting other departments within the emergency plan context.

B.2.- Action plan

It should include definitions, organisation and instructions that the whole plant/facility should assume in case of emergency. Generally, the action plan should include the following aspects:

B.2.1.- Emergency level

The following emergency levels should be defined:

- Near emergency: an anomalous situation that can be neutralised with the means available where it happens, by the personnel usually present.
- Partial emergency: an emergency situation that cannot be neutralised immediately, unlike near emergencies, forcing those present to request assistance from the rest of the plant/facility;

- General emergency: an emergency that overcomes the self protection means set in the plant/facility, and forces to alter the usual organisation and to replace it by an emergency organisation, requesting outside assistance.

B.2.2.- Chain of command

In any emergency situation it should be known who is in command, and with what competences. It is recommended to establish a Single Command and a hierarchical organisation for simplicity's sake, for which the following should be defined:

- Emergency command: it shall hold command on all human and material means that participate in the emergency. Directly depending from it:
- Task command: it will handle all teams working against the emergency, keeping close continued contact with the Strategic Command.
- Strategic command: it will handle the facilities operations, advising the Task Command on where to direct its effort.
- Logistic command: it will be responsible for covering the necessary supplies and support organisation for the task teams.

Responsibilities and available means should be clearly defined for all of them. The established Chain of Command will be the backbone of the plant/facility emergency organisation.

B.2.3.- Emergency organisation

In front of every emergency situation (near, partial or general), the organisation and means for facing it should be set.

In case of a near emergency, the personnel present should react; a task group should be called preventatively, which should be permanently on standby to assist with further mobile equipment and the appropriate personal protection equipment.

Composition and characteristics of this task group will vary depending on the plant/facility size and characteristics. It may be a professional firefighting and emergency team, or personnel that, while normally carrying out other activities, are qualified through special training; these should be permanently present at the plant/facility. When the situation involves a partial emergency call, a part of the plant/facility personnel will enter the emergency organisation, while the remainder will stay on alert.

In this case, the Emergency Command, the Task Command and the Strategic Command will take action. The task team will be in action, but it will require reinforcement by the firefighting and emergency group (FFE Brigade, FFE Team, etc.).

The so called FFE Brigade represents the largest share of human resources that the plant/facility counts on for self protection. Depending on the nature of the plant/facility's activity, it may consist of volunteers (volunteer firemen), or of all positions that may be left without creating a serious hazard for the production process.

The presence of an adequately trained and equipped FFE Brigade is a key element in a plant/facility's Emergency Plan.

The Emergency Plan should explain the summoning mechanisms and the FFE Brigade members' obligations. Each and every one of them should have their tasks defined for the moment a partial emergency is called.

Lastly, the risk may develop in such a way that all internal resources plus external assistance are required. This is the general emergency case.

In the Emergency Plan, little detail of general emergency actions can be given; however, it should at least define clearly the Chain of Command.

The rest of the personnel will remain strictly subject to a paramilitary structure and discipline, and should organise rapidly, adapting themselves to the type of major emergency they may have to face.

Task, strategic support, logistic support and external relations brigades should be created, including command posts, commands, liaisons and other mechanisms that may allow running the organisation according to circumstances.

Public assistance bodies (Fire Brigade, Red Cross, Police, etc.) should act under the instructions of the Emergency Command when in the facility's premises.

If the emergency affects or may affect the outside, Civil Protection will take over the command.

In such general emergency organisation, a new agent is defined, namely the external relations manager, who will centralise all the information, being the only authorised person, except for the Emergency Command, to make declarations.

B.2.4.- Alarm signals

The plan should include alarm signals that are known by all personnel. Alarm communication should follow the sense: detector ==> communications control.

In response, the Communications Centre shall either call an alert, in case of near emergency, or shall call a partial or general emergency. Lastly, an "All is Safe" or end of emergency signal should be available, which will also be used for system checks.

B.2.5.- Emergency communications

A communications code should be established, embedding the highest level of discipline. Every communications should answer to an essential reason. Telephones should not be used unless there is an imperative need, and external communications should only take place to request assistance or information from the authorities.

The plan should consider an alternative courier system, in case of failure of the usual communications. An Emergency Control Centre should be in place, or a Communications Centre. All communication systems (telephone, radio station, couriers, alarm centre, etc.) should be available there, as well as the instructions for their use.

A key personnel list should be available, including usual location (telephone, address, pager, etc.), at the location(s) from which external calls will initiate, as well as the telephone numbers of the external assistance sources, such as Civil Protection, Fire Brigade, Police, Red Cross, close by companies and main public authorities that should be informed.

The Communications Centre should be manned by competent and adequately trained personnel, since its function is essential to the appropriate development of actions in the first moments of an emergency.

B.2.6. - Evacuation and transport

A plan for evacuating the facilities should be in place. It may be dangerous giving a general signal for evacuation; it is more advisable to signalise evacuation appropriately, and to have personnel instructed on how to direct evacuations or evacuate themselves. Evacuation points should answer to people's instinct of conservation and their everyday habits; clearly visible mustering points should be provided in low risk areas, from which evacuation to outside safe areas will be led.

It is worthwhile keeping a record of injured people and their initial destination. It will avoid many worries from relatives of workers and people involved in the emergency.

All vehicles available at the plant/facility should remain at the Emergency Command's disposal; each one should have a fixed driver allocated.

B.2.7.- Summary table

The Emergency Plan should include a summary table showing very clearly the highest amount of information possible, the most significant being the communications flowchart and the emergency organisation chart.

This table should be attractive and noticeable; both its colours and its size should facilitate reading.

B.2.8.- Annexes

Amongst all aspects included in the Emergency Plan, some require a detailed development that is not interesting to most of the workers at the plant/facility. These developments will be included in plan annexes. The following may be mentioned as examples:

- Composition of the FFE Brigade,
- FFE Brigade operating methodology,
- List of key telephone numbers,
- Drawings of risk areas,
- Drawings of access ways,
- Guide on moving injured people,
- List of available FFE resources,

- Others, depending on type of plant/facility.

In this way, the general rules in the Emergency Plan will not extend more than five to ten pages with double spacing, although the complete Plan may extend to fifty or more pages, annexes and emergency procedures included.

C. Emergency plan implementation and maintenance

In order to implement and keep the emergency plan alive, several techniques should be applied:

- Creating emergency groups encompassing one or several plant/facility departments, with the mission of developing emergency procedures; charging the emergency group leaders as integral components of the Emergency Plan development.
- Having the emergency procedures to get to the detail of defining, by means of personal cards, the immediate automatic tasks of every employee in case of emergency.
- Running FFE Brigade drills at the operating areas, with all problems involved.
- Running emergency drills at the operating areas, coordinating FFE operations with production process operations.
- Widely and accessibly disseminating information received on emergencies at similar plants/facilities.
- Analysing to the last consequences those incidents that might have caused an emergency and, by applying some imagination, expose the consequences should the risk have materialised.

2.2.5 Relationship between IEP's, External Emergency Plans (EEP's) and Mutual Assistance Plans

Introduction

As discussed previously in this study, it is the duty of the Administration's competent bodies to prepare and approve the External Emergency Plans for industrial facilities and centres that are obliged to prepare Internal Emergency Plans.

The existing legislation refers to the necessary and mandatory interrelation between Internal Emergency Plans and External Emergency Plans.

Article No. 7 of RD 886/88 of 15th July[10], states that industry owners are obliged to declare to the competent bodies in their Autonomous Community information regarding eventual major risk situations; more specifically, and literally: "... Internal Emergency Plans ...Mutual Assistance Plans between industrial establishments, if any... All the necessary information that may enable the competent Authority to prepare the External Emergency Plans, including the associated Safety Study comprising an Operativity Functional Analysis, when it has been determined that consequences may exist outside the facilities. In extraordinary cases, the competent Authority may require a Risk Quantitative Analysis."

---

[10] BOE of 5th August, 1988 (No. 187)

Article 11 of the referenced RD states that the competent Authorities may require from industry owners additional information to that of the mandatory, particularly for preparing the External Emergency Plans.

A more precise example is found in the regulations for admission, handling and storage of dangerous goods in ports[11]; Article 124 states that "the Internal Emergency Plan of each port shall integrate in the associated External Emergency Plan for port areas, which will be prepared, approved and authorised by the Authorities competent in this subject.../...

.../... The Internal Emergency Plan and the External Emergency Plan in port areas shall constitute an Integrated Plan. Integration of these plans shall be carried out by means of a common document in which procedures for liaison and information between both will be established, as well as the corresponding joint actions."

Furthermore, existence of other nearby facilities should be carefully considered. The way in which emergencies at one site may impact other facilities, and vice versa, should be addressed with their managers, and the necessary measures should be set in a Mutual Assistance Plan.

Mutual Assistance Plan

The most advisable practice for developing Mutual Assistance Plans between close by facilities is creating a committee.

This committee will be composed of those responsible for safety at the participating facilities. It should be set up depending on the number of workers, size and internal organisation of each facility.

Independently of the particular measures that each facility may establish, the committee should:

- Study the potential risks of each facility, and the organisation each facility has for controlling them;
- Analyse the possibilities for integrating the procedures designed for each facility, and recommend the most suitable ones;
- Recommend methods for minimising damage, should a serious emergency occur.

The committee will only be effective if it continues existing after preparing the plan, following up the tasks assigned to each member.

As a minimum, the Mutual Assistance Plan should comprise:

- A list of the foreseeable emergency types (fire, gas leaks, etc.);
- Alarm and communication systems: how, what, and in which order is the emergency reported to the other facilities;
- Designation of key personnel: lists with addresses, telephone numbers and identification system in emergency;

---

[11] RD 145/89 of 20th January, BOE of 13th February, 1989 (No. 37)

- Inventory and location of available assistance equipment (firefighting means, personal protection equipment, etc.);
- Available assistance services (medical, nurses, security, etc.);
- Training and drill procedures.

External Emergency Plan (EEP)

The External Emergency Plan shall be based on those events identified by the facility operators that might subsequently affect the population and the environment.

The Authorities[12], which would be responsible for preparing the Plan, should be notified through a mandatory[13] statement by the industrial facility managers.

Those responsible for preparing the EEP may plan as appropriate in accordance with the contents of the declaration[14]. The complexity of the EEP will depend on the diversity of potential events considered.

The general principles applied for preparing an External Emergency Plan are the same as for the Internal Emergency Plan. However, due to the likely diversity of events or accidents to consider, the main concern is ensuring coordination of the public assistance services (already in place) and preparing them to address the specific risks and problems that may arise in an emergency at the facility.

During the first stages of the External Emergency Plan preparation, the following should be taken into account:

a) Emergency Plans of each facility, as well as Mutual Assistance Plans between facilities of the area, should be part of the External Plan; therefore, they should be compatible one with another. Participation of authorities' representatives as well as of their emergency services in the Mutual Assistance Plan is more than advisable.
b) Whatever its structure, the Plan should be as flexible as possible.
c) The Plan should establish a command structure and identify the respective responsibilities of the personnel involved. It should designate a coordinator who, whilst keeping in contact with the emergency manager at the affected facility, organises and directs all outside activities. Including an Emergency Control Centre is essential.
d) All emergency services and organisations that may become involved in a major emergency should be consulted, in order to define their roles and include them in the Plan (Police, Fire Brigade, hospitals, ambulance services, electric boards, transportation services, schools, etc.).

The following list (although not comprehensive) gathers some aspects to be considered when preparing the External Emergency Plan for port facilities.

---

[12] Competent bodies of the Autonomous Communities, according to Art. 4 of RD 886/88 of 15th July
[13] Art.6, "Obligation to declare", of RD 886/88 of 15th July
[14] Art. 7, "Contents of the Mandatory Declaration", of R.D. 886/88 of 15th July

Organisation

- Details of the Command Structure (names, telephone numbers, addresses, etc.)
- Coordination
- Alarm systems
- Implementation procedures
- Emergency control centres

Communications

- List of key telephone numbers
- Identification of personnel involved
- Means of communication

Special equipment

- Availability and location of cranes, bulldozers, fire protection equipment, etc.

Specialists

- Information on institutions, companies or persons with which contact may be useful

Volunteer organisations

- Description, location, resources, etc.

Chemical products

- Information on products with associated potential risks, stored or processed in each facility

Weather reports

- Procedures for obtaining weather conditions and forecasts

Evacuation measures

- Transportation, evacuation centres, supplies, first aid, ambulances, etc.

Information

- Contact with the media; reporting to relatives

End of emergency

- Procedure to declare emergency termination

Investigation

- Procedures for gathering information on the emergency causes
- Effectiveness review for all aspects of the Plan

Annexes

- Emergency and Mutual Assistance Plans of each facility
- Data sheet forms
- Drawings, maps, etc.

2.2.6 Activating the EEP from the IEP

Although all aspects affecting the preparation and development of Emergency Plans (both Internal, External and Mutual Assistance) are significant, maybe prompt action is in many cases a determining factor to achieve full control of the event. When addressing the relationship between Internal and External Emergency Plans, activation of External Plan procedures initiated by the Internal Emergency Plan is also decisive in order to accomplish the set objectives.

Classification of the various emergency situations in a facility and their impact on the External Emergency Plan should be defined taking into account the following concepts:

Personnel emergency: an accident at a site, which requires treatment of one or more individuals with complicated injuries, caused, *e.g.*, by pollution or burns.

Emergency alert: corresponds to an internal or external situation posing a previously nonexistent risk, with no alteration in the plant/facility's operation, which could produce other types of more significant emergencies if not dealt with. It would correspond to Situation 1 (PRE-EMERGENCY) of the External Plan.

Local emergency: a situation caused by an accident, the consequences of which would remain confined within a limited area of the facility; evacuation of that area may be required, although no external damage would be derived. It corresponds to Situation 1 (PRE-EMERGENCY) of the External Plan.

Facility emergency: a situation caused by an accident causing a significant degradation in terms of facility safety, which may degenerate into a serious risk for the whole facility. It corresponds to Situation 2 (EMERGENCY - ALERT) of the External Plan.

General emergency: a situation caused by an accident leading to, or potentially causing, uncontrolled risks outside the facility. It corresponds to Situation 3 (EMERGENCY - ALARM) of the External Plan.

Correlation between the emergency levels in the Internal Emergency Plan and the action phases in the External Emergency Plan should be the following:

The Emergency Control Centre at the facility should report to the (External) Emergency Control Centre all emergency situations that correspond to any of the levels described.

Table 2.1 Relationship between emergency levels and action phases

IEP	EEP
Personnel emergency	---
Emergency alert	Situation 1 (Pre-emergency)
Local emergency	Situation 1 (Pre-emergency)
Facility emergency	Situation 2 (Emergency - Alert)
General emergency	Situation 3 (Emergency - Alarm)

The communication of an emergency should include the following information:

- Circumstances of the accident;
- Involved hazardous substances, in order to assist in assessing the possible accident impact on people and the environment;
- Report of necessary measures to mitigate the effects of the accident in the medium and long term;
- Necessary measures to prevent accident recurrence.

2.3 Essential components with an operating character in a fictitious PFSP

Available personnel

- Total personnel: 7 people on a 24 hour basis, plus 4 people during normal working hours.
- Subcontracter maintenance: 12 people during normal working hours.
- Security and surveillance: 6 people on a 24 hour basis.

Physical security systems

- Perimetral concrete fence, crested with jump proof metal blind fence and anti intrusion barbed wire topping.
- Closed circuit TV with 24 hour surveillance and recording system.
- Hourly perimeter patrols, with a guard tour patrol system including watchstations at various perimeter locations.
- Perimetral detection and alarm systems.

Access control

- Access with gate barrier and armoured door.
- Fence under 24 hour surveillance with 2 guards.
- Access allowed only to persons previously summoned, identified and checked.
- Checkpoint with archway metal detector and scanner for baggage and control of parcels and mail.

Communication equipment and systems

- Communications with ships: VHF fixed and portable transmitters.
- Communications between personnel: VHF fixed and portable transmitters (includes security personnel and emergency and surveillance channels).
- Communications with the company: private and public telephone network.
- Communications between the control tower and the Port Authority.
- Computer network: the corresponding intranet.

Internal transportation

- Internal private railway, connected to the public network.
- Underground supply lines, under the company's surveillance.
- Single surface access through a vehicular traffic road. An alternative access is available for emergencies; it would be closed in normal circumstances and made available in case of blockage of the main access.

External links

2.3.1 Risk evaluation

Risks should be evaluated in accordance with the established tables.

Anchorages and moorings

- Ship seizure and grounding against a strategic target
- Explosive laden suicide craft
- Impact of remotely fired projectile
- Explosive laden remote control craft
- Boarding, using another ship
- Divers attaching explosive charges on the hull below the waterline

Storage structures: Silos and tanks

- Impact of remotely fired projectile
- Explosive laden suicide craft against the port facility
- Explosive laden remote control craft
- Explosives attached by divers on berthed ships
- Impact on port facility using another ship

Dock water surface

- Explosive laden suicide craft
- Remotely fired projectile
- Remote control craft
- Ship grounding against the facility

Risks on mobile equipment

- Explosive laden suicide vehicle
- Explosive laden remote control vehicle
- Impact of remotely fired projectile

Limiting and access control barriers

- Explosive laden suicide vehicle
- Strike against entering or exiting persons
- Long range weapon fire against guards

Corrective Measures

Goods and infrastructures subject to higher vulnerability, and therefore to a higher risk, are fences or limiting barriers and access checkpoints in case of personal or close attack. Possible corrective measures would involve increasing allocated personnel and perimeter patrols.

Within the facility, goods with the higher risk are those in the dangerous goods area, pipe and transport racks, and assistance equipment. Integrity of this equipment depends directly on the perimeter surveillance, since the highest risk is the impact of a grenade remotely fired from the surface.

Areas and aligned windows with highest risk should be protected with a metal fence; it should be understood that long range external surveillance is beyond the responsibilities of the company being considered.

Other formalities for implementation

It is not necessary go further into the applicable particularities, since they coincide with those set in the ISPS Code; they would therefore be, to a certain extent, very theoretical. A possible specification for a fictitious port facility has been highlighted, although very likely coinciding in whole or in part with an actual case, as working margins are tightly limited.

2.4 Partial conclusions

The following items have been identified:

- Design, procedures and contents similar to the available emergency plans for ships.
- However, risk assessment models are used, which, to this date, are not used for ships.
- Much larger operating and personnel organisation.
- Largely dependent on assistance from outside the port public domain, it being wide and diverse.
- As for ships, it is mainly applicable to safety items.
- Strong organisational chart for the Chain of Command on emergencies; possible problems due to the lack of a Single Command.
- Need for consistency and harmonisation between IEP's and EEP's.

3 Security team

3.1 Current crews in national ships

One of the consequences of evolution in the maritime industry has been a downsizing of crews, basically based on the Gross Register Tonnage (GRT), and trimmed depending on the technological advances it may exhibit.

This balance, otherwise unstable with regard to its strict definition, is the result of applying the Ministerial Order on the Indicator Chart of Minimum Crews, as well as several Resolutions from the Merchant Marine Directorate General, under the request of the interested shipping companies, having been reviewed on a case by case basis, particularly considering the type of sailing (Northern Europe, high seas, etc.), type of engine (totally or partially attended, level of automation, etc.), percentage of multi-purpose sailors in the total crew.

Composition of average crews, both maximum and minimum depending on these applications, which may be considered as normal in our dry bulk and polyvalent fleet, were and may still be deemed as acceptable, according to the crew rolls consulted for a research study[1]:

- For 500 to 1 000 GRT ships:
    - Maximum 10:
        - 2 Deck officers
        - 3 Engine room officers
        - 3 Deck personnel
        - 2 Catering personnel
    - Minimum 8:
        - 2 Deck officers
        - 2 Engine room officers
        - 3 Deck personnel
        - 1 Catering personnel

- For 1 001 to 1 600 GRT ships:
    - Maximum 11:
        - 2 Deck officers
        - 2 Engine room officers
        - 3 Deck personnel
        - 2 Engine room personnel
        - 2 Catering personnel
    - Minimum 10:
        - 2 Deck officers
        - 2 Engine room officers
        - 3 Deck personnel
        - 1 Engine room personnel
        - 2 Catering personnel

---

[1] "Merchant Ship Crews and their Impact on Operating Costs", CETEMAR, 1989.

- For 1 601 to 4 000 GRT ships:

  Maximum 15:
  3 Deck officers
  3 Engine room officers
  5 Deck personnel
  2 Engine room personnel
  2 Catering personnel

  Minimum 10:
  3 Deck officers
  3 Engine room officers
  3 Deck personnel
  ---
  1 Catering personnel

- For 4 001 to 10 000 GRT ships:

  Maximum 16:
  4 Deck officers
  3 Engine room officers
  6 Deck & engine room personnel
  3 Catering personnel

  Minimum 14:
  4 Deck officers
  2 Engine room officers
  5 Deck & engine room personnel
  3 Catering personnel

- For 10 001 to 25 000 GRT ships:

  Maximum 26:
  4 Deck officers
  4 Engine room officers
  8 Deck personnel
  6 Engine room personnel
  4 Catering personnel

  Minimum 22:
  4 Deck officers
  4 Engine room officers
  7 Deck personnel
  4 Engine room personnel
  3 Catering personnel

- For ships above 25 001 GRT

  Maximum 29:
  4 Deck officers
  4 Engine room officers
  8 Deck personnel
  9 Engine room personnel
  4 Catering personnel

  Minimum 24:
  4 Deck officers
  4 Engine room officers
  8 Deck personnel
  5 Engine room personnel
  3 Catering personnel

This same classification, based on the ship GRT, shows a composition lower by 3 to 6 crew members, depending on the class, when applied to other international fleets, although this is mainly due to the high level of automation and technology that is incorporated on the general equipment in any of the departments of the ship.

3.2 Influence of personnel and action plans

Several assessment methods are available in the productive and service processes for those parameters that may be present and therefore influence the final outcome of an emergency, both from its initial stage through the final stage, this outcome being measured by the level of success attained.

In terms of the human team that acts in emergencies, this has been widely analysed through several assessment methods, mostly for cases of fire, which in the majority of cases are the main concern in any emergency, and require the best coordination possible of the task group through the action plans.

The following have been selected from amongst them:

3.2.1 E.R.I.C. method

This method takes into account the importance of the training and qualification level of the company's (the ship's) internal personnel, if available.

The coefficients used in the method are:

For an in house task service	0.65
No in house service	1.00

This turns into a very positive evaluation (33 %) for companies with in house personnel that is specialised in the safety of their production system.

Considerations on the method and its application to a ship

It should be noted that an in house task group involves a significant level of knowledge, when compared to the remainder of the personnel that may normally assist them, which can almost compare to that of the professional personnel in an official emergency body (except for the lack of a larger experience, which is nevertheless compensated by the more extensive knowledge of internal circumstances and conditions).

It becomes obvious that this availability scores high, since it constitutes an effective component for an immediate response with full knowledge of the situation.

A ship has this personnel available, specialised by type, transit and cargos, and, in principle, they should contribute a significant level of safety to her integrated system.

3.2.2 M. Gretener's method

This method addresses the availability of personnel that is ready for the task, without considering individual actions that may develop in such circumstances, as its approach is general, taking into account the permanent availability of professional personnel that is external to the company, this being easily understandable when on shore.

However, it offers a distinction between the company's professionals, a very interesting classification regarding their numerical composition that links perfectly with a possibility criterion regarding the possible and the desired control of the emergency.

Filtered levels for a ship would be:

Level 1   Task group composed of at least 10 people trained for the emergency type.
Level 2   Company safety body composed of at least 20 people, with an organisation of its own.

Depending on the ship's tonnage, both circumstances may even concur, fitting therefore into a deep organisation of action in internal emergencies.

Considerations on the method and its application to a ship

For this parameter, relevant to the "company specialist" concept, the same considerations as for the E.R.I.C. Method may be applied.

Nevertheless, the criterion contributed by the level in which the available personnel may be classified represents and additional possibility for the overall approach to the emergency and its effectiveness.

This is directly related to and supported by the *Indicator Chart of Minimum Crews and Current Crews in National Ships*.

3.2.3 K.A.O. method

Although this method has little application to a ship, it nevertheless shows certain criteria that allow a more specific approach to the parameter for its consideration on ships.

These considerations refer to the relationship existing between human teams and the available equipment, as follows:

- When in house teams are numerically sufficient, but there is no knowledge on the use of emergency equipment, the teams should be considered as insufficient.

- If in house teams are sufficient and they know how to use the equipment, but they are not organised because a specific emergency plan is not available, these are partially sufficient teams.

Considerations on the method and its application to a ship

The criteria provided by this method allow adjusting the human component capability for the task more tightly, since it has been proven by and large that even having available the equipment required by conventions, in many cases it has not been appropriately or most effectively used.

For this reason, such criteria should be taken into account for quantifying the parameter and, particularly, for insisting on the need of having available the appropriate equipment to the types of risks that are inherent to the ship, under the principle that not everything is good for anything, but rather that which is specific and has been assessed, therefore a maintenance programme being required, not only for the operation of the ship herself, but also for all the safety equipment, in order to attain the best preventative, security and action results in emergencies.

3.2.4 Summary of the personnel and action plan parameter

This parameter depends on the number of crew members available, on their knowledge and on the internal organisation that stems from an approach to the actual needs of the ship for an appropriate action in case of emergency.

The minimum number of crew members for the national fleet is defined between 8 and 25, depending on tonnage and other details as stated in Section *Current Crews in National Ships*; its upper limit could decrease to about 20, if applied to ships under other flags.

Minimum needs for human resources for a normal action in case of fire, this being the case for the maximum availability of human resources, in order to provide certain assurance of safety to their components, as well as to ensure secondary operations supporting the overall operation, would be of 8 people, with the following roles:

- · 4 people to handle 2 hose lines and carry out rescue operations.
- · 1 person to support the former for communications, valves, etc.
- · 1 person to direct the firefighting group operations.
- · 1 person to control the facilities.
- · 1 person to control the ship and the surroundings.

This detail coincides with the minimum crew that may be expected in any ship, whatever her tonnage, when related to another aspect of the emergency, namely the time for executing tasks.

However, considering the higher degree of control that may be exerted on a fire on a low tonnage ship, a higher percentage of average crews with about 16 members, and the need for commanders with a more extensive knowledge in order to direct the operation successfully, it would seem appropriate, in order to proceed with the approach used for the parameters that should be quantified, to set some percentages of trained crew members, based on which the actual condition of the ship would be penalised.

This should generate a positive reaction in those responsible for personnel (the ship owners), so that they foster their crews to attend training courses, in order to normalise the current deficient situation, since meetings, information and sometimes training sessions and onboard drills are not always sufficient to match the evolution of tactics and procedures and the training on simulated cases, much closer to reality, that may be reproduced in suitable onshore facilities.

If availability of action plans is considered, lack of organisational planning becomes apparent for most of the many cases that may happen on board any ship.

In this respect, a ship has the *Indicator Chart of Minimum Crews*, a document stating the functions allocated to each crew member, in a generic and basic manner, in accordance with the most frequent causes of marine accidents, without a direct application to specific cases for each one of them. Should a real emergency occur, improvisation of tasks fits within the most basic schemes, with an eventual loss of time, divergence or repetition of roles, reduced effectiveness and high risk of not controlling the emergency.

On one of our most modern ships, which also has one of the highest risk ratings due to her cargo, broad and unspecific roles such as *"prevent ignition, stop effluent, contain fire, evaluate situation, direct, assist, etc."* are allocated to officers in charge, or such as *"assist, responsible for detecting leaks, under charge of, additional equipment, etc."* to the remainder of the crew, all of them requiring a higher level of detail and specificity in order to avoid doubts, hesitation or inappropriate actions that may need subsequent correction, etc.

These details may only be defined if previously analysed through simulations in which the personnel is acquainted with the different variables, so that in the real case the surprise may be smaller and decisions may follow a logical and known order, leaving improvisation aside; at the same time, the roles being available in writing, they can be analysed at any time, and knowledge may be updated as practical experience may require it.

The formal method that allows their execution are the so called *Action Plans*, which should be used in the periodic drills that ships are obliged to complete, by which every crew member should undergo a firefighting[2] drill once a month as a minimum.

The purpose of the action plans is to qualify the crew so that in a real case they may gain control over the emergency in as short a time as possible, with minimum damage, thus ensuring ship integrity.

They should comprehend a theoretical section, in which specifics of the subject are presented, in combination with visits to the locations referred to; appropriate tactics and procedures for the subject case shall be included.

The practical section may be done with or without prior notice. With these drills, errors or negative aspects are corrected, as required by the simulated case. After the drill, all participants should debrief to analyse impressions, details and modifications resulting from the plan.

The level of the drill should adapt to the average level of knowledge of the crew for a trouble free comprehension by the majority; complexity should be increased up to the highest possible level of reality.

For an appropriate design of the action plan, the following data require formalisation:

1. Since multiple situations may occur, those of highest risk and concern are selected previously, and they are combined with the desired level of difficulty. A comprehensive complex plan should include several emergency consequences, starting from an initial one, followed always by rescue and succour of injured people, with application of first aid, continuing with collateral consequences in secluded areas, their control, control of spillages, and any others that appear as logical and possible in relation to the type of ship.

2. Establishment and selection of environmental conditions as severe as possible, in order to expose weaknesses in the plans, data that will, in any emergency, require definition, and which will differ from the ideal conditions where paper "holds anything" and creates a false security that leads only to the crude and disastrous reality.

---

[2] Rule 18, Chapter III of SEVIMAR/83.

3. Specifying locations that will be affected and therefore products and materials present. Based on this, fixed systems, portable equipment, watertight doors, section limits, resistant divisions, etc.

4. Defining the number of crew members and their distribution within the various groups that may be created, matching the indications in the organisational chart.

5. Controlling timings in the drill case, as well as any incidents that may be detected during its course, correcting some on the run and leaving others to develop freely in order to expose more clearly inappropriate actions.

6. Analysing everything that has happened with everyone's participation, drafting final results on schematics, so that they may serve as guidelines for further drills and as source for real cases that may occur in the same location and due to the same cause.

3.3 Influence of time and difficulty in acting

The parameter related to the impact of the estimated necessary time for gaining control during a task action follows a similar procedure to that of the impact of the number of crew members; it refers mostly to the most extreme cases considered for emergency types, which generally encompass the highest number of factors that will require attention and control.

3.3.1 ALPHA factors method

Values provided by the quantification method for the parameter (influence of the time required for initiating task actions) are represented by factor α_5, related in turn to the training level of the participants in the task.

These values are:

- For non professionals (little experience and knowledge)   0
- For in house specialised personnel   −7

as long as they act within a period of time not more than 10 minutes.

In other words, it scores high on the availability of personnel with specific knowledge on the risk associated with the ship due to her type or traffic, thus guaranteeing task effectiveness.

This method provides α values for responses of no more than 5 minutes or more than 20 minutes, which, nevertheless, are deemed highly insufficient in order for the team to attend fully protected and equipped, or excessive, due to the constant presence on board, whatever the ship length being considered.

Through factor α_6, the method shows how special conditions and circumstances weigh on a task.

The procedure consists in calculating the minutes considered necessary for overcoming difficulties, until reaching an action directly applicable to the control of the emergency, *i.e.*, including certain parallel operations for ensuring success, or for operating equipment or mechanisms that may assist in controlling the event.

Every 2 minutes of this necessary period are penalised with a +1 value. Therefore, it will be sufficient to know the task in detail, to quantify it in minutes and to divide it by 2. The value obtained is α_6.

Considerations on the method and its application to a ship

The method does not define a number of possibilities, as each calculation is the result of the time that should be used; for example, it could happen that a task in a cargo area with direct access in the initiation of the emergency would take 10 minutes, resulting therefore in a coefficient of +5; or that, in the same cargo area, but with access through a scuttle, the task might take from 30 to 40 minutes, resulting in a coefficient of +20; or that a task in the engine room would require 20 minutes, resulting in a coefficient of +10.

Task difficulty may always be reduced to a minimum, depending on the best training of the participating personnel, and on the availability of equipment that compensates for human limitations.

3.3.2 K factor method

This method, along with many others, defines as a good task that which may be initiated in less than 10 minutes after the event is known; therefore, when it happens within this period of time, it scores with a factor value of –5.

A task within a 15 to 20 minutes interval is considered to be normal, and scores a neutral zero value.

If any difficulty is present during the task, due to access or other causes, it is penalised with a factor, its value ranging from 0 to +3.

Considerations on the method and its application to a ship

It is applicable to the same extent as for the α factors method, according to the respective discussion.

3.3.3 G. Purt's method

It applies, in a similar way to the former methods, an (L) coefficient that corresponds to the time required for initiating the task; for our purpose, this takes a value of 1 for task times of 10 minutes (with in house professionals).

Considerations on the method and its application to a ship

It is applicable to the same extent as for the α factors method, according to the respective discussion.

3.3.4 E.R.I.C. method

This method sets some weighing coefficients, depending on the type or level of knowledge and on the expected time for the task.

The values for these coefficients have a very low specific weight under the more normal conditions, for their eventual onboard application; for a task below 10 minutes (the usual case) and a body specialised as would be desirable (that of the ship), values are 0 and –0.1, increasing from here on as knowledge level decreases or task time increases.

3.3.5 M. Gretener's method

As with the previous method, the normalised value for the coefficient (s_4) is 1 for task times below, in this instance, 15 minutes. However, it is also related to the participation of highly specialised professionals, which prevents a determination of its value.

Considerations on the method and its application to a ship

In any case, it becomes obvious that the most important thing in any method, regarding task time, is that it should stay between 10 and 15 minutes, rather than the type, class or level of the participants in the task; this consideration becomes further justified when taking into account emergency evolution.

In cases affecting ships, response times fall within the acceptable limits, or are even shorter, from 5 to 10 minutes; therefore, the coefficient that is used will only be influenced by the knowledge of the crew.

3.3.6 Summary of the personnel and action plan parameter

In order to establish more accurately the necessary time for the crew members to be ready for carrying out an effective task, the worse case should be considered, coinciding with nighttime, when only the usual bridge and engine room night watches can be counted on; this means there is only an officer and a subordinate in each department, unless the extreme situation of having a ship with unattended engine would be the case, when only the two persons on the bridge would be on watch.

The response time breakdown would be:

Personnel on watch (officers)

- Detecting the emergency type and assessing the situation, relating it to the rest of the ship   1 minute
- Making decisions and giving out the required orders to the subordinate assisting him/her   1 "

- Issuing alarm signals and establishing internal communications as required 1 "
- Actions related to safety equipment 2 "

              Total time: 5 minutes

Personnel on watch (non officers)

- Time for receiving orders 2 minute
- Getting to the equipment stowage area 2 "
- Getting equipped for the task 1 "
- Getting to the established mustering point 2 "

              Total time: 7 minutes

Personnel off duty

- Waking up and interpreting the alarm signal 1 minute
- Dressing the minimum 1 "
- Getting to the equipment stowage area 2 "
- Getting equipped for the task 1 "
- Getting to the established mustering point 2 "

              Total time: 7 minutes

Depending on times required by both officers and subordinates on watch for initiating the operations for controlling the emergency, it may be said that within the first 5 minutes significant tasks may be already executed, and within the 2 following minutes field operations may be initiated that are required in order to ensure control positions. A very well trained crew may reduce these times by 1 or 2 minutes, although allowance should be made for small problems that may appear after the alarm signal, which will have to be compensated for with some additional time for their resolution; therefore, 7 minutes is a time that may well be assumed as normal.

Furthermore, if the part that may be applied to each emergency type is considered, depending on the difficulties that the task may pose, each ship will show her peculiarities that differentiate her from others, the same as shape and size do; therefore, these aspects need to be compensated for by a higher degree of specialisation of the crews, aimed at the ship.

3.4 Crew level on security training

Responsibility for security enters the civil and labour scopes, with hardly any adaption time to new approaches.

This situation is unthinkable in any other industrial and/or tertiary activity, as well as that personnel should assume security responsibilities.

From the dawn of navigation, merchant ship crews were harassed by pirates; they saved the day with cunning and craftiness, applying deceit and dissuasion, like painting black squares that, from a distance, would resemble the gun ports of a warship, rather than looking like a civil ship for transport; in any case, it they were caught, if they lost the cargo or even the ship due to an armed attack, they had no further responsibility than having done all they could.

With the ISPS Code coming into force, and the creation, amongst others, of the position of Ship Security Officer (SSO), responsibilities may now be demanded from such position.

Currently, the crew should not only seek to survive those actions considered in the ISPS Code (many of which are typically related to terrorist strikes), but also assume the load of responsibility and consequences.

Questions arise as to how to achieve this, and with what means to attain effectiveness in such handling and responsibility.

It is quite well known that criminal actions at most times precede preventative actions, since those seeking to do harm use creativeness and invention in order to design how to proceed, changing every time the method to be exposed.

Ship security depends no longer on its own preventative procedures, since criminal actions mostly do not originate in the marine medium, but rather on shore, while security risk control does not depend only on the measures set in the Ship Security Plan (SSP), but responsibility for it does.

The vast amount of parameters that play a role in security and their great variety exceeds the risks of maritime safety accepted so far.

Safety has always used training in order to address those cases of novelty and, at the same time, need, as they have arisen with time, particularly in recent years.

In this respect, the following proceedings and training subjects are worth noting:

- Resolution MSC.66(68) of 4th June, 1997, in force since 1st January 1999, approval of amendments to STCW, 1978, as amended.
- Ro-Ro Passenger Ship Crews. Training on Multitude Control, Emergency Management and Human Behaviour.
- Resolution A.855(20) of 27th November, 1997, on applicable standards for onboard helicopter facilities.
- Resolution A.865(20) of 26th November, 1997, on minimum training requirements for personnel nominated to assist passengers in emergency situations on board of passenger ships.
- In Spain, Order MFOM/2296/2002 of 4th October, 2002, which regulates training programs and professional degrees for bridge and engine room sailors for the merchant marine, and specialty certificates.

- Specialty courses:

  - Basic training
  - Advanced firefighting
  - Survival crafts and rescue boats (excluding speedboats)
  - Rescue speedboats
  - General operator of global maritime distress and safety system
  - Restricted operator of SMSSM
  - Tanker familiarisation
  - Oil tankers
  - Gas tankers
  - Chemical tankers
  - Basic on passenger ships
  - Passenger Ro-Ro ships and passenger ships other than Ro-Ro
  - Automatic radar plotting aids (ARPA)

To these should be added those subjects that are prescribed by the ISPS Code; due to their newness and the scarce references available, the model courses recommended by the IMO may be mentioned:

- Following Model Course 3.19 (SSO), the grouped objectives would be:

  - Inspecting and supervising the SSP implementation
  - Coordinating loadings, supplies, personnel
  - Proposing modifications to the SSP, etc. together with the CSO
  - Maintaining onboard security and surveillance
  - Ensuring appropriate crew training
  - Reporting security events, coordinating with PFSO
  - Ensuring equipment operability

- If Model Course 3.19 (SSO) is followed, teaching parameters would be:

  - Minimum duration: 14 hours (2 days)
  - 11 units of 1 to 1.5 hours, *e.g.*:
  - Weapon detection, dangerous substances (1.5)
  - Actions required for each of the three levels (1)
  - Preparation of drills, simulations, etc. (1)
  - Protection equipment (1)
  - Introduction (historical background) (1.5)

- Considering the recommendations of Model Course 3.20 for the Company Security Officer (CSO):

  - Minimum duration: 18 hours (3 days)
  - 11 units of 1 - 1.5 - 2 - 2.5 hours, *e.g.*:
  - Weapon detection, dangerous substances (2.5)
  - Actions required for each of the three levels (1)

- Preparation of drills, simulations, etc. (2)
- Protection equipment (1)
- Introduction (historical background) (1.5)

• When considering Model Course 3.21 for the Port Facility Security Officer (PFSO), it can be seen that it is very similar to the two above, changing ship for port where appropriate.

Generally, all courses (3.19, 3.20 and 3.21) show the same bibliography and references, and also the statement that, at the time of printing, there are no recommended publications on the subject.

3.4.1 Crew functions according to the ISPS Code

- The Officer of the Watch shall assist the Captain/SSO as required.
- Officers shall be knowledgeable of the SSP, in order to apply it to what it may concern.
- Subordinates shall carry out security tasks as required.

In turn, the crew shall be knowledgeable of:

- Current ship security level.
- In emergency, shall follow instructions from the SSO.
- Shall participate actively in drills and exercises, as set on the SSP.
- Shall be watchful, and report any event.
- Shall pay attention during training lectures related to the SSP.

3.5 Partial conclusions

Seeing the training requirements defined in the Code, when comparing them to the minimum requirements, which generally are assumed as maximum, it is worth considering the following questions:

- If for so many years training, making aware, and increasingly technical and sophisticated care has been given towards occupational risk prevention and accident reduction, and nevertheless this has not prevented accidents from occurring, how can appropriate crew training be ensured, starting from minimum, little operative knowledge, with such short teaching times?
- How can confidence created by a properly executed job be passed on to the crew, thereby achieving their full participation, when there are more doubts than knowledge?
- How can positive results be attained when facing real security cases that require such a complex resolution?
- How can SSOs maintain psychological control and over their state of mind, if their responses do not prevent or minimise the tragic and traumatic consequences of a security related event?

In any preventative approach, particularly in those applied to safety, the worst belief is to reckon that one is safe, and it is possible that a large number of responsible persons (SSOs), having undergone 14 hours of training, may have assumed overnight (from 24:00 hours of 30th June, 2004 to 00:00 hours of 1st July, 2004) full responsibility on security.

Although it may be alleged that we are at the beginning of implementation, and that, of course, everything leaves room for improvement, still a mariner's responsibility reaches 100 % since the ISPS Code came into force; faced with a problem with such a large, unpredictable scope, training on security cannot consist on merely covering the minimum requirements for possessing a certificate and continuing to operate the ship.

An innovative spirit must be created, by providing specialised publications and more comprehensive contents, in accordance with the magnitude of the risks addressed by security functions, and taking into account the circumstances under which the activities develop, which, unlike other activities, prevent from fleeing danger and force performing in a tragic play, from the beginning of the event to its conclusion, following an unconvincing script.

Therefore, intensive work is required, by providing practical solutions that result from a wide comprehension of the theoretical principles that have the greatest bearing, which may in turn allow to progress from "paper that holds anything" to the closest, as well as safe, reality, towards an effective management according to security's prescriptions.

With respect to action, crew size and response, the following is observed:

- Onshore industry provides criteria for assessing the response capability, allowing the quantification of the degree of effectiveness.
- Theoretically, a ship has a very advantageous position, in terms of effectiveness of emergency tasks from the first call, warning or alarm.
- Size of task brigades for controlling any emergency is limited to the ship's role, which varies highly depending on tonnage; considering that in every emergency type, consequences of different natures will occur, small deadweight ships have their success very limited, whatever the task may be.
- The aforementioned circumstance limits, firstly, the contents of each crew member's functions, and secondly, the implementation of the safety and security plans themselves.
- Such shortcomings may be covered in part, either by a high level of crew training, or with the incorporation of a larger number of sophisticated equipment.
- Training and level of knowledge are not difficult to attain, while being equipped with certain technologies may prove impossible (financially), the lower the deadweight of the ship.

4 Organisation of emergencies on board

4.1 Organising an emergency

In the previous chapter the importance allocated to both the number of available crew members to participate in an emergency, and the response time to initiate and to attempt closing an undesired situation, was justified.

For a long time, organisation of emergencies on board has been standardised by means of the Chart of Duties and Instructions for Emergency Cases, or Indicator Chart, or Organisational Chart.

This chart shows the functions allocated to each crew member for the various maritime accidents, mainly referred to fire, stranding, abandonment, and others, depending on the type of ship and the transit she operates, as may be the case with chemical tankers, for which this should be extended to spillages, toxic gas leaks, etc., as the Captain of the Ship Owner may deem necessary to include, towards the safety of the crew and of the asset the ship represents and constitutes.

In this manner, the procedures to be followed are established and recorded; in most cases, they are extremely brief in content, casting an image of simplicity that does not correspond with reality when the emergency occurs; therefore, a large part of the crew community have resolved that papers hold anything, and that in most cases, when the application to emergency situations has become necessary, it has been proved that it was mostly inappropriate, thus creating a loss of confidence in the value of the document.

Training delivered in the strict sense of contents, explained and presented in the most realistic terms, while seeking the involvement of the attendees when they find themselves introduced into the emergency, generates radical changes in crew members' aptitudes and attitudes, until reaching conviction and acceptance of their respective responsibilities.

4.2 Synthesis of emergency actions (bridge officers)

Without pursuing an extreme rigidity in presenting those actions required from part of the crew, namely the Captain and the Deck Officers, some contents are detailed, extracted from real ships in full operation.

4.2.1 General

When an emergency is detected, alarm bells are activated. The Officer of the Watch at the bridge contacts the personnel on watch in the engine room, in order to place the engine in alert. The Captain moves to the bridge and, once the emergency type has been defined, the personnel assembled at the mustering point are informed. The Captain delivers the due orders to initiate the response; the personnel proceed to cover their posts, which have been previously defined, together with their duties, in the organisational chart of each ship.

Furthermore, there is usually in each cabin an individual card with specific instructions for the crew member occupying it. Excess personnel remain at the mustering point, waiting for orders.

Personnel teams are made up, which normally consist of a *Team* or *Emergency Brigade*, composed of selected personnel from among the officers, foremen and subordinates, who are supported by persons who have special tasks assigned to them. There is also a *Support Team* or *Auxiliary Brigade*, composed of the remainder of the personnel, excluding those on watch (these will stay at their posts until relieved). The duty of this brigade is to assist the emergency brigade, ensuring the supply of the necessary materials and carrying out supplementary tasks such as: closing venting lines, skylights, watertight doors, assisting and moving injured persons, ensuring communications with the emergency brigade by means of two way radioelectric sets.

If during an emergency, the Captain deems necessary to have all the non essential personnel to abandon ship, the emergency team should remain on board, in order to act as required. Presence of cadets on board is totally random, and they cannot cover a specific post, therefore their roles will be those assigned to them by their Captain or officer.

4.2.2 Stranding

In case of involuntary stranding, the Officer of the Watch at the deck will order the engines to be stopped, and will warn the Captain. In case of imminent stranding, the Captain should manoeuvre and apply all available means in order to avoid stranding or minimise its effects. If this is not possible and the ship is to ground, therefore without manoeuvring possibilities, the engine should be stopped and the hazard signal sounded, in accordance with SOLAS. The Captain is fully responsible for the ship, and should keep to his/her post at the bridge. The First Officer, in charge of the reconnaissance brigade, shall carry out the first inspection, which will consist in: a visual inspection, making sound all cargo and fuel tanks, all compartments adjacent to the sea in order to ensure their integrity, comparing ballast tank soundings to recent ones to check for possible leaks, and any heeling should be recorded and included in the assistance report. Furthermore, damage extent should be verified, if impact is not in an engine area. The Captain should be briefed, and any necessary action in order to face damage and stop water intake should be initiated.

After assessing the cause for stranding, determining the hull areas in contact with the ground and evaluating the effects of wind, current and tide, the Captain should calculate the impact of damages on ship stability and resistance, prior to ordering a weight redistribution.

The Chief Engineer, on hearing the emergency signal, should order the shutdown of essential services and report to the Captain propulsion, steering, electric power, bilge levels, and should also seek to restore all possible services.

If the impact point is within engine areas, the Engine Room Officer should take charge. The Chief Engineer should take charge over the bailing devices and of reporting to the Captain.

The Captain should then initiate the corresponding procedure, deciding either to manoeuvre to regain floatability or consolidate the stranding. Depending on the result, the Captain will resume voyage to the destination port, or will initiate the towing or salvage procedure.

The Captain should also warn the company and the authorities, all being recorded in the Navigation Log.

The following hazards should be taken into account, therefore taking measures to prevent them:

- Ship breakage due to the action of the sea
- Pollution hazard
- Fires due to the spillage of flammable substances and uncontrolled ignition sources

The Captain should also assess the possibility of environmental damages. If the assessed risk of subsequent damage to the ship is higher for attempting to restore floatability by her own means than for remaining stranded until professional assistance is provided, the Captain should seek to maintain the ship in that position, as long as the assessment of the situation makes this advisable.

4.2.3 Boarding/collision

If the ship is in alert situation due to a possible collision, the Captain should manoeuvre and use every visual and acoustic signal in order to avoid collision or minimise its effects. If this were not possible, after the collision, the Captain, being the main responsible person, should take command. The alarm signal should be called, and engines stopped. First Deck and Engine Room Officers should make up a damage assessment team, together with a deck crew member and an engine room crew member; this team should carry out a visual inspection, searching for injured people, people fallen overboard, and eventual water ingress, fires, etc. The team will report to the Captain, who should evaluate the damages. The Captain should communicate with the other ship, and separation of the two should be addressed, if such manoeuvre was required.

Apart from calculating the effect of damages on ship stability and resistance, if the impact is on the engine area, the Engine Room Officer should take over. The Chief Engineer should take charge over the bailing devices, and keep the Captain informed. Emergency situation should be called, due to the possibility of fire or ship abandonment. The Captain should report to the company about the situation of the ship and her damages. And then the Captain should make the final decision.

4.2.4 Abandon ship

This decision is made by the Captain, and should be carried out in the shortest time possible, and with the minimum accidentability. Prior to abandonment, a number of preparations should be made. The

Captain should sound the alarm. All personnel, except those keeping watch, should assemble at the mustering point. The Captain should issue verbally the abandon ship order. A general radio call is broadcast, stating such action as well as the position of the ship, requesting immediate assistance. The crew should act in accordance with the Organisational Chart of the ship. The Chief Engineer, prior to abandoning the ship, should shutdown engines, boiler, equipment, close fuel valves, fans, etc.; furthermore, he should leave the ship in the best possible condition for abandonment or, if it were possible, for getting aboard again or for towing.

When the Captain orders to do so, rafts, life rings, floating materials, etc., should be eased. All personnel should move to the assigned boat, where the First Officer should check that everybody has assembled at the mustering point with the appropriate attire, and life jackets properly worn. Then the boat should be appropriately unlashed and checked. Painters should be secured, davits operated to the boarding deck, and personnel boarded.

The Captain, who should be the last to abandon the ship, should use the rescue boat and carry the radiobeacon, radar transponder and GMDSS radiotelephone. The Captain should have collected the Patent of Navigation, the Crew List and the ship's documentation.

Once on water, details should be reported by means of the salvage equipment, in order to facilitate search and recovery. It should be ensured that survival measures aboard rafts are complied with. A personnel headcount should be obtained, checking their physical condition and assisting those in need. The Captain should assign roles to everyone aboard.

Ship abandonment and rescue boat

Safety measures:

- Wear all clothing, including footwear and some type of head covering to avoid sunstroke.
- Non inflatable life jackets should be fastened tightly onto the body. When height is over 10 metres, or there is oil in flames on the surface, the life jacket should be thrown overboard first. Inflatable life jackets should not be inflated until in the water; this type of jacket should be inflated as soon as the person is in the water or away from the flames.
- Weather permitting, abandon the ship overboard using a rope, ladder or net. If there is no other way but jumping, check first for people, floating materials or wreckage remains on the water.
- Never dive (head first), but jump in (feet first). Keep nose pinched with one hand, and pull life jacket down with the other hand.
- Try to abandon the ship as far away as possible from the affected area.
- Check wind direction, swim against the wind in order to dodge flames, oil or current deriving from the ship.
- When in the water, keep calm and avoid panicking. Stick to the following instructions:
    o Spare your energy by moving as little as possible and by keeping in foetal position.
    o Avoid oil patches as much as possible. If possible, protect eyes and nostrils by keeping head up or by swimming under water. After swimming under water and before coming to surface again, shake vigorously the water surface in order to remove oil, flames or any debris.

- o When in the water, keep close to other people, in order to avoid as much as possible shark attacks, and to facilitate rescue tasks.
- o If the ship sinks rapidly, swim fast and help injured people to abandon the area as soon as possible, in order to avoid suction.

Rescue boat

A ship's rescue boat is yet another means for survival in case of shipwreck. If it is used for other purposes, this may become a potential source of risk, if the appropriate safety precautions are not applied during operations. It is therefore required, for the safety of the boat and of the crew members, that the following basic precautions be strictly followed during any operation with the rescue boat:

- Life jackets should be always worn if weather conditions are unfavourable, including reduced visibility.
- Smoking or using lighters is forbidden.
- Engines should not be started if there is excessive smoke or vapours. Check for leaks, damaged pipes or loose connections. All defects should be corrected.
- If excessive leaks are observed during the engine operation, it should be immediately stopped, and the cause for the malfunction should be corrected before restarting the engine.
- A lookout should always stand at the prow when sailing in restricted waters.
- The boat crew should be appropriately trained in its handling. Circumstances permitting, it should be manned by the Second Officer and an experienced sailor.
- The rescue boat should not sail close to a berthed or anchored ship, or close to dock edges, unless this is unavoidable. Skippers should keep the boat at low speed until no there be no danger of collision with any other boat or ship that is difficult to see.
- The rescue boat should be kept at low revs when crossing with other boats that are moored to ships or docks, when sailing on waters with many boats, or when sailing close to heavy laden boats.
- Easily accessible floating life jackets should be available aboard the rescue boat for all crew members and possible castaways. Personnel boarding the boat should not exceed the number of available life jackets, except in those exceptional rescue cases in which castaway safety may call for a prompt rescue.
- When applicable, it should be ensured that the gas bottle to right the boat is in its place and charged.
- It should be ensured that fire extinguishers are in their places and charged.
- Safety devices should be kept dry at all times; if they become wet, they should be dried.
- Electrical systems should be inspected for loose connections or worn insulators prior to starting the boat, and at any time there may be any hint that these systems may be damaged. The boat should not be started until the damaged part is repaired.
- All instructions on engine and boat operation should be carefully followed and complied with.
- The boat should not be overloaded.
- The boat should not be started if bilge pumps are damaged.
- Lights prescribed by regulations should be placed on the rescue boat when sailing between sunset and sunrise, or in reduced visibility.
- All rescue boats should include fog signalling equipment, in accordance with the type of boat.

Rescue boat davits

Boat davits are exposed to the corrosive action of weather and seawater splashes. Due to this, appropriate maintenance is one of the most important safety precautions. Frequent inspections and appropriate lubrication may prevent degradation and failures leading to accidents.

Davit facilities should be inspected weekly as a minimum, to ensure that all operating parts, falls and safety devices are in proper working condition. Any defective components should be immediately reported. Safety precautions as listed and the associated checks should apply to the use of pulleys, weights, drums, hooks, etc. Particular attention should be paid to:

- Electrical components mounted at weather exposed locations
- Winch brake settings
- Excessively worn cables, or with warped or broken wires
- Bearings on strut turning supports and block lashing mechanisms
- Tightening of all bolted couplings
- Length adjustment of boat falls
- Blocks, pulleys, rollers and other moving parts

Prior to beginning any rescue boat handling operation, all non involved personnel should keep away from the area. Is should be ensured that qualified operators are present for each operation. Keep personnel aboard the boat to the necessary minimum for the lowering, hoisting and stowing operations.

When the boat is secured due to bad weather, the bowsing tackles on stays and slings should be set at the appropriate tension to avoid damaging the davit heads.

- Limit switches should not be used as stop switches.
- Proper condition of hoisting hooks should be checked prior to hoisting or lowering the rescue boat.
- Winch motor should not be energised while gravity lowering a boat.
- When lowering a boat into the water, the prow hook should always be loosened first; when hoisting the boat, the prow hook should always be fastened first.
- Extreme care should be always applied when fastening or loosening the rescue boat hoisting falls. Hands should be kept clear from blocks. Lanyards should always be used when fastening or loosening rescue boat falls.
- It should be ensured that retaining bars are withdrawn prior to hoisting the boat.
- When boat hoisting falls are unrolled with no load, winch motor should not be stopped with the brake blocking switch; the main switch should be used instead.
- Swivel shackles on hooks, cables or fibre ropes on any part of the hoisting falls are not permitted and should be removed (this is not applicable to radial or turning davits with fibre rope falls).
- Prior to and during boat hoisting and lowering, the winch cable drum cover should be opened and cable condition should be checked for proper coiling.
- When possible, boat lowering and hoisting should be done with the ship stopped.
- When using radial davits, the following safety procedures should be applied to manoeuvring fibre rope hoisting falls, in addition to general procedures for pulleys, blocks, cables, etc.:

- All hoisting falls should be inspected.
- It should be ensured that there is no overloading, and that davit and hoisting falls capabilities are not exceeded.
- Quick release hooks or appropriately secured hooks should always be used.
- No rings should be worn while handling ropes or cables.
- Prior to lowering the load, the hauling section should be tied to a cleat with one turn. While the load is lowered, it should be kept under control by holding the hauling section that goes through the cleat.
- Safety loops should be tied to the boat hoisting rings when davits turn inward or outward.

4.2.5 Fire

Any crew member detecting smoke or fire should call the alarm, reporting to the Officer of the Watch its location and seriousness. The fire alarm signal should then be called. The Captain should take over command at the bridge, and the whole crew should act rapidly, following the ship's Firefighting Plan, thus making up the firefighting, support and medical teams that should analyse fire type and extent and prepare the appropriate means of extinction.

Adjacent areas should also be inspected, seeking to avoid fire progress; if necessary, combustible materials should be removed from them. In turn, all fans and air conditioning should be stopped, and all watertight doors and scuttles closed. The ship course should be altered so that wind may have the minimum influence on the fire. Fire extinction tasks shall be carried out as quickly as possible.

Due attention should be paid to ship stability conditions and to the volume of water used for firefighting.

If the fire occurs at a location that is protected with the fixed CO_2 or Halon system, the area should be isolated, having previously checked that all personnel have left, and then the system should be triggered. Only the Captain or his substitute may order this trigger. The Officer in charge of radio communications should keep external communication equipment available, reporting the position of the ship to coastal stations and other ships, remaining throughout the emergency at the Captain's command for transmitting or issuing general distress calls as required.

Bridge watch should be maintained, and deck lights turned on if required. If applicable and possible, signals for "ship not under command" and others as required by the regulations should be exhibited. Firefighting should continue, and depending on the results of previous actions, the Captain should decide whether it can be controlled without external assistance, or whether this is required; eventually, the possible need for abandoning the ship and requesting assistance by radio should be considered. If the fire can be extinguished, cooling down adjacent areas to the affected location should not be overlooked, using fire hoses as sprayers.

Fire in the engine room

If fire starts with personnel inside, the person discovering the fire should call the alarm and try to extinguish the fire with dry powder extinguishers or, if the fire is in the electric panel, with Halon extinguishers. Doors and air intakes should be closed, and electric supply should be interrupted. If the fire is too serious, the Chief Engineer should confirm activation of the automatic fire alarm at the bridge.

Personnel should muster in the control room, where the highest rank officer should decide whether to fight the fire with hoses and foam, or whether to evacuate the chamber and use the CO_2 system. The officer should keep in contact with the bridge through the telephone, loudspeaker or walkie-talkie.

Usually, the Chief Engineer is in charge of closing the flame screens and of the main engine and generator emergency shutdown in the affected chamber. The Chief Engineer should also see to the firefighting pumps startup and select the sprinklers pump automatic startup. If the CO_2 system is used, the alarm will sound; nevertheless, it should be ensured all the same that nobody remains inside the chamber in which it will operate.

If fire starts in "unattended engine room" condition, the standby officer should not go to the chamber; in accordance with the ship's firefighting system, the corresponding emergency team will be in charge of extinguishing the fire. The team leader, assisted by the Chief Engineer, should decide on the required action.

The support team should be in charge of organising the supply of additional equipment, foam generation, fire propagation prevention measures, and evacuation of eventual injured persons. The Chief Engineer should check the emergency power unit and the emergency pump.

Fire at the accommodations

If fire starts at the accommodations, storerooms or the galley, the emergency team should consider: firefighting progress capability, breathing equipment, required protective clothing in order to access the area, and knowledge of the area layout. Water should be sprayed.

Ventilation systems and remaining equipment should be stopped. Electric circuits should be isolated. Firefighting should be carried out in pairs. Cooling down the surroundings should not be overlooked, once fire is extinguished. The First Officer should keep the Captain informed.

Fire in cargo tanks

When fire is detected, the alarm triggers; the First Officer of the Deck should lead the investigation on fire seriousness and decide how to fight the fire (hoses vs. fixed system).

The emergency team should prepare and connect hoses around the tank and cool down the deck. If the fixed system is used, the tank should be closed and the CO_2 system connected.

The Chief Engineer should in turn stop the void ventilation, if required, and disconnect electric supply to the equipment of the affected void, stop non essential services, start firefighting pumps and select automatic start for sprinkler pumps.

When at sea, if fire is external, the Captain should order to moderate engine speed (if possible) and turn the prow so that flames are directed towards free spaces.

Firefighting (documentation from another ship)

A firefighting brigade shall be designated aboard all company ships, which should be permanently renewed, depending on embarkments and disembarkments. The Captain is responsible for designating the brigade components; for this purpose, qualifications and knowledge of the crew members should be considered. The firefighting brigade should undergo weekly trainings on task development and equipment handling.

Any crew member detecting a fire should immediately call the alarm and report it to the Officer of the Watch.

Upon hearing the fire alarm signal, the whole crew should equip themselves with the protection helmet and carry out their duties as assigned in the Organisational Charts.

If the fire occurs in a closed area with an Inert Gas system, the person responsible for its activation should check previously that the area has been left by all crew members.

The three steps to be followed in case of fire are, in this order: location, confinement and extinction.

If fire occurs in an electrical panel or equipment, the first step should be to disconnect it.

When entering a confined space to extinguish a fire, the crew members should be using autonomous breathing equipment.

Prior to firefighting using an extinguishing agent, its adequacy for the type of fire should be tested.

The means of extinction to be used should be tested prior to approaching the fire.

When possible, fire should be approached from the windward side.

It should be prevented that the extinguishing agent itself should increase the fire.

The extinguishing agent should be directed to the base of the flames, with a horizontal sweeping motion if required to cover the whole base.

4.2.6 Actions in case of contact with the sea bottom

When the ship experiences unusual jerks or vibrations coming from the hull, or inexplicable movements or changes in the engine revs, it may be suspected that the ship has touched the sea bottom. Engines should be stopped and any unexpected speed reduction should be watched; charts for the area should reviewed and draught data checked.

The exact position should be obtained by fixed point delay. Presence of hydrocarbons around the hull or on the wake should be visually checked during daytime; by night, a white, absorbent cloth should be lowered. All tanks should be sounded and, if required, perforated tanks should be isolated.

4.2.7 Actions in case of hull failure

If a ship looses one or more side plates, or significant damages occur on the hull, the Captain should sound the general alarm. The crew should assemble at the allocated points. The Captain should make an estimate of the situation, and hear the opinion from the highest ranking officers.

If the ship is in imminent danger of sinking, a distress message should be sent, and the ship owner should be informed; if there is hydrocarbon spillage, the competent authorities should be informed, and the ship should be abandoned.

4.2.8 Actions in case of excessive heel

If this happens during loading/unloading, tank cleaning or bunkering manoeuvres, all operations shall be cancelled until the cause is determined. The Officer of the Watch should alert the terminal, the Captain and the officer, reporting to them about the situation, and should activate the emergency signal.

The Captain should take measures towards its corrections, by using ballast pumps, sounding and preventing pollution. If risk is present, the ship should be abandoned. If the situation is placed under control, all parties affected should be informed.

4.2.9 Engine room flooding

When the bilge high level alarm is activated, the emergency brigade, after carrying out a visual inspection, should confirm flooding to the bridge. The Captain should manoeuvre in order to reduce roll and pitch, issue the appropriate instructions to the crew, and evaluate ship stability and structural stresses.

The Chief Engineer should shutdown all non essential services. The emergency brigade should act, securing the closure of the jet chamber door, and should verify startup of bail pumps, as well as the eventual setup and installation of the portable bail pump, for the subsequent repair of the water ingress.

The Captain should report to the company and the authorities, and proceed to the destination port. The bridge should be informed if water level threatens to reach the engine flywheel. The Captain should consider the towing or salvage options. The affected chamber ventilation should be shutdown from the bridge, as well as the main engines in that chamber.

4.3 Organising emergencies at the port

If emergency alarms sound while the ship is at port, the crew members should assemble at the mustering point. The Captain and the officer in charge of radiocommunications should stay at the bridge. If the Captain is on shore, the highest rank officer should take command.

The Engine Room Officer on duty should secure water supply, additional electric power and the engine chamber. The engine room personnel on duty will stay. Supernumerary visitors or shore workers should disembark. The emergency team leader should inform the bridge and contain the emergency inasmuch as possible.

4.4 Terrorism and piracy

The objective is to prevent alien persons from boarding the ship during navigation or at port, since they may have the intention of seizing the ship or her load, or crew belongings. The regulation covering this is the *1988 Convention for the Suppression of Unlawful Acts against the Safety of Maritime Navigation*, of 1st March, 1992 (BOE No. 99). This defines the crimes of those unlawfully seizing or destroying a ship, committing acts of violence against persons on board, or threatening with committing such crimes.

The Captain of the ship is in charge for the organisation of, and compliance with, the obligations defined in the convention.

Rounds watching for stowaways, as mentioned in the convention, should be carried out with utmost care, since terrorists or pirates may hide until the moment arrives to act. There are navigation areas (anchorages and ports) that are renowned for pirate and terrorist strikes; therefore, the Captain should not leave the ladder or ropes on the side, and should lock ramps, doors, storerooms and access doors to accommodation.

The Captain should inform the crew about the danger, so that doors are kept locked. A reinforced watch should be designated, in order to keep a special watch, frequently patrolling the deck. When the ship is moored or anchored, ropes and chains should be watched for climbers.

The fact that strike operations may take place at sea with speed boats, and that any ship may be boarded should not be overlooked. If required, the watch auxiliary sailor should be posted at a location from which the whole aft deck may be watched, undertaking surveillance of the area and the bows. The side should be lit, and firefighting hoses should be ready, in order to contain strikers.

Any act or attempts by terrorists/pirates should be reported to the competent authorities and to the consignor. If terrorists/pirates succeed in entering, nobody should oppose them; the Captain and the officer should obey their demands without any delay.

N.B.: As may be observed, this ship had not implemented the ISPS Code as yet, maybe because at that date it was not mandatory.

4.4.1 Other sources

- Terrorists and pirates may board like stowaways do, in order to hide until the moment to act arrives. It is therefore very important to carry out the round for stowaways with utmost care, as mentioned above.

- There are some sailing areas, anchorages and ports that are renowned for pirate and terrorist strikes, although the latter, in particular, may appear anywhere. Therefore, when the ship is in such areas, the Captain should adopt the following precautions.
- No ladders should be left hanging on the side.
- No ropes should be left hanging on the side. If it is necessary to keep towing lines on the side, the authority should be consulted.
- Scuttles, storeroom doors and access to accommodation should be locked.
- The crew should be informed about the danger, so that all doors are kept locked.
- A reinforced watch should be designated for a special surveillance, with frequent deck rounds.
- When the ship is moored or anchored, ropes and chains should be carefully watched for climbers.
- When the ship is sailing, the Officer of the Watch should not lose sight of the stern.
- The fact that pirates/terrorists operate with speed boats and can board any ship should not be overlooked.
- If necessary, the watch auxiliary sailor should be posted at a location from which the whole aft deck may be watched, undertaking surveillance of the area and the bows.
- A distress call procedure should be agreed upon, in case such type of people would approach the ship.
- The side should be lit and firefighting hoses ready for use against eventual strikers.
- Any acts or attempts of terrorism or piracy should be reported with no delay to the competent authorities, the consignor and the safety management department.
- If pirates or terrorists succeed in boarding, nobody should oppose them; everybody, starting with the Captain, should comply to their demands with no delay.

4.5 Stowaways

The company calls attention on the fact that the risk of stowaways boarding may be present in any port of call. Even in European ports there is the risk of stowaways getting aboard, bound overseas or to countries with higher standards of living.

- In some ports, stowaways are involved with drug trafficking.
- P&I Clubs, which are greatly concerned with the solution to the problems generated by the presence of stowaways on board, have issued preventative measures against stowaway embarkments, of which the Captain will become responsible for compliance; these may be summarised as follows:
    - Keeping a permanent gangway watch.
    - Inspecting empty containers.
    - Inspecting container latches prior to loading.
    - Inspecting open, tarpaulin covered containers prior to loading.
    - Properly locking accommodation (it is a good measure to hire a port watchman).
    - Carrying out an inspection round on the whole ship prior to setting sail.
    - Requiring container sealing by the dock entrance watch; the container seal number is stated in the container receipt form that the First Officer should sign when receiving it on board.

- o Requiring from the terminal that containers making up the first layer of the deck cargo should be stowed door against door.
- o Stowing open containers in the uppermost layer.
- o Requiring in written form from the competent authority (usually the Port Police) that an inspection round should be carried out on the ship prior to setting sail.
- o Making an entry in the Navigation Log, stating that all these measures have been taken.
- o Sending the safety management department a report stating that all these measures have been taken.

When, in spite of all these precautions, a stowaway embarks and is discovered during the voyage, the following shall be done:

- Entering in the Navigation Log, with as much detail as possible, the time, place and other circumstances surrounding the discovery. The stowaway should be required to declare embarkment port and method.
- Entering in the Navigation Log an inventory of the stowaway's personal belongings and money in his/her possession when discovered; this entry should be undersigned by two crew members bearing witness, and by the stowaway if possible.
- Entering in the Navigation Log whether the stowaway carries any personal documents, as well as his apparent state of health.
- Reporting immediately the incident to the safety management department.
- Reporting immediately the incident to the consignee at the destination port.
- Writing a report to be issued to the P&I club representative, in order to activate proceedings.
- The stowaway should in no case be forced to work, neither authorised to work at his/her own request.
- The stowaway's freedom of movement should be restricted inasmuch as possible; extreme precautions should be adopted by locking all cabins, storerooms, workshops, etc.
- The stowaway's personal data should be included in the crew lists.

In general, the Captain should suspect that the stowaway is carrying a certain quantity of drugs; therefore, a thorough search of the areas to which the stowaway may have gained access during his/her stay on board should be carried out, in order to locate it.

Even when no drugs are found in the search, the Captain should record in the Navigation Log that this was done, the personnel involved and the method used.

If the search result is negative, it should be recorded in the Navigation Log that the possibility still exists of finding drugs by personnel who are more skilled in this type of searches, and that if it so happens, the drugs would be the stowaway's.

If the search result is positive, details on the finding should be recorded in the Navigation Log and reported to the consignee at the destination port and to the safety management department, who should adopt the appropriate measures.

When the stowaway disembarks, the Captain will require from him/her to sign a declaration specifying:

- that the stowaway has been properly treated, and has been provided with food and accommodation;
- that the stowaway has not been forced to work;
- that the stowaway is disembarking with all personal belongings and money that he/she declared to possess on the date he/she was discovered aboard.

If the stowaway would refuse to sign such declaration, the Captain should record this fact on the Navigation Log, together with the signature of two witnesses, who should state the truthfulness of the declaration being refused by the stowaway.

5 Principles and considerations towards a response

5.1 Response

It is important to carry out a previous investigation and an evaluation of vulnerability that may serve to identify weak points in the safety system and allow making recommendations for improvement. Such risk analysis should be carried out by a Safety Consultant who is not directly involved in the implementation of this safety. Once done, the ship owners should adopt the required measures, not falling back on their luck, but not overreacting in a way that may harm their interests.

The overall response may be thought of as composed of two distinctive elements. Any requirement regarding Maritime Safety should be divided in a preventative response and a reactive response.

Preventative aspects in any safety programme should issue from within. The industry should bear the main responsibility of insuring itself within reasonable and cautious terms and under a preventative focus.

Regarding the reactive response, as a general rule the industry should not assume the responsibility of providing a response in front of a criminal strike. The basic division of responsibilities is clear: the industry takes preventative measures, and when a reaction is required, it should be in principle the responsibility of governments to act both at a national and international level.

The issue may be also analysed from two main separation lines that divide responsibilities (see fig. 5.1):

Firstly, there is a division established on the distinction between method and motive. For criminal groups, strategic considerations will be drawn over the motives, while methods will be a reflection of the tactical needs. Maritime industry as a whole operates on a safety level in which the analysis and establishment of the method is more important than the analysis and establishment of the motive.

Secondly, there is a division between the preventative and the reactive responses.

By using these divisions it becomes possible to prepare an illustrative matrix that may assist in locating the maritime industry within the generic context of the fight against criminal violence at sea.

5.2 Strategies (motives)

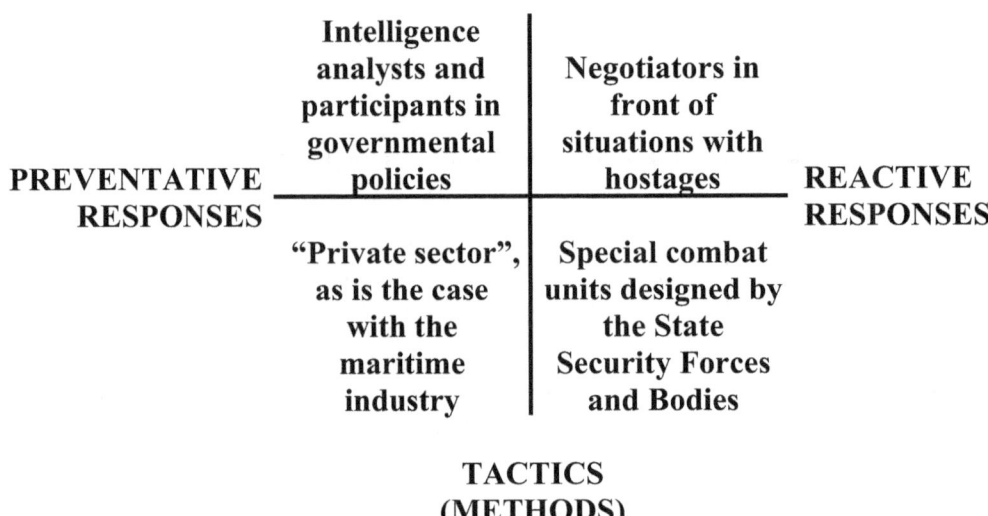

Figure 5.1

5.3 Tactics (methods)

This simple matrix shows plainly the division of responsibilities. The main reason for designing it is locating the maritime industry; as a private sector, it should be located in the lower left quarter. In other words, the main commitment of the maritime industry should be with a preventative response, essentially aimed at aborting the tactical development of criminal groups.

Besides illustrating this basic message, the matrix also fulfils another purpose in that it highlights those items that are prone to create a certain level of controversy. If it is accepted that responsibilities of groups within the private sector fall within this one quarter in the matrix, then it should be also accepted that the public sector (*e.g.*, governments and their agents) is in principle responsible for the other three quarters. It is likely that controversy will be stirred when a government interferes excessively in those areas of main involvement of the private sector, or when the action of the private sector falls within areas that are mainly under the responsibility of governments.

In the context of violence at sea, nothing illustrates the difficulties better than the question of whether merchant ships should or should not have some form of armed force or security protection available. This is an issue that is often raised within navigational circles, brought forth by ship owners who are anxious to protect themselves by their own means when no preventative measures are available that would represent an effective alternative.

There is a generic question about arming merchant ships, and another specific question about whether maritime police should or should not be deployed. These two separate questions cover two different approaches to the fact of granting merchant ships the capability of arming themselves. On the one hand, having light weapons available for use by the crew means that the private sector adopts an armed position (potentially reactive). On the other hand, presence of maritime police may be considered as an attempt to maintain the reactive response within the public scope. Maritime police could be better managed by governments than by shipping companies, and could represent an extension of the public power (presumably of the flag state, although possibly of the coastal state).

Whichever the selected method, the fact of arming merchant ships might become a two edged sword. At first instance it is a preventative response, in the sense that it is presumed that the knowledge of ships being armed would dissuade criminal groups from attacking them. If such were the case, and potential aggressors would be effectively dissuaded, then everything would be solved. The problem comes when a criminal group decides to strike notwithstanding. If this were the case, the ship would be forced to trigger a reactive response. The success of the dissuading posture depends on whether the potential aggressor is convinced that the target will set the battle. This means the target should show a disposition to fight if it became necessary.

If, on the first occasion that a strike against an armed ship takes place, the crew surrenders their weapons on becoming convinced that they do not fulfil their dissuading role, then the whole policy of arming ships as a preventative response topples. No *effective* dissuasive policy can be based on "cardboard figures".

Therefore, an almost unavoidable consequence of arming merchant ships is that, upon being attacked, they would become involved in a reactive response. The question to be addressed, both by governments and by shippers, is to what extent would that be desirable. This question goes beyond a mere consideration of immediate benefits and disadvantages.

Whichever method is applied for solving the issue of weapons on board, there is no doubt that it would be highly irresponsible advocating for untrained individuals to handle a reactive response to a criminal strike. There is only one possible option for untrained and unprepared personnel facing a ruthless criminal attack: not opposing physically, and obeying basic instructions, avoiding also any possible action that might favour the strikers.

Nevertheless, use of weapons is not totally unfavourable. Weapon availability for use by an untrained crew is one thing, while the constitution of a well trained maritime police force is another very different thing.

The idea of a maritime police force is inspired on the deployment of the air police, the task of which is both to dissuade and to respond reactively to a hijack threat. The development of forces specially trained in security of the airlines operating under their flag is known in some states and assumed in others. The FAA (Federal Aviation Administration) of the USA licensed their first air police team in early autumn of 1985. Their origin is based on the hijack of a TWA flight to Athens in the previous summer, which resulted in an American citizen murdered while the aeroplane was in the Beirut International Airport.

The American administration runs since then a number of five week courses in order to qualify these air policemen. Although this is a confidential portion of the air police program, the FAA is getting ready to reveal that trained personnel have been secretly deployed on selected international flights. As additional steps, a security coordinator might be designated for each flight, and new regulations could force airways to include security as part of their crews' training.

When the promotion of a maritime police force system is suggested, it is assumed that this concept represents a maritime equivalent of the air police program as introduced by the United States government. By using the FAA air police as a prototype, the maritime police would not be deployed on all ships, nor would it be necessarily visible or manifest. Obviously, the most similar case to an aeroplane is a cruise ship, and it is certainly possible to imagine the various states separately deploying maritime police on cruise ships, disguised amongst passengers. If this would be considered to be acceptable, there should be no objection in principle to boarding armed personnel on other types of ships, mainly merchant ships that have to sail through high risk areas, or the cargo of which is particularly interesting to the criminal community, for whatever reason.

A brief reference to the comparison between an aeroplane and a cruise ship, regarding the problem faced by the security forces when deploying, has to do with selecting the appropriate reactive response. A shootout in a plane at 30,000 foot between air police and hijackers, with passengers trying to cover themselves behind their seats, may not be the most adequate response. Likewise, a shootout on the upper deck or the recreational or accommodation areas in a cruise ship might cause a larger destruction than that originally intended by the strikers.

In every analysis for an appropriate reactive response it should be kept in mind that such response should be controlled and coordinated, when possible, with any external response. In this sense, not only a daring crew member may create danger, but also a carried away maritime policeman may cause problems. Selection of adequate candidates for training is a difficult task, whatever the selection criteria. On the one hand, it is a matter of recruiting individuals for turning them into trained licensed killers (a maritime police force would not be constituted if it was not prepared to shoot to kill when circumstances would demand it). On the other hand, these individuals trained to kill would need a perfectly adjusted sense of responsibility; such particular qualities are difficult to combine.

Obviously, comparison with air police force should not be taken too far. The maritime environment has its own specific problems, and differs on significant aspects from the air travel world. If the maritime police force proposal continues to be examined, it would be considered as an extension of the civil power of the state deploying it; therefore, some jurisdictional issues appear.

If, in general terms, a maritime police force is an extension of the civil power that deploys it, the problem is in establishing who should deploy it. Since not long ago, there is a tendency for the coastal state to control the adjacent waters, even though, for instance, it could be a responsibility of the flag state to provide the ship with maritime police coverage.

Under certain circumstances, there are more than enough arguments favouring the coastal state to assume such responsibility, as it is more knowledgeable of the local threats and has its own interest in maintaining law and order in its coastal domains. Maritime police would then be an actual extension of the coastal state's civil power, and therefore would be automatically assigned with the organisational task (the importance of controlling and coordinating the reactive response must be borne in mind) in the face of a crisis situation created by a hijack and the subsequent hostage negotiation.

However, terrorism and piracy threats in a specific area are in many cases a symptom of inland trouble. It is also highly likely that the concerned coastal state is already very busy with its internal problems, for having to enforce order in its waters.

Furthermore, measures that might be adequate in Western Europe coastal waters might not be very prudent on Africa's western coast or in the South China Sea; it all depends on the circumstances.

If the maritime police force were to be deployed by the flag state, a problem that many states would be facing (particularly western states) would be the probability that a good number of their ships would be left with no protection, unless governments using flags of convenience would facilitate agreements for taking the necessary actions. If this were not the case and the threat would show itself sufficiently serious, the tendency might be that ship owners or shippers would take justice into their own hands and would contract private security companies in order to deploy armed agents instead of officially designated maritime policemen, which would cause jurisdictional problems of their own. When coming into port, for example, there should by some sort of agreement in place between the flag state and the state the port belongs to on security and weapon possession.

If a common agreement is intended, it would be also reasonable that all maritime policemen, irrespective of their nationality, should act on similar basic Standard Operating Procedures.

Initial implementation of a maritime police force is highly problematic, and actually it is not possible to reach "rapid" conclusions on its respect. All that may be said is that, at this point in time, the global threat does not seem to ensure a wide deployment of armed security guards. A maritime police force option should not be discarded as a general concept; it could become useful in the future, and if this were the case, it would become necessary to refer to the aforementioned issues.

Another item to be addressed on the armed response subject is the legal status of armed merchant ships within the Public International Law. The above discussion focused on the consequences of deploying light weapons (personal use weapons), to be used by ship crews and by officially designated security personnel, without considering the eventual provision of military forces for the defence of merchant ships. However, for jurists the problem exists of precisely defining where the legal line should be drawn of up to which point the possession of weapons turns a merchant ship into an armed merchant ship.

The fact that the Captain of a ship should keep an automatic pistol and some ammunition clips in the safe does not mean that the ship should be considered as an armed ship; this would be absurd. Therefore, the difficulty is in establishing the condition of a merchant ship the crew of which is supplied with personal weapons, the ship herself being equipped with light weapons that may be fitted onto the deck should the need arise.

What seems to be clear is that the proposal for armament on merchant ships is such a controversial matter that it would be discouraging that the maritime industry should develop it without cooperation from governments. However, some measures exist that may be adopted by the shipping companies themselves, which would give less opportunity to disagreement between state authorities and ship owners or shipping companies. Some of them fall entirely within the competences of the maritime industry (*e.g.*, designating a Security Officer in each ship; installing TV monitoring systems; modifying internal design characteristics; introducing training on security; and implementing on board some reasonably basic, simple security measures). Notwithstanding, preparing some type of threat alert system, establishing some method to facilitate information flow (including an authentication system) and providing redundant communication systems are examples of measures that might require some governmental support and participation.

Governmental action may not be restricted to unilateral action either. Decidedly, it should include participation at international level, but one of the problems on this respect is that the high number of governments involved in preparing a practical threat response hinders a positive outcome.

The dilemma lies in that governmental participation and involvement are essential previous requirements in order to make completely effective some of the measures that have been mentioned.

The navigational industry and the maritime community have been, in general, reasonably well treated by the International Maritime Organisation (IMO) that serves them. This body may not always seem to act swiftly enough, but compared to a large number of other international organisations, it exhibits a highly commendable history. Governments have come to recognise IMO as the most appropriate international forum for addressing a wide scope of maritime matters.

While the maritime industry progresses by acting by itself in developing certain security measures, some matters may raise anytime requiring multilateral agreements. If such were the case, it would be convenient for the industry to work together with IMO and not on the contrary.

The International Maritime Organisation has played an important role in coordinating the prevention of unlawful acts at sea. Guidelines drawn by a small group of experts were unanimously approved by the Maritime Safety Committee, and constitute nowadays a valuable guide on which the industry may base itself for adopting practical preventative procedures and, where required, obtaining governmental support and participation in order to ensure measures that, due to their nature, would fall outside their competence.

It is absolutely impossible to address any matter with the purpose of preparing security instructions for the navigational industry without having beforehand some idea on what these instructions are supposed to be a response to.

In many places in the world, ships may be forced to rely on the cooperation of authorities onshore, having no control on their security mechanisms. Under such circumstances, it is important that the ship's own security measures may be as effective as resources may allow and threats may require.

Nevertheless, the industry trend is to defer or, if possible, reject any expenditure that may involve a budget increase. If consequences of criminal violence at sea seem insignificant and do not represent an immediate threat, shipping companies will hardly be ready to adopt measures against it.

If the appropriate reaction from the maritime industry is sought, the real need of reinforcing security measures should be shown.

It is therefore of the utmost importance to define the security threats for ships and, prior to proceeding with the *reasonable* cautions that shipping companies should adopt against all forms of criminal violence at sea, it is worthwhile to focus on some of their kinds.

5.4 Piracy

5.4.1 Introduction

The increase in maritime commerce and the birth of piracy are almost parallel: in fact, the practice of seizing a ship's cargo was much extended in ancient times, particularly in the Mediterranean area, where tradesmen, like the Phoenicians, concerned with salvaging their trading centres, did not hesitate to use similar methods to those of the pirates. Also in the Greek and Roman worlds the activity of sea thieves registered particularly high periods, and numerous attempts to fight it were made. During the Middle Age, piracy in Europe intensified under the conquering activities of the Vikings and the Arabs, this leading to the constitution, under the protection of the Turkish Empire, of several true pirate states, the Barbary, which lasted until the 14th century.

It was however the New World discovery and the formidable transit of valuable cargos between America and Spain that determined the development of an overwhelming pirate fleet.

The golden age of piracy may be established more or less between 1690 and 1720. For a long time, the Caribbean was a sanctuary for sea thieves, but on 1689 England and Spain became allies momentarily, and for a short period of time the impunity of pirates in that area was restrained.

They were mostly English people, ravening on the Spanish. They then moved their field of action on to the Indian Ocean, and established bases in the North American ports, where people of influence were ready to financially support capture expeditions, obtaining in return a profit share. They provided also a superficial cover of legality by issuing authorisations that, as opposed to a "Letter of Marque", were valueless.

The latter would express the authorisation by the Crown or the government for privately owned armed units (corsair ships) to operate during wartime with license to strike and seize enemy merchant ships, setting at the same time the limits to their attributions. The first "Letter of Marque" was issued in England in 1293, but it was not until the end of the 16th century that the maritime capture system became a true institution, by which the Crown received 10 % of the cargo value, while the rest remained with the corsair. Other countries adopted the same system and used it until 1856, when privateering was abolished by the Paris Declaration.

Strangely enough, corsairs have come back to the scene in Southeast Asia, where some countries find themselves incapable of watching their territorial waters. Although nowadays corsairs do not operate under any actual Letter of Marque as in the past, they seem to have permission and even cooperation from some governmental officials. Recent complaints from ship owners suggest that some components of the Chinese security forces and the Indonesian navy may be involved in piracy acts.

Nowadays piracy coexists next to us, and even though their actions are not as notorious as in the Age of Sail, they are still as cruel. Globally, theft at sea continues to be a concern for national and international authorities. Often, criminals focus on passengers on board that carry highly valuable electronic instruments and materials, which are also supposed to have enough cash on them as to encourage theft. But they are not the only ones in danger; any ship, from a small boat to a large oil tanker, may be the target of a piracy act, a violent act that involves theft or hijack of a ship, sinking her, taking hostages on board, smuggling or even privateering.

In some countries and ports, theft of personal belongings from unlocked cabins, unoccupied while the ship is berthed, are frequent; however, during the past two decades, a significant, continued increase has been observed of organised strikes against ships while sailing.

There appear to be two clear categories of pirates that operate in high seas: one of them is the professional pirate, and the other one is what could be called an amateur or "chance pirate". Their objectives are totally different; the former seeks continued gains, while the chance pirate makes use of the opportunity of stealing some cash and items that may be easily resold. However, while neither pirates, nor corsairs have ever had any claim for honesty or righteousness, and have always acted illegally, they are not particularly interested in violence for the sake of it. This does not mean that they would harbour any doubts about using it in order to attain their objectives; they may respond with firearms to any resistance to a strike, and do not usually contemplate hostages within their plans. Both groups of pirates intend a rapid strike and a clean escape, with the minimum possible turmoil. In this respect, the sea thief is no different than the land thief.

Some changes may be seen in the world piracy models in the past twenty years, this not implying a move away from the illegality of the act. Twenty years ago, the main drive for piracy was drug smuggling. Dealers often hijacked comfortable and well equipped yachts in order to carry drugs in disguised voyages from South America to Caribbean ports, even to the United States. Yacht and crew disappearances began to raise suspicions; but since drug dealing benefits were so generous, drug dealers could afford to change their operating mode, by using their own vessels. Yachts were replaced by fast and powerful motorboats that would collect at sea from a large private yacht or a small ship and carry the cargo swiftly to a safe port, in which to make a rapid and lucrative sale.

These vessels are normally bought for this precise function, and it is suspected, although it is hard to prove, that some of these powerful boats are specifically designed for such illicit enterprise. However, the risk for theft or hijack of smaller vessels has not disappeared completely, since there are still small scale dealers, or even beginners in drug dealing, that, while not invading the territories of the big cartels, carry on their small business.

Therefore, nowadays drug dealing has become just one more of the reasons for chance piracy, its main drive being mere theft.

Meanwhile, professional pirates keep on harassing both smaller vessels and large ships, and their actions span from common theft of cash, personal belongings and equipment to hijacking the ship herself and stealing her cargo. According to the *IMB Regional Piracy Centre* bulletin, during 1995, just within the January to September period, a total of 100 piracy incidents were recorded, more than during the whole of 1994. In 1996, piracy related incidents continue, and are particularly violent.

Knowing the locations where they operate will allow an advance in the planning of an eventual voyage through such areas.

Following a simple classification, there are four categories or definitions of piracy:

1. Ship administrators and Captains refer to the international law on piracy that originated from the Convention on the High Seas of 1958, which was reiterated in 1982 in the United Nations Convention on the Law of the Sea. Article 101 of the 1982 Convention establishes the definition of piracy, this being the objective of the law:

"Article 101 - Definition of piracy

Piracy consists of any of the following acts:

(a) any illegal acts of violence or detention, or any act of depredation, committed for private ends by the crew or the passengers of a private ship or a private aircraft, and directed:
(i) on the high seas, against another ship or aircraft, or against persons or property on board such ship or aircraft;
(ii) against a ship, aircraft, persons or property in a place outside the jurisdiction of any State;

(b) any act of voluntary participation in the operation of a ship or of an aircraft with knowledge of facts making it a pirate ship or aircraft.

The international community uses, through its governments, this law for fighting piracy when such acts occur within the boundaries of national jurisdiction over the sea.

2. National laws of coastal states determine and govern over piracy acts within their internal waters and territorial seas, based on the sovereignty of the coastal state over those waters. However, depending on the coastal state's particular laws, what constitutes piracy within such areas may be different to what constitutes piracy on high seas.

3. The community of maritime underwriters establishes and changes their rules on what constitutes piracy from their business' standpoint, and their definitions may vary with respect to the international law and national regulations or any other. Their system works well, except when lawsuits reach the court and they have to meet remedies as set by national and international laws, as the case was with the "Andrea Lemos" [1].

4. General public or press perception is that any act of violence in any place of the ocean is an act of piracy; nothing less may be expected from a term with such a wide background over the centuries.

5.4.2 Strike methods

Normally, but not always, strikes take place overnight, and they may be generally classified in two groups:

A) Strikes while the ship is anchored or berthed

Attacks while the ship is berthed in the port or at anchor awaiting entry into the port may be carried out by pirates climbing the mooring lines and anchor chains, or scaling the ship side from small vessels. Thieves may also enter the ship through the accommodation ladder or accesses used for bunkering or loading provisions.

---

[1] In 1978, its case caused a redefinition of piracy in the context of war clauses.

B) Strikes during navigation

While the ship is sailing, strikes are carried out by taking advantage of the dark hours of the night, from small swift vessels or sampans with six to eight people on board that approach the quarter or lie alongside the ship. Pirates board the ship throwing a grapnel tied to a line over the side wall, or climbing up a bamboo pole fitted with a hook at the top.

Another system is using a larger ship as a "mother ship", which releases several inflatable boats tied together with a line over forty metres long; they manoeuvre in order to place themselves ahead of the ship; the ship's bow catches the line and leads the boats to the sides as desired; the pirates then climb to the ship with lines or bamboo poles.

Pirate attacks against sailing ships are very frequent in Southeast Asia waters, particularly in the South China Sea, where the intersection of several countries and the existence of countries made up of many smaller islands make it easy for pirates to operate with impunity. These pirates do not appear to be organised, and are loyal to none but themselves; they operate close to international waters boundaries and in territorial waters, thus having quick access to a safe port in case of being pursued by another country's armed patrol. They will occasionally operate far from the coast, but rarely on open seas.

The bridge is their first target, since it constitutes the control and steering centre, while other pirates disperse all over the ship, intimidating the crew. It is better not to resist pirates; often, they will be armed with knives and machetes, but occasionally they will carry firearms.

The most dangerous even possess automatic weapons, typically AK-47s, easy to acquire in the arms market, particularly in the Far East.

The frightening part of the pirates' operation when assailing a navigating ship is that frequently they will tie up the crew and abandon the ship, leaving her to sail on the automatic pilot. In very busy waterways like the Malacca Strait, this creates a hazard for potential collision and environmental disaster.

5.4.3 Purposes of piracy

The main purpose of piracy is theft of cash and valuables, and particularly of the Captain's Safe, but they can also seize all type of supplies from the ship, including the content of the upper deck storerooms and the boatswain's kit. Pirates also loot those cabins in which they reckon valuables may be found, seizing any money and objects they may come across.

Although not commonly, a ship's cargo may also be part of the pirates' loot; however, it would be reasonable to think that, for this to happen, connivance of maritime authorities or local customs would be necessary.

In such a case, the ship is hijacked and taken to a "favourable" port, where the merchandise is often sold including a percentage for local officials. This purpose is frequently cloaked under the charge that the ship was discovered committing smuggling, and was therefore delivered to the custody of the authorities.

The cargo, however, simply disappears, and the ship is released later on. In other more dramatic cases, pirates have completely seized the ship, stolen the cargo and slaughtered the crew, subsequently selling the ship. The case of the "Anna Sierra" represents a clear example of such acts[2].

5.4.4 Piracy acts and armed robbery

Currently, the IMO is regularly informed by the IMB about the number and characteristics of piracy acts, but doubtlessly the actual figure is much higher. Nature of the strikes varies from those on which pirates just strip crew members from money and valuables, in addition to the ship's safe, to those cases in which the whole cargo is stolen (occasionally, also the ship). Normally, violence does not go beyond threatening, although injuries have occurred, and sometimes crew members have been murdered.

The first time the IMO was made aware of piracy acts was in 1983, when Sweden requested from the Maritime Safety Committee (MSC), the main technical body in the organisation, to investigate a situation that was described as "alarming".

The Swedish notification identified the West African coast as the most affected one. Ships anchored at sea awaiting berthing were the targets of strikes, normally overnight, by armed bandits that sailed in fast motorboats.

The International Maritime Bureau, created in 1979 by the International Chamber of Commerce (ICC), with the original purpose of fighting maritime fraud, declared that the attacks taking place in the West African coast could date as far back as 1970. In Southeast Asia, specifically in the Phillip's Channel between Indonesia and Singapore, other incidents had taken place, and some other acts had been reported in other regions like, for example, South America and the Caribbean.

After debating the matter, the MSC prepared a text draft that was subsequently submitted during the thirteenth period of sessions of the IMO Assembly (the governing body of the organisation), which was held in November 1983; it was approved and adopted as resolution A.545(13) of the Assembly.

The resolution notes with great concern the increasing number of incidents involving piracy and armed robbery, and recognises the grave danger to life and the grave navigational and environmental risks to which such incidents can give rise.

Next, the resolution "urges Governments concerned to take, as a matter of the highest priority, all measures necessary to prevent and suppress acts of piracy and armed robbery against ships in or adjacent to their waters, including strengthening of security measures".

The resolution "invites Governments concerned and interested organizations to advise ship owners, ship operators, shipmasters and crews on measures to be taken to prevent acts of piracy and armed robbery and minimize the effects of such acts". It "further invites governments and organizations concerned to inform the Organization [IMO] of action taken to implement the aims of the present

---

[2] This case was discovered because the crew was rescued alive, after being left on a raft and a pontoon. "Saga of the Anna Sierra. Planned Piracy.", *Fairplay*, 30th of November, 1995.

resolution", and "requests governments concerned to inform the Organization of any act of piracy or armed robbery committed against any ship flying the flag of their country, indicating the location and circumstances of the incident.

Finally, it requests from the IMO's Council (meeting twice yearly), "to keep this matter under review and take such further action as it may consider necessary in the light of developments."

Even though the number of piracy acts and armed robberies has decreased in some areas, in others the problem has worsened. For this reason, in November 1991, the IMO Assembly adopted a second resolution on the matter, A.683(17). It notes that "with great concern the still increasing number of incidents involving piracy and armed robbery against ships and the increasing violence against persons on board such ships."

Later on, the resolution "invites governments to increase their efforts as a matter of the highest priority to suppress and prevent acts of piracy and armed robbery". Neighbouring states are invited "to co-ordinate their actions", and urges governments to ensure that "information on incidents involving piracy and armed robbery against ships and the modus operandi of pirates and armed robbers is made available to ships transiting their waters". Governments are urged "to encourage ships entitled to fly their flag to ensure that information on threats or attacks by pirates or armed robbers is promptly conveyed to the coastal authority concerned" and "to take appropriate precautionary measures when entering waters where there is a record of attacks by pirates or armed robbers".

The IMO is also requested "to disseminate any information received on acts of piracy or armed robbery against ships to Member Governments and non-governmental organizations by means of regular circulars", and "to seek means of providing support for Governments requesting technical assistance on the prevention of acts of piracy and armed robbery against ships by such means as national or regional seminars and workshops".

Since May 1991, IMO analyses all reports on piracy acts and armed robberies and submits the corresponding summaries to the MSC for review. Although this has contributed to determining the areas in which the problem is more serious, the number of cases that have occurred is still alarming; in April 1992, the MSC pointed at the increasing ferocity of the attacks.

Besides the danger incurred in by the victimised crews, it seems impossible to exaggerate on the dangers it poses to navigation and the environment. In some cases, the crew were tied up and the ship left to sail at full speed without any control while the bandits fled. Under such circumstances, the ship represents a threat for everything coming across her, the possibility of colliding becoming very real. If perchance it were a fully loaded tanker, there is also a big likelihood of a huge environmental catastrophe occurring. Where this danger is more real is in the Southeast Asian waters, where navigational waterways are quite narrow and shallow, and transit is high (the Malacca Strait sees about 40,000 ships every year).

At the MSC meeting, governments were invited to participate in organising regional seminars, in order to adopt joint action plans, and they were requested to designate within their administrations persons in charge of handling the reports received.

In August, the Secretary-General, Mr. William A. O'Neil, sent to the 136 member states of the IMO a circular (MSC/Circ. 597) proposing complementary measures. In particular, it was requested from governments that they should use the communications system created under the International Convention of 1979 on Maritime Search and Rescue (SAR), in order to assist attacked ships; this may be attained by allowing the Captains of threatened ships to contact the closest Rescue Coordination Centre (RCC) that, in turn, may relay the information to the nearest authorities in charge of suppressing piracy and, if required, warn neighbouring states of the threat.

The circular further recommends using the SafetyNet service, created by the International Maritime Satellite Organisation (INMARSAT), in addition to the other communication means that, provided by the Global Maritime Distress and Safety System (GMDSS), came up in February 1992.

In spite of such actions, piracy kept posing a serious threat; therefore, in November 1992 the Secretary-General reported to the IMO Council, which acts as the governing body of the organisation between an assembly period and the next, that he intended to create a special workgroup in order to address the Southeast Asia problem.

In 1991, a loaded VLCC was hijacked by pirates and held in the Malacca Strait for 25 minutes, sailing uncontrolled since the crew was being held at gunpoint.

In December 1992, it was reported to the Maritime Safety Committee (MSC) that the workgroup would prepare a report that would detail the situation at the Malacca Strait, would specify the required navigational techniques and would recommend the safety precautions and the adequate means in order to enforce compliance with the regulations. The workgroup would be composed of experts on prevention of illicit actions (UK), search and rescue (USA), navigational safety (Greece), radiocommunications (Norway), maritime transit organisation, navigational aids and ship transit services (Australia and Japan), and financial consequences (Netherlands).

Representatives from the three coastal states (Indonesia, Malaysia and Singapore) also participated, and several renowned nongovernmental organisations joined the group as consulting bodies in front of the IMO. Amongst them are the International Maritime Bureau, the International Shipping Federation, the International Confederation of Free Trade Unions (ICFTU), the International Association of Lighthouse Authorities (IALA) and the International Federation of Shipmasters' Associations (IFSMA).

Reports by the various experts were submitted to the IMO Secretariat towards the end of May 1993; a final report was subsequently prepared by the Secretary-General, who, in turn, submitted it to the MSC, the main technical body within the IMO; they reviewed it during the 62nd period of sessions (MSC/circs. 622/623), and the IMO Assembly adopted resolution A.738(18) dated 4th of November1993 (see Annex IV).

5.4.5 Illicit actions against passengers and the crew

The saying goes that the "Achille Lauro" has meant for *security* what the "Titanic" meant for *safety*; this answers to the fact that, while after the sinking of the "Titanic" international cooperation gave place to the drafting of an agreement on basic levels of safety, after the attack against the "Achille Lauro", also thanks to international cooperation it became possible to reach an agreement on basic levels of security.

When the "Achille Lauro" was attacked in 1985 and the United States, along with many other countries, expressed their rejection and concern, it represented a natural step to them to request from the IMO a consideration of the matter. The proposal was plain: "review the issues of terrorism on board or against ships, with a view to make recommendations on the appropriate measures to be adopted".

Upon receipt of this request, the IMO reacted swiftly and skilfully. The Secretary from the Maritime Safety Committee (MSC) prepared a document drafted by the USA Coast Guard and submitted it to a specifically selected subcommittee for consideration. Thus, seven experts sat together in IMO's conference room in London, and wrought a resolution that has become one of the most significant of those produced by the organisation.

The subcommittee was chaired by a Norwegian, and composed by an American, a Russian, a Greek, an Italian, a Canadian and a German. The USA representative had little participation, since the document being considered proceeded from his country; since Perestroika and Glasnost were emerging, the Russian representative was favourably bold in its approval.

The response from the Maritime Safety Committee was in the form of a document titled "Measures to Prevent Unlawful Acts which Threaten the Safety of Ships and the Security of their Passengers and Crews". To everyone's surprise, the resolution was approved immediately and unanimously by the 136 member states during the fourteenth assembly (the governing body of the International Maritime Organisation); it was numbered as resolution A.584(14), adopted on 20th of November 1985.

In the resolution it is noted "with great concern the danger to passengers and crews resulting from the increasing number of incidents involving piracy, armed robbery and other unlawful acts against or on board ships, including small craft, both at anchor and under way".

The MSC was instructed to prepare on a priority basis detailed and practical technical measures, including measures applicable both on shore and on board, in order to effectively safeguard passengers and crew members aboard ships. These measures would take into account the task carried out by the International Civil Aviation Organisation (ICAO) with respect to the establishment of standards and recommended practices for the safety of airports and aeroplanes.

In December 1985, the United Nations provided also their support, by exhorting the IMO to study the problem of terrorism aboard or against ships, with a view to submit recommendations for appropriate measures.

The MSC completed the preparation of measures during their 1986 period of sessions; they fall within a sufficiently wide framework that allows administrations to adequately use them in accordance with their local conditions and circumstances. These measures establish that governments, port authorities, administrations, ship owners, captains and crews should adopt the appropriate measures in order to prevent unlawful acts that may threaten passengers and crews. Measures are intended for cruise ships on international voyages at least 24 hours long and for port facilities servicing them. Although they are not intended for ferries and other short crossing passenger ships, they could also be applied to them if deemed suitable.

The MSC, while eager to vote for the proposal, was very cautious and provident in setting the resolution with the term "guidelines", which implied that even though governments would be pleased to show their satisfaction in cooperating in the fight against terrorism, there was no requirement towards them with regard to the costs involved in such fight. The implementation task for those "guidelines" was left in the hands of port authorities and ship owners.

All this happened very quickly, but it was really consequential. From the moment that the resolution was adopted, the existence became evident of an internationally approved and recognised formula clearly and comprehensively establishing what ports and ships should do in order to provide the adequate protection against terrorist acts. Since the 26th of September 1986, a document is available that may be used by politicians, jurists, journalists and the general public to judge whether a given port or ship has actually taken "reasonable measures" in order to protect their passengers and crews; this is MSC 53/24, Annex 14, "Measures to Prevent Unlawful Acts against Passengers and Crews on board Ships".

These measures highlight the need for port facilities and ships to have a security plan in place and to designate a Security Officer. They subsequently describe very much in detail how security inspections should be carried out and what security measures and procedures should be adopted. In another section, security training is addressed, and lastly, the importance of exchanging information is underlined.

Later on, in 1986, the governments of Austria, Egypt and Italy proposed that the IMO should draft a convention on the matter of unlawful acts against the safety of maritime navigation. They declared that the intention of such convention was to fill the gap existing on the suppression of such acts and that, as a matter of fact, while three universal conventions were addressing the safety of air navigation, no similar international instrument addressed maritime navigation.

Those governments explained then that the convention draft envisaged a wide suppression of unlawful acts against the safety of maritime navigation that endanger innocent human lives, threaten the protection of people and goods, seriously impact the performance of maritime services, and are therefore a cause of grave concern for the international community as a whole. Due to this, and in tune with the aforementioned conventions, the convention draft submitted by those governments contemplated the absolute and unconditional application of the principle of punishing the offenders or granting their extradition.

The proposal was unanimously approved, and work on the project began immediately. The Council convened unanimously that the matter required urgent action. In March 1988, a conference was held in Rome that adopted the *Convention for the Suppression of Unlawful Acts of Violence against the Safety of Maritime Navigation*, which included provisions contemplating the absolute and unconditional application of the principle of punishing persons committing or being suspected of having committed the offences described in the convention, or of granting their extradition. By a protocol, the scope of the provisions of the convention was extended to *unlawful acts against the safety of fixed platforms located on the continental shelf*. Both instruments came into force on the 1st of March 1992.

Finally, after the hijacking of the ferry "Avrasya" in the Black Sea by Chechen rebels in January 1996, a set of comprehensive measures aimed at fighting terrorism and other safety threats against passenger ships was proposed; they were addressed by the Maritime Safety Committee of the IMO during its 60th session.

The main recommended measures were:

- Passenger, baggage and vehicle search
- Preventing unauthorised access to the ship
- Actions in order to prevent carriage of weapons and explosives on board
- Setting restricted areas at ports and aboard ships

The most argued clause was related to the implications of checking and displaying on a screen everything boarding the ship, in terms of cost and delays, and the precision was made that inspection of passengers, baggage and vehicles should adjust to "the level of risk for unlawful acts": "at a high threat level, security checks/displays should increase, the required trained personnel, equipment and facilities being made available".

5.4.6 Anti piracy contingency plan

All ships operating in areas in which pirate strikes happen often should have an anti piracy contingency plan in place. Such plan should be drafted taking into account the risks to be faced, the available crew, their capabilities and training, the possibility of establishing secure areas aboard the ship, and the surveillance and detection equipment provided.

A) **Scope**

Malacca Strait, Singapore and South China Sea.

B) **Preparations**

1) Weather decks that should be lit:

- main aft deck, around accommodations
- boat deck

Outside lighting should be reinforced with portable screens where required; lights hindering normal navigation should be removed.

2) Four firefighting hoses coupled to hydrants, ready for use. They should be placed covering the whole bow, two on port side and two on starboard side. All remaining hydrants (including those of hawse holes) should be left closed.

3) Except for one, all outside doors, including that of the servo, should remain locked. One door should be left open for use by the deck watch. Doors should be locked in a way that they may not be opened from the outside, but may be easily opened from the inside in case of fire or emergency.
4) Both rudder hydroamplifier pumps should be running.

5) Radars and VHF operating.

C) Watches

1.- Bridge and deck

    2000 - 2400, 1 officer and 1 watchman

    0000 - 0400, 1 officer and 2 watchmen (1 on deck with a walky talky)

    0400 - 0800, 1 officer and 2 watchmen (1 on deck with a walky talky)

2.- Engine room

    1 watchman in communication with the bridge by walky talky or telephone

D) Development

The plan should be in force while sailing through waters as detailed in "A", and should be applied daily from 22:00 hours to dawn.

1.- At dusk, all outside lighting should be switched on in accordance with "B-1".

2.- At 22:00 hours the watchman should start a round, checking that all outside doors (but one) are locked from the inside, in accordance with "B-3". From that moment on, no crew member, except for the watchman, should go outside, in order to prevent that any door is left open.

3.- From 00:00 hours on, a man on watch should be permanently detailed on the main deck, at the bow, in communication with the bridge with a walky talky. The other watchman should keep watch at the bridge; posts should be rotated hourly ("C-1"). A watchman should be detailed in the engine room until dawn ("C-2").

4.- Should any vessel approach the ship in a suspicious manner, the first watchman to spot it should report it to the Officer of the Watch, and they should stay alert. If suspicions are confirmed, the watchman should report it to the bridge, should move on to the accommodations, lock the last door and go to the bridge. The Officer of the Watch should:

    a) Switch on the general alarm

    b) Start up the firefighting pump

    c) Switch rudder to manual in order to facilitate "full port" or "full starboard" manoeuvres, should they be required for escape

    d) Issue a general call on the VHF, Channel 16.

On hearing the general alarm, engine room crew members should report to the engine room, and deck crew members should report to the bridge. Appropriate messages should be issued through any available means of communication.

In the extreme situation of pirates boarding the ship, no resistance should be offered.

5.4.7 Partial conclusions on piracy

Acts of piracy, like any other crimes that devastate society, may happen anywhere in the world, although the most susceptible areas to suffer it are those where poverty of the littoral cities contrasts with heavy maritime transit and scarce protection given by authorities.

Since 1983 and under a request by the IMO, the International Maritime Bureau, constituted by the International Chamber of Commerce (ICC), is the organisation in charge of collecting and publishing reports on pirate strikes.

Their number is alarming, more so because their reports clearly expose that many attacks are not reported, either out of concern about eventual delays at port while the investigation is carried out, or for fear of calling attention towards themselves, thus favouring new attacks, or for fear of possible diplomatic offences, because of being considered as "denouncing party" by the local authorities, or because the Captains may be worried about it reflecting their lack of discipline and attention during the watch.

It should be expected that every ship and shipping company would provide all available means for preventing that their interests and property would be harmed by the actions of organised groups of robbers or mere petty thieves, and it is preferred that they would always act within legality and patterns adequately defined by the international organisations that regulate maritime transportation.

5.5 Terrorism

5.5.1 Introduction

It is difficult to reach a consensus on what this phenomenon means specifically. What is agreed by most, if not all, of the analysts is that terrorism involves the use or a threat to use violence; beyond that, controversy is entered.

In general, it is thought that it is instinctively known what terrorists do and how they operate, but when it comes to providing an updated definition for the term "terrorism", we come across insurmountable obstacles.

Maybe usage of the term "terrorism" should not be restricted to descriptions of actions carried out with an essentially political or religious purpose. By doing this, all actions related to purely material ends would be automatically excluded. This not taking into account whether such actions may involve or not the use of terror tactics (*e.g.*, extortion under threats, kidnapping, hijacking, blackmail, protection payments, armed robbery, etc.), nor considering the essential purpose of the groups committing such actions. For example, an armed robbery done by a terrorist group with the only purpose of raising funds or acquiring "essential" equipment (weapons, explosives, etc.) would be difficult to classify.

Although the trend of establishing a clear distinction between the politically driven terrorist threat and other kinds of violent threats is understandable, this could lead to adopting dangerous simplistic assumptions. For example, it could lead to overlooking the infinity of basic criminal means that extreme political groups have used and still use to support their politically motivated activities.

Another dangerous assumption that may occur is that people on board run a greater risk in case of terrorism than in other criminal cases. While this may be undoubtedly true for many cases, actually it is not always so. When, for example, the Provisional IRA boarded and subsequently sunk the MV "Neille M" and the MV "St. Sedan" (on February 1981 and February 1982, respectively), in none of those cases they had any intention of harming people on board. In actual fact, they did everything necessary to ensure that the crew could reach the coast safely.

These comments intend merely to illustrate the statement that politically driven terrorist groups use different tactics on different occasions for a different number of reasons, occasionally committing offences for purely materialistic reasons, often not harming individuals when not convenient. It is therefore daring to apply strict distinctions, since then a very likely risk is incurred of adopting an inappropriate and inadequate response to the predominant threat. The terrorist is flexible, as is the pirate. They mould their tactics in order to adjust to the prevailing conditions. Anyone with the purpose of restraining or fighting any kind of violence at sea, no matter how minor, should act in this same manner, paying no regard to what motivates it.

Maritime industry should avoid this confusion because of another very good reason. Knowledge of the reason is, admittedly, of considerable importance when trying to solve a crime or dismantle a criminal group (whether politically or economically driven). But a shipping company's management, a ship's Captain and her crew are not involved at this level in the response to the criminal element. This is up to the governmental and international agencies, not private individuals.

When trying to review protection means for ships and ports, and when referring to the maritime industry's response to the reasons for the offence, while they hold certain interest, they will be granted less significance than *methods*.

No one may deny that sabotage and placing bombs indiscriminately are procedures more close to politically driven criminal groups than to those acting under materialistic motivations. Nevertheless, there are always exceptions, and some methods are used indistinctly by both, irrespective of their motives. Thence, if maritime industry adopts a range of security measures aimed at responding to a set of tactics (or methods) adopted by criminal societies (leaving motivations aside), it will find itself restraining and/or fighting not only the so called terrorists, but also that traditional scourge of mariners, *i.e.*, pirates.

From the maritime industry's standpoint, there is practically no difference between a pirate and a maritime terrorist. For the Captain of a hijacked ship it is of no moment whether attackers are terrorists driven by politics or pirates driven by money; the end result is very similar (plus, pirates may be as ruthless as their terrorist counterparts). This could then really stimulate the industry to work on preparing security instructions for ships that would include considerations on all *methods* likely to be used by criminal societies.

There is still one more reason for adopting a combined approach. It is based on the analysis of the incidence of *politically* driven maritime crime with respect to the total amount of all other forms of violent offences committed at sea in recent years.

Maybe the most remarkable conclusion that any objective analysis of maritime terrorism incidents should produce is that its relevance has been low by far. Politically driven criminals seem to have neglected for some reason the maritime environment (or otherwise have thought about it and decided that other environments suit their goals better). However, such latent threat demands attention.

5.5.2 Terrorist methods and objectives

Although hijacking a ship may become a rather complex operation, hijacking an aeroplane also has its difficulties. In some cases of air hijacking, the initial success of the operation turned into the hijacker's failure, being with too many people in a confined space, therefore finding it impossible to handle the situation he himself created.

The larger accommodation space of a ship may solve this inconvenience. However, it is not possible to keep under constant surveillance every area of a ship without a numerous strike force.

Air terrorism, independently of its motivation, has capitalised the achievement of its goals over two main factors: raising the awareness of those intended to have the pressure put on by endangering such number of innocent people, and by the urgency of the problem. However, terrorist activities have seen a change of direction, from the acute, emotional situation produced in the air to a more sustained pressure that may be created by other means.

Terrorist actions may pursue two possible objectives. They may destroy or cause damage for the mere sake of publicity, or they may seize facilities and hold people with the purpose of using the threat of such destruction or damages in order to achieve another goal. Many examples exist of the former. Indiscriminate bomb placing or murder, subsequently recalled by a particular terrorist group "claiming responsibilities", are examples of the desire of exhibiting power.

The second goal may be also easily identified in many examples of aeroplane hijacking, embassy assault, kidnapping and other acts in which hijackers offer the cessation of the violent action in exchange of certain demands.

In order to attain any of the two objectives, personnel are required, which generally need to be infiltrated. Such infiltration may be achieved violently, surreptitiously or deceitfully, although it may also take place with people who, once they have obtained a job and have earned a relationship of trust, make their ideology manifest and declare their motives. This second kind is the prevailing one, and the hardest to fight.

Many hijackings taking place are carried out by "trusted" personnel. The highest responsibility with regard to the safety of the ship lies with the ship owner, who in turn delegates it to the Captain. But even though ultimate decision is in the hands of the Captain, a Captain of a ship may, or is able to, obtain the advice and practical assistance in any port at which the ship may have called. In such matters, there should always be the highest level of coordination between the Captain of the ship and the police or other on shore security forces.

5.5.3 Impact of terrorism in passenger ships

Murder of a disabled senior citizen in 1985 during the "Achille Lauro" hijacking led the Mediterranean cruise industry to an absolute, sudden standstill. Passenger ships found themselves either indefinitely moored in front of Piraeus, or queuing, trying to call at St. Thomas, Virgin Islands. Official figures from the Greek government after the murder showed direct losses of 300 million US dollars: 200 million from tourism and 100 million from cancelled cruise ship reservations. This enormous impact on maritime industry was not caused by a major escalation of destruction and bloodshed, but by the action of four men that carried out a terrorist strike.

During the Gulf War in 1991, while the Allies' military power was devastating the Iraqi forces from warships and bombers, people from all nationalities ceased to travel. Flights were cancelled, reservations for cruise ships plummeted, and some ferries were even withdrawn from service in order to cut down on costs.

The cause for such immediate, devastating impact on the passenger transportation industry was not the issue with Iraqi tanks, missiles or poison gas, but the possibility that maybe five or six men or women could be planning a terrorist strike.

Every day, one hundred violent deaths occur in New York; many murders are not even mentioned in the press. However, back in 1989, when an unidentified group murdered Colonel Higgins, an American, in an alley way in Beirut, the United States President himself made his aeroplane "turn round" and return to Washington in order to "address the crisis". Reservations for cruisers fell dramatically, and many seamen lost their jobs.

Therefore, there may be no doubt that acts of terrorism have a large impact on the passenger transport industry and on the profitability of passenger ships. Deciding what a passenger ship company should do in order to avoid possible terrorist actions, or what a passenger ship should do to prevent them, is nonetheless an arduous task. The natural function of a military ship is to provide protection against violent acts, but this is a very inappropriate function for a ship that is designed to provide some relaxed holidays or a fast ferry crossing.

5.5.4 The nature of terrorism

The fact that this technique known as "terrorism" may have had such an impact on maritime life, and that such tactics may have had such an immediate and drastic effect on the profitability and redundancy level of crews, lies on the unique nature of terrorism, as compared to other violent acts.

Somebody killing their neighbour or injuring a person during a robbery is clearly regarded as a criminal; however, if the same crime is committed under the allegation of political, religious or even environmental motives, a delusive impression seems to be created that this is not so any more, and it may even seem to have a justification. The excuse given is that terrorism is an act carried out for a "cause" rather than for personal benefit, and that in order to achieve such selfless "cause", participants are risking their own lives towards a goal that does not pursue economical gain.

This combination of "cause" and apparent "self sacrifice" is not sufficient in itself in order to call on the attention of the whole world. Other elements are necessary: innocent victims, horror and, most important, good communications. Without media coverage, terrorism would not exist.

It is by means of this combined formula of cause, innocence, horror and communications that the situation has been reached where a small number of men or women with a limited amount of weapons or explosive can immediately call on global attention. In 1972, the Palestinian issue was brought to the knowledge of eight million people after the massacre of Israeli athletes during the Munich Olympics, where the world's media were concentrated and ready to give a wide coverage of the tragedy.

It would be therefore rash to assume that such powerful and often successful tactic would not be still used by an increasing variety of people that feel exceptionally strong about their own particular convictions and wish to obtain global notoriety. Terrorist acts will not cease. Terrorism will stay forever, and it will need addressing on a routine basis, not dramatically. This applies also to the maritime industry.

5.5.5 Maritime terrorism

Navigating has always been fascinating and exciting, but passengers that travel by sea often feel vulnerable; after sailing off, they feel like having lost a degree of their sovereignty and being in the hands of others; they feel they are at the mercy of the elements. Therefore, the ideal ingredients for a terrorist strike are in place: an exciting, potentially dangerous situation, innocent people in a vulnerable position, and excellent communications.

In the past decade, except for some bloody terrorist operations (*e.g.*, the Irish IRA, the Spanish ETA and the Tamils of Sri Lanka), Americans and American interests have been the most attractive terrorist targets. Given the volatile situation in the Middle East,

American travellers are still at risk. For a terrorist selecting a target, there is a proven psychological benefit in choosing as victims of their attack the rich rather than the poor, and, amongst them, members of the Jewish religion are regrettably those running the highest risk, together with American citizens.

But it is important to keep in perspective the fact that the current level of risk is low. It is much more likely that a ship may have to use her inert gas system to extinguish a fire in the engine room, or that she may have to lower the lifeboats after a collision, than having to deal with a terrorist incident. Nowadays no passenger decides not to travel by sea under the unsubstantial thought of maybe suffering a terrorist strike.

5.5.6 Maritime terrorist strikes. Case history

Fortunately, although some maritime criminal and piracy acts have occurred, and they are increasing in numbers and brutality, besides the sinking of the Greek line cruiser "Sanya" back in 1973, which sank after striking a mine laid by Beirut's Black September terrorist organisation, there have been only three major acts of terrorism at sea: the "Santa María" in 1962, the "Achille Lauro" in 1985 and the "City of Poros" in 1989. It is interesting to note that none of them attained the results originally intended by the attackers. In the three cases, they were military incompetent and proved to be "professional" failures. Nevertheless, they achieved a vast and persistent global publicity, which should not be surprising since the sea provides a perfect stage for a terrorist drama.

5.5.7 Parcel and letter bombs

Over the past years several examples have occurred of ships receiving explosive devices under the disguise of letters or parcels. Such artefacts do not usually come from terrorist groups, but it is rather more likely that they be sent from ex-employees who are either resentful or dissatisfied with their dismissal or with the company's policies; notwithstanding, besides conveying the message to the company, letter bombs may maim the innocent persons that open them.

If a parcel raises suspicion, the best solution is to take it to the bow, to an upper deck, keeping it away from people. If an explosion suppression blanket is available, it may be placed over the parcel; otherwise, wet mattresses may be used for the same purpose.

The best protection against letter/parcel bombs is natural suspicion against any unexpected element, or coming from a strange place, or written in an unusual form.

Once suspicion is raised, other indicators may assist in deciding whether the object may indeed be dangerous:

- A letter that, beneath the external envelope or cover has in internal wrapping indicating "Private" or "Personal".
- Greasy stains on the envelope or cover.
- Distinct smell, similar to marzipan or almonds.
- Evidence of wires or metal foils, particularly when the wrapping or cover is damaged.
- Small hole or perforation on the envelope or container.
- Excessive weight related to size.
- Irregular weight distribution, content appears to be stiff while wrapping is flexible, or something under stress is perceived.
- The parcel or envelope has excessive wrapping.
- Written indications are scant or not very legible.
- Incorrect address; parcel or letter arrives unexpectedly.
- Quantity or amount of stamps does not correspond to the parcel's weight.
- Personally delivered from an unknown source.

If based on the above, suspicion about a letter or parcel received on board prevails, DO NOT OPEN IT.

5.5.8 Check and bomb search plan

Even though it is true that possibilities of a ship experiencing a terrorist attack are scarce, the same may not be said about the possibility of receiving bomb warnings, *i.e.*, somebody stating that a bomb has been placed on board. In such occasions, the Captain may decide either to ignore the call or to take measures about it.

Given the small number of occasions in which bombs are actually found with respect to the frequency of bomb calls, temptation to do nothing about it is great. However, if the warning is ignored and a real explosion occurs, with the subsequent results, such decision will be highly criticised and judgment will be hard.

Therefore, the principle to be followed is to do something about it, and this is to search.

There are so many ways in which a terrorist may disguise a bomb that it is virtually impossible that a crew member may determine that what is being seen is actually an explosive device.

The secret is in checking the area, not in searching for the bomb, thus looking rather for some item (like a parcel, a box or a bag) that is not usually found in that place. Search, therefore, should be carried out by somebody who usually works in that area and is capable of deciding whether there is any object placed there irregularly.

This implies that the existence of an emergency plan is of little use if crew members are located in places they do not visit frequently, or if a team made up of officers and the boatswain is chosen, which, though often the most trustworthy and competent people in the ship, are not really effective, since they are not familiar with the general layout of certain areas or the contents of some of the storerooms.

Thus, the ship's safety plan should include a chapter detailing clearly who is responsible for checking each area of the ship, and how to act if anything is found.

The second principle is to use eyes rather than hands.

It should be very clear to any crew member finding a suspicious object that it should not be touched, but reported. The Captain, upon receiving the report, should decide what to do, such decision not being conditioned by any indication from the company.

If the call was received, *e.g.*, from the police, and something suspicious has actually been found, it would be reasonable to return to the closest port and request assistance. If the message was received in a not very convincing way, *e.g.*, from somebody sounding drunk calling from a bar, then it may be decided to continue the voyage, having evacuated the area and taken precautions as detailed in the ship's emergency plan for such kind of emergency.

Many ships carry aboard an explosion suppression blanket, to be used in such situations. For the specialist, this may look like merely delaying the problem, but for the people on board it means certain protection against the explosion and glass projections.

5.6 Drugs

Although countries producing drugs are known, and identifying their markets is relatively simple, the high demand for drugs, the enormous profits they generate and the impotence of administrations notwithstanding the laws in force lead to the conclusion that few ports in the world may be considered safe.

However, certain countries are seen in connection with drug problems more often than others, amongst them: Aruba, Bahamas, Belize, Bolivia, Brazil, Chile, Colombia, Curacao, Dominican Republic, Ecuador, Spain, Haiti, Honduras, Jamaica, Morocco, Panama, Peru and Venezuela.

5.6.1 Assessment of vulnerability to drugs

When assessing the level of precautions to be adopted in front of the possibility of drug traffic, the Captain should collect as much information as possible in order to evaluate the threat level.

- Whether the port itself is related with drugs, this being recognised.
- Whether the port is catalogued as a port of call for drugs.
- Whether the port is in a country typical for drug transits.
- Whether any of the adjacent countries are catalogues as a drug producing country.

5.6.2 Involved persons

Something common to all drugs is that they do not hide with provisions or cargo, neither are they disguised around the body, or go into hand or cabin baggage, or slip behind a false bulkhead, all by themselves. Drugs need people to move them about.

There are basically two methods for using ships for drug smuggling. The first method is an organised conspiracy.

Organised conspiracies generally handle large amounts of drug, between tens and hundreds of kilograms; they include several, if not all, crew members. Disguise techniques are usually rather sophisticated, since conspirators have ample time to carefully hide the drugs. Detection will probably require considerable time and effort, in addition to the use of tools. Place of hiding is likely a main ship component, such as the engine room, tanks, cofferdams, compartments, or other internal or external ship areas.

The second method has to do with a corrupt crew member. They normally handle small quantities of drug, from a few grams up to five or six kilograms, and usually operate on their own or with one or two accomplices at the most. Hiding techniques are usually not too sophisticated, since here the smuggler does not have much time to act without being observed. Detection does not take long, neither does it require much effort, sometimes a screwdriver or a spanner being all that is required. Places of hiding are usually common access places, not only visited by the smuggler, but by anyone.

Crew members involved in drug smuggling tend to exhibit certain features:

- Nervousness or suspicious behaviour
- Unusual ostentation of large amounts of money
- Wears and uses unusually expensive items
- Wears out of season clothing
- Loose or bulging clothing
- Shows uncommon interest in some ship areas, certain cargoes or some particular equipment

5.6.3 Drug trafficking

Nowadays, drug commerce is at a peak in many countries; more drugs are used, and other offences increase also as drug addicts resort to violence in order to obtain the needed money to pay for them.

The most lucrative drug markets are in the European and North American developed economies. As for drugs, they are produced in South America and some places in Asia. But for drugs to get from supplier to consumer, complex operations are required that involve several means of transportation, many drugs being forwarded by sea.

Drug smuggling constitutes an offence virtually in every country in the world; there are indicators showing that more and more seamen use drugs.

One of the most interested organisations on drug traffic increase is the Customs Cooperation Council (CCC), which, along the years, has worked on various international measures in order to fight it. It cooperates closely with the United Nations Division of Narcotic Drugs, the United Nations Fund for Drug Abuse Control and the International Narcotics Control Board.

In 1985, the CCC addressed itself to the IMO suggesting to look into new ways in which both organisations might draft measures in order to counteract drug trafficking. It was agreed to include the item in the agenda for the next meeting of the Facilitation Committee. Meanwhile, the IMO Secretariat began to probe into the feasibility of drafting guidelines for seamen about how to avoid drug concealment and how to act when drugs are discovered on board. Another organisation, the International Chamber of Shipping (ICS) (recognised by the IMO as a consulting body that attends meetings regularly) was also working jointly with the CCC.

The Facilitation Committee, in its meeting in March 1986, noted with grave concern the alarming increase in drug abuse, in unlawful drug trafficking worldwide and in the use by traffickers of commercial transport, including ships, for drug smuggling. The Committee agreed to work jointly with the CCC and the ICS in the subject of guidelines for fighting against the unlawful traffic of drugs.

The guidelines, published in early 1988, contain:

- Measures for preventing drug smuggling on board
- Measures for improving the detection of drugs concealed on board
- Measures for dissuading seamen from using drugs or participating in its smuggling
- Information on kinds, nature and characteristics of those drugs most frequently smuggled
- Education and training on risks attached to smuggling and drug abuse
- Measures to be adopted by ship owners and their employees when discovering drugs

Work on the drug problem progressed, paying attention to drug and alcohol abuse by seamen. IMO's Subcommittee on Standards of Training and Watchkeeping drafted guidelines that were approved by the Maritime Safety Committee, and disseminated in May 1992, through a circular.

They point out the importance of selecting seamen prior to recruiting them; the need for rehabilitation, education and counselling is also highlighted. Next, they set forth seven guides to be followed when establishing a review program for drug and alcohol abuse.

There are other United Nations bodies that also participate in prevention programmes on drug consumption, the circular making reference to some of them, *e.g.*, the International Labour Organisation, the World Health Organisation and the United Nations International Drug Control Programme. The circular states that any work or research activity initiated by the IMO within this field should be shared with those organisations.

An indicator of the significance of narcotics control is the number of measures being taken by some other organisations in the maritime transportation industry that attend IMO's meetings. The International Chamber of Shipping, the International Association of Independent Tanker Owners (INTERTANKO) and the Oil Companies International Marine Forum (OCIMF) have all published guidelines on the matter, to which member states of the IMO and other maritime transportation related organisations have had their attention called.

5.6.4 Protection measures against drug traffic and consumption

Checks

The best protection against drug trafficking is trying to avoid them boarding, this meaning that models should be implemented of random checks on people boarding, in order to detect any eventual entry of drugs.

Also on a random basis, or as a response to a particular drug threat, a search of the ship should be carried out in order to locate eventual drug packages, disguised with the cargo or in the ship's structure.

Every time a drug search is done, it should be recorded in the Navigation Logbook.

Drug check procedure

The drug search team should be made up under the direction of the Ship's Security Officer, and it should be composed of veteran representatives from all departments; participation of the Chief Engineer should always be requested, in order to carry out the search in the most practical and least harmful manner for the facilities.

Inasmuch as possible, search team members should not inspect areas where they specifically work or live and, when possible, they should search working and living areas of crew members belonging to professional categories different to theirs.

The team should have the following equipment available:

- Torches and spare batteries
- Screwdrivers, spanners and levers
- Mirrors and probes as those included in the IMS approved search equipment.
- Gloves, hard hats and non slip footwear

- Bags/envelopes for exhibit collection
- Form sheets

Following is a sample of areas used in the past for drug concealment, classified by department:

Deck department:

- Navigation bridge and radio station
- Lifeboats and swimming pool
- Paint lockers and spares storerooms
- Stowing materials
- Pumps, pillars and cranes

Supply Department:

- Galley, mess and common areas
- Passenger cabins
- Own materials storerooms and waste compartments
- Freezers and cold storage compartments
- Food storage compartments
- Crew accommodations and officers' cabins.

Engine Department:

- Maintenance materials storerooms
- Lift shaft and machinery areas
- Bilges
- Propeller shaft log
- Servomotor
- Tanks and cofferdams
- Ship spares storerooms

Some of the most used places for drug hiding are:

In cabins:

- On the rear and bottom of drawers
- Under mattresses
- Inside radio receivers and similar devices
- In ventilation conducts
- On or under lamp fixtures
- On ceiling panels or behind bulkheads

In stairways and corridors:

- Under hand railings
- On fire extinguishers
- In fire hose boxes

- On the top rim of watertight doors
- In ventilation conducts
- On ceiling panels or behind bulkheads
- Behind or even inside chilled water fountains

In toilets and shower rooms:

- Underneath or behind wash basin pedestals
- Behind the WC
- In shower sprinklers
- In heaters
- Inside toilet paper rolls or towel dispensers
- In ventilation conducts
- On or under lamp fixtures
- On ceiling panels or behind bulkheads.

On deck:

- On superstructural ledges
- Inside switchboxes or winch commands
- In lifeboat compartments
- Inside paint cans
- Beneath the swimming pool or inside its conducts
- In holds, battery rooms and chain boxes.

In the engine room:

- Under floor plates or in bilges
- In motor bases and pedestals
- In emergency staircase and lift shafts
- In ventilation conducts
- In spare part and equipment boxes
- Inside tanks
- Under the propeller shaft

Galleys and pantries:

- In flour boxes or similar
- In vegetable bags or food tins
- Underneath or behind conventional fridges
- Inside fish or mixed with the meat in the freezer
- In materials storerooms or waste rooms

5.6.5 Indicators of assistance for identifying drug abuse

In such a reduced and confined community as a ship's crew, presence of a person abusing drugs may have a devastating effect on the morale and efficiency of the rest of the crew.

Drugs create an ever increasing dependence, and a drug addict is often incapable of financing such addiction with the normal earnings. It is therefore vital that drug abuse indicators be recognised as early as possible in order to adopt the required corrective measures. Some early indications are:

- Dramatic theft increase
- Empty medicine bottles or boxes, even used syringes found in waste bins or liners
- Burnt rope smell in toilets or corridors
- Sudden behaviour changes in hitherto stable crew members
- Emotional changes in hitherto stable personnel
- Functional effectiveness level degradation in a crew member

5.6.6 Physical symptoms

Some of the physical symptoms which supervisors and officers should be watchful about and capable of recognising include:

- Unnecessary use of sunglasses, to cover dilated or contracted pupils.
- Use of long sleeves when it is hot, to cover evidence of injections.
- Addicts to depressives such as barbiturics normally show alcohol intoxication signs: jabbering speech, staggering walk.
- Those abusing stimulants, such as amphetamines, show symptoms of excessive activity, excitability or irritability, as well as accelerated breathing. Eye pupils may also be dilated, even under bright light. These drugs may also cause loss of appetite and cracked lips; a person that does not stop talking, scratches continually and chain smokes is to be suspected.
- The most obvious symptoms to heroin addiction are injection marks and contracted pupils; frequent visits to the toilet and to the cabin and excessive secrecy on possessions are also grounds for suspicion. After an injection, the individual enters a state of drowsiness, practically lethargic.
- Marihuana is normally smoked in groups, and can be told by its characteristic smell, similar to that of burnt hemp. Symptoms shown by consumers include chatter, exaggerated bursts of laughter and time and space distortion, in addition to loss of coordination and reddened eyes, finally ending in a state of drowsiness and weakness.
- Those abusing hallucinogens usually seem to be in a trance, the most common characteristic being dilated pupils, uncontrollable emotional changes being also possible, from the highest happiness to a fierce panic, or even an unstoppable desire of self destruction. The possibility exists also of a flashback effect some weeks after the dose, even not having taken any more drugs.

Both officers and supervisors should be aware of the fact that some of the symptoms described may answer to diverse causes, amongst them mere tiredness or fatigue due to working conditions. Therefore, when a person may be suspected of drug consumption, a second opinion should be sought before considering drug addiction.

5.6.7 Drug search plan

One of the main objectives of the Initiative Program for Maritime Transportation is showing the authorities that the ship signing the agreement has placed a continued interest on her part in drug traffic prevention.

In order to show it, certain basic procedures should be implemented on board, such as carrying out random searches with varied frequency, which should be included in the ship's security plan.

A search aimed at finding drugs is completely different to that done after a bomb call. In this case, both sight and touch may be used; nevertheless, particular care should be taken when handling contaminated syringes, due to the risk of infection.

While a bomb search does not require that bulkheads should be unscrewed or that hands should be put in water cisterns, it is not the case with a drug search.

Such searches require a team of specially trained people, including, if possible, engine room officers and electricians, who will require search tools and knowledge about places where drugs have been concealed in the past.

It is also worth mentioning that when a cabin is searched, its occupant should be present.

5.6.8 Actions to be taken when drugs are found at sea

Existence of guidelines for action

When drugs or suspected substances are found on board, and when no specific guide is provided by the company, instructions should be requested from the company prior to initiating any action. Furthermore, the finding should be reported to the authorities at the port of destination by radio, prior to entering territorial waters.

Safety considerations

All drugs are extremely dangerous; some may even be absorbed through the skin. Therefore, if any suspicious substance is discovered, the following steps should be followed in order to ensure personal safety:

- Do not shake, hold or touch the substance without wearing skin protection and breathing mask.
- Do not inhale dust, smoke or vapours.
- Do not act hurriedly.
- Do not smoke near substances, or expose them to heat or flame.
- Under no circumstance try, eat or drink the suspect substance.
- Clean from hands and brush from clothing any contaminant as soon as possible.
- When storing large quantities of the suspect substance in a safe place, ensure proper ventilation of the area.

Use of a specific guide

The basic scheme for any guide of action when finding drugs at sea should include the following aspects:

- Called another officer to witness the place where the parcel or suspect substance was located, and, if possible, take photographs of the substance as found.
- Touch as little as possible, and keep in mind that fingerprint tests will be carried out. Move the substance to a safe place, handling it with care, to be locked and sealed, setting a watch if necessary.
- Record any findings in the Navigation Logbook, including as many details as possible: date, time, finding location, approximate amount, people who found it, names of witnesses, etc.
- Collect wrappings and any other item found in the location, and consider the possibility of searching other similar areas and locations.
- Write an event report as soon as possible, covering any occurrence. It is often helpful to draw a sketch of the location space and area, and also to record why the specific area was searched (noting whether there was any warning of suspicious activity). The report should be signed by the witnessing officer and the Captain or department head, including time and date.
- Nobody should be allowed to leave the ship until the competent authorities have acted at the port of arrival.

5.6.9 Partial conclusions about drugs

There are certain cases in which unlawful action of people on board seriously impacts the company, and it is therefore in its best interest to establish all available means to avoid that, while ignorant of it, drug smuggling may occur aboard its ships.

In a positive effort to reduce the amount of drugs introduced into the United States, Customs authorities in that country have prepared an Initiative Program for Transportation, designed "to prevent smugglers the usage of commercial shipping as a means of transportation and introduction of illegal drugs".

This provides that shippers may avoid or reduce their exposition to being fined by showing that they have exerted "the highest degree of care and diligence" to prevent the ship from being used for drug smuggling. A company that may show that the required steps have been made to implement the commitments of the signed agreement will have higher probabilities of this influencing the Customs authorities in the final decision for any penalty, if drugs were found aboard.

In order to back this Initiative Program for Transportation, the 1986 decree against drug abuse established serious penalties for those found guilty of transporting illegal drugs into the United States.

Many efforts are made to end the violent phenomena associated with drug commerce; with respect to their illegal traffic, there are already a large number of countries that have passed similar regulations.

5.7 Other forms of criminal violence at sea

Ships, as a means of transportation that include human lives and goods, are also the victims of all those other types of crimes and damages that affect on shore entities.

Whether for economical reasons, or due to particular ends, occasionally ships find themselves involved in diverse violent actions, amongst them extortion, kidnapping, sabotage, labour conflicts, etc.

Such subjects do not have a specifically maritime character; therefore they will be addressed briefly, by showing small illustrative examples that reflect in some measure how ships also become involved in the human conflict of violence.

5.7.1 Extorting passenger ships

Extorting passenger ships derives undoubtedly from the success of similar tactics applied to companies and aeroplanes.

Either operating actively or passively (with anonymous threats), the extorter seeks always an economical benefit, but it becomes obvious that in the case of direct action, as with kidnapping, the veracity and urgency of the action will be greater than in the case of an anonymous bomb threat.

There have been several cases of requesting a ransom under the threat of causing an explosive device hidden in a passenger ship to explode. There is one example dating back to 1973, when the American citizen Jerry Priddy demanded the sum of 250,000 $ from Princess Cruise Lines, threatening to destroy their ship "Island Princess", which was sailing with 850 people on board.

This particular case was a bluff. The ship's Captain, having been informed, carried out a discreet search for explosives, in which only two parcels were discovered, of the size of a cigarette packet, wrapped in Manila paper. The voyage continued uneventfully; meanwhile, the FBI arrested Priddy in the location agreed for delivering the money. He was imprisoned and sentenced to a nine month term.

Nevertheless, there have also been attempts to hijack ships for economical reasons, like back in 1978, when four people were arrested by an agent pretending to be an arms trafficker, while they were plotting the seizure of Eastern Steamship Lines' "Emerald Seas"; their plan was to sail from Miami to South America holding passengers and crew, and obtain a six million dollar ransom.

5.7.2 Sabotage

Fortunately this is an infrequent case, but it is still of concern, since actually a ship is literally in the hands of her crew.

In 1982, such type of case took place in a United States Coast Guard ship, which gave the act greater publicity than what in many instances similar actions get.

While patrolling the Gulf of Alaska, Coast Guard patrol boat "Boutwe II" captured a 39 foot sail ship, the "Orea", which was carrying 1,240 kilograms of marihuana. On the trip back to Kodiak towing her prey, the "Boutwe II" started experiencing a number of mechanical problems that eventually were identified to be acts of sabotage. A 19 year old Coast Guard man was formally accused under two charges of damage to machinery, one charge of damage to military property, one charge of conspiracy for endangering the patrol boat and one charge of attempting to steal the sail ship. The conspirators had planned on immobilising the "Boutwe II", putting on protective clothing and fleeing on the "Orea" with her cargo. Another crew member was involved, while a third, found drowned in his diving suit, could also have been involved.

5.7.3 Protection measures against sabotage

There is the threat that someone may want to sabotage the ship causing an explosion, a fire, or damage to specific equipment. The difference with a terrorist strike is that in this case there are no hostages. The target is therefore a ship of a given nationality that may have caused offence to some individual, or a ship carrying someone in particular.

The saboteur is probably reluctant to risk his own life or freedom when committing his crime, and will attempt to introduce the instrument on board together with the kit or provisions. It is extremely difficult to protect against this type of attack; precautions should be kept at the level of the threat. The adequate response to this type of risk encompasses both a sense of awareness and an ability to recognise anomalies, without neglecting random searches.

It is comforting that attacks of this kind are usually but clumsy instruments for claiming demands. Therefore, their effects are often more symbolic than real, although a ship carrying a very sensitive or flammable cargo will obviously run into greater risk.

Even though it is normally an internal aggression, there have also been cases in which saboteurs have attacked ships from the outside, gaining access to the hull from another vessel lieing alongside, from a small passing boat, from the dock, or underwater. Most likely targets are main engine water intakes, propeller shaft or rudder. Such attacks are not easy in practice, and require some technical skills, not available to most terrorist groups. Nevertheless, if any concern is raised in this respect, precautions should be taken such as sending divers to inspect the hull, patrolling the surrounding waters to the ship, keeping the propeller turning and adding external lighting.

In the cases of acts of sabotage from within by someone aboard, opportunities are considerable, and attaining the goal is easier. Introduction of sand, stones, abrasives, contaminants or adulterating materials in fuel lines or filters, starting a fire or a spillage, cutting cables or introducing a virus in the computer, are relatively easy actions, and protection against them is difficult. This would be an example of the greatest concern professional Security Officers have: "having the enemy within".

Routine surveillance of sensitive areas may assist in protecting against internal sabotage, but the actual solution is vetoing employees, this posing no little trouble to shipping companies.

On the one hand, knowledge of a person's background is of great assistance prior to offering a position, but more and more, legal restrictions prevent damaging people's civil rights, which make it much more difficult to uncover data on prospective employees.

However, when dealing with experienced people, references should be checked, by ensuring that data are reliable.

IMO guidelines establish also that ships should have contingency plans in place so that in an emergency situation both on shore and on board personnel know at all times how to proceed.

Emergency plans are a necessary portion of ship management, and should be reviewed periodically both internally and by competent authorities.

5.7.4 Assaulting

It may seem inadequate for ships to have detailed contingency plans when dealing with terrorist assaults. However, certain principles need to be included in the ship's safety plan. Firstly, experience from previous terrorist strikes shows that an initial violent reaction against armed terrorists is not only highly dangerous, but totally useless. Once it is found that the attack is committed by a group of armed terrorists and not by an individual under the effect of alcohol or drugs, the best thing to do is to follow the orders given by the terrorists.

This is not the natural reaction of many seamen who, although logically alarmed by the shouting and shooting of the terrorists, show an immediate, logical desire to avoid those ill intentioned people to seize their ship.

It is nevertheless not the most sensible policy. Very likely, terrorists will be quite excited and eager to show that they intend to seize the ship by force, and will be carrying automatic weapons and be experts in their use; an officer running to the safe to get hold of a pistol (which may have not been fired for several years) will place himself in a very vulnerable position. Even if an eventual shootout would abort the terrorist attack, the probability of a passenger or crew member becoming injured is high, therefore making it unadvisable.

Another relevant factor is that the ship is a part of the territory under the sovereignty of the flag she flies, and is subject to the laws of the country of registry. That country may have strict laws on the usage of fire arms and, even though the ship may be sailing in international waters, the eventuality of an officer shooting a terrorist might imply his indictment on a manslaughter charge.

Commercial considerations may even be at stake, such as the huge amount of legal and financial demands that are raised by an armed incident.

The question is with the fact that not carrying arms on board may imply that one single armed person may be able to hold a large ship. One possible solution would be having professional security officers on duty, trained and equipped to handle an armed situation, although this could be expensive. However, the best alternative is providing the Captain with the best training and security equipment to assist him in ensuring that no weapon comes aboard the ship.

Actions in case a ship is seized by force

In a passenger ship, it is likely that terrorists would attempt to seize the ship by boarding as innocent passengers, then choosing the ideal time to act.

On a non passenger ship, terrorists would attempt to seize the ship either through craftiness, *e.g.*, creating a "ship in danger" situation, or through a manoeuvre that would force the ship to stop; while possible, it is not likely that a ship would be seized by an armed forced while at port.

However, in any of the above cases, the following recommendations should be effective:

- Firstly, ensure the ship's safety in accordance with good marine practice.
- Next, if possible, issue a distress message, preparing in advance authentication procedures in order to warn on shore authorities and the company of the possibility of radio messages sent under coercion.
- Offer a reasonable cooperation. Terrorists will be probably very tense and "trigger happy" at the beginning of the incident. Tension may decrease largely by the Captain and officers acting normally.
- Danger associated with provocation is real. Leading the hijackers may be a psychopath looking for a pretext to kill. Such pretext may be deliberately created, or caused by a misinterpretation. Abuse or aggression should not be returned.
- It is not likely that hijackers understand fully how a ship operates. They may suspect even of routine operations, such as the simple procedure of changing course; trust will need to be reestablished that no subterfuge is being planned against them. It is also unlikely that they would be totally aware of safety requirements associated with the cargo.
- At an early stage of the incident attempts should be made to establish what terrorist group is striking.

It may not be suggested that the hijacker, who may only be a stowaway or someone with a mental disorder, will have political or economical claims, or any specific objective. Nevertheless, if the hijacker is a terrorist, it will be vital to know which are the claims, and what conditions should be satisfied in order to fulfil them. Demands may be being dictated by accomplices on shore, and the incident may be linked to some other elsewhere.

It should be assumed that the incident will be lengthy. And so it should be, since data show that incidents with hostages extending over time have higher probabilities for a conclusion with no victims among hostages.

The Captain and all the crew will feel alone during the incident, as they will not be updated on the steps taken by the company or government behind their backs. Such feeling of forlornness may lead them to an antagonism against their own authorities and to sympathy towards the terrorists, unless those involved prepare themselves psychologically against such feelings. Even so, all efforts should be channelled to ending the incident, the highest emphasis being placed on preserving life and personal safety of all the affected innocent parties.

On the other hand, establishing a reasonable harmony between hostages and their captors will probably reduce the possibilities for the terrorists acting violently against their hostages.

A confrontation between the terrorists and the authorities should be expected at any time. Prior to such confrontation, an opportunity may appear or be raised for providing information on the terrorists. Authorities will want to know their number, description, gender, how they are armed, how they are deployed, how do they communicate between themselves, which language do they speak and which do they understand, their ability and their level of survcillance.

Establishing a safe, direct channel of negotiation between hijackers and government negotiators is an essential step for successfully concluding an incident in a peaceful manner. Ideally, the Captain and the crew should avoid getting directly involved in the negotiations, but if they are forced to participate, they should act as mere mediators. The Captain will probably need to explain the difficulties in establishing and maintaining long range communications at sea and the problems associated with the various time zones, etc. Besides being true, such kind of arguments assist in imposing real delays that benefit hostages.

Where and when possible, hijackers should be encouraged to surrender peacefully and dissuaded from mistreating either passengers or crew members.

After concluding the incident, the Captain and the crew should avoid talking personally with the press or other media about the methods employed by the government for solving the conflict.

If an armed action takes place aimed at recovering control of the ship, and even anticipating it if possible, the Captain and the crew should instruct the passengers on the following issues:

- Not reacting to call the attention of the newcomers, commandos that may have a rather impressive aspect.
- Not paying attention to any unusual activity perceived.
- If shooting is heard, or the order to "GET DOWN" is called out loud, everybody should immediately lay themselves on the floor, face down, ears covered, eyes shut and in silence. Everyone should stay in this position without getting up or moving until the assault is over and the "all clear" message is called out.
- If the order "STAY STILL" is called out loud, everyone should freeze in position not to run the risk of attracting the shooting.
- If the location of the terrorists is known, or where a bomb has been placed, or any other information that may assist the assaulters, it should be reported immediately to them.
- Never cover up or hide the terrorists. Do not take photographs of the assault force.

Nevertheless, it should be mentioned that these kind of warnings, given in order to limit the impact of an assault by an antiterrorist commando, are also known by terrorists themselves.

Amongst other aspects, the plan should cover:

- The need to intensify surveillance and use of lighting and surveillance and detection equipment.
- Crew response when detecting a potential attack or once it has been committed.
- Alarm procedures and communications to follow.
- Reports to be issued after an attack or attempt.

Measures in front of an eventual intended boarding

- Sound the ship's steam whistle and the general alarm bells.
- Establish contact on the VHF with coastal stations and other nearby ships.
- If possible, increase speed.
- Launch distress flares.
- Switch on all the external lighting.

- Use reflectors to light and dazzle the suspect vessel.
- Stay alert and maintain a consistent outside watch.

Actions after a pirate boarding

- If possible, barricade the bridge and the engine room.
- If possible, make the crew strong in safe areas.
- Report the situation by radio as soon as possible and request immediate assistance.

Obviously, Captains may initiate any action that they may deem reasonable under the circumstances of the case in order to repel the boarding. However, at no time should they risk either their own safety or their crews'.

Reporting the incident after the attack

Immediately after an attack, a report should be sent to the corresponding RCC, and through it to the public forces or maritime authorities of the coastal state. The report should identify the ship, her position, damage to the crew or ship, escape direction of attackers, their number, description of their vessel, as well as any eventual capture of any attacker by the crew, or whether anyone was injured or dead aboard or the ship became seriously damaged.

Lastly, the Captain may decide to throw overboard a suspicious object, although this is not recommended at all, and to do so the IMS specifically designed system should be used, which includes a line for keeping the artefact fastened.

5.8 Hijacking yachts, and other violent acts against smaller vessels

Many people and vessels have vanished in certain areas where, at times, poverty and a lack of security at sea, as well as the occasional smaller scale drug trafficker, cause recreational navigation to become too risky an adventure.

It is unlikely that professional pirates would dedicate their efforts to smaller vessel assaults, but as with street crime, anywhere in the world an opportunist wishing an increase of income may be found.

An example of a piracy incident to a recreational vessel would be one which happened back in 1994 in the South China Sea to the 36 foot sloop "Tara". Sailing from Fremantle to Honk Kong, the vessel left Singapore, and in front of the coast of Vietnam it was harassed by several local fishing boats until, after a two hour pursuit, a freezer ship appeared on the horizon and the pirates decided to give up, not to be identified during such an adventure. They were obviously would-be pirates, mainly theft driven.

Security measures that travellers should consider when planning a trip range from trying to avoid dangerous areas to using methods to prevent boarding (remotely controlled reflectors, dogs), amongst which firearms are not recommended due to the legal issues involved with related incidents in foreign countries.

Except in areas where drug trafficking prevails, chance piracy is sporadic, and occurs on careless travellers that provide for an easy strike by sailing or mooring by night close to the coast in dangerous areas, travelling on their own or mentioning inconvenient data over the radio, etc.

Nevertheless, the majority of serious cases of disappearances and hijackings have much to do with drug trafficking. Traffickers make use of the simplicity of robbing or hijacking the means of transportation, then getting rid of their owners and even the vessels after the operation.

In the Caribbean Sea, several professional importer networks were broken up, but they were swiftly replaced by beginners operating in Central America, Mexico, and on the United States East and West Coasts. Following these changes, numerous vessels began to vanish in those areas. Due to the long distances involved in such enterprises and the intention of sailing without calling at any port, the chosen vessels were, and still are to a certain extent, motor sail boats. With the increasing demand, the loading limitations of sail boats forced a change towards a larger displacement ship type, fishing boats or luxury yachts, thus increasing the loss of such vessels.

It was found that many of the disappearance cases showed hijacking evidence, such as the following common traits:

- A seaworthy vessel, capable of carrying large loads over a considerable distance.
- One or more crew members with a questionable identity.
- An owner crew member known to be carrying a large sum of money on board.
- A ship kitted for a reasonably long voyage.
- A ship leaving her last port unobserved.

In many other cases, hijacking takes place at high seas by some recently recruited crew member.

In August, 1974, the "Kamalii" was boarded and seized by two Vietnam veterans (Mark Maynard, aged 27, and Kerry Bryant, aged 25) and an ex-member of the Coast Guard (Michei Melton, aged 24) in Honolulu's harbour.

With the actual crew (Bob Weshkeit, aged 49, Frank Power, aged 47, and John Freitas, aged 52) on board and gagged, the ship set sail for Thailand to collect drugs. Two days after sailing deep into the Pacific, the original crew were forced to jump overboard, in spite of their pleading. The hijackers only stopped to throw them a raft. Although they were away from the main navigation routes, the castaways were rescued five hours later by the Italian freezer ship "Benadir". After sending a warning message by radio to the Honolulu Coast Guard force, and after being pursued by the patrol boat "Point Corwin", the "Kamalii" was caught and the hijackers arrested.

Cases are innumerable: the possible hijacking of the "Tecumseh" and the "Kat Mei", both well equipped vessels, which vanished after leaving Caribbean ports at which they had recruited crew members.

The "Lupita", hired in Mexico by two American couples, was later found dismantled in the San José Island. It is believed that the enrolled crew murdered them and then used the vessel for a sending of drugs.

The "Peregrine" was scheduled on a crossing from Acapulco to the Grand Caiman Island through the Panama Canal; to that end, six crew members from Southern California were enrolled. The ship vanished without a trace, but investigators determined that extra quantities of supplies had been boarded before departing. Again, a drug connected affair is suspected.

Maybe the strangest cases are those of the "Puerto Limón" and the "Cómo No". The former left Houston bound for Costa Rica, after becoming known that drug traffickers had been spotted aboard. The ship and her crew of twelve never reached port, and, most surprising, their radiobeacons (which activate automatically when in contact with water) never indicated any position at all. Federal agents considered this disappearance as a drug driven hijacking. The "Cómo No" should have been sailed by a retired couple from Fort Lauderdale, Florida, through the Panama Canal to their residence in the West Coast. In Nassau, a German citizen was hired for working aboard and, following his recommendations, an Indian citizen was also hired in Barbados.

As the vessel called port at Venezuela and at the Canal, the letters home from the lady began to show her fears and concerns regarding the crew. The "Cómo No" never reached port. Subsequent investigations revealed that the identification documents from the crew members were forged, and it was suggested that a drug driven hijacking might have taken place.

Some cases have been even brought to the screen, like the disappearance of the ketch "Seawind" while moored in the Palmira Island in the Pacific. While at anchor, its owners did not establish a previously agreed radio communication with a radio ham at Hilo, Hawaii. In former contacts, the couple had expressed their concern about another couple aboard the yacht "Iola". After waiting for three weeks, the radio ham reported the disappearance of the "Seawind" to the Coast Guard. In late October, an off duty Coast Guard boat spotted in Honolulu a vessel, the "Lohaki", which matched the description of the "Seawind", and requested an investigation.

When the Coast Guard and FBI agents approached the vessel, a man jumped overboard and swam his way to the bank; however, the agents arrested a woman, Stephanie Sterns, who was sentenced for drug trafficking. The man, who was caught later on, was Buck Duane Waiker (alias Roy A. Alien), an escapee from a federal prison, a bank robber and a drug trafficker. With respect to the yacht hijack, both were sentenced for major robbery; some years later, after finding unearthed Mrs. Graham's bones, Waiker was sentenced for murder.

Thus, even though it would seem that the sole concern of yacht owners should be the theft of inflatable boats or outboards, personal violence is something common amongst seafarers, and therefore a matter to be considered when it comes to safety at sea.

5.9 Labour conflicts

Other acts of violence similar to piracy may be caused by subjacent tensions in labour conflicts, manifestations of dissatisfaction or resentfulness because of poor living conditions aboard.

In 1980, two incidents occurred, highly representative of these kind of acts.

The first one happened on the 12th of January aboard the "Easy Rider", while at anchor at about 25 miles Southeast of Morgan City, Louisiana. Crew member Robin Stansbury suddenly decided that he wanted to get home immediately, because of an urgent issue that could not be solved on the radio. Armed with a pistol and a rifle, he forced Captain Jack Waiker to lift anchor and set sail to Brownsville, although the latter managed to send a warning that he was doing so at gunpoint.

The Captain and another crew member were locked in a storeroom overnight, during the pursuit by a Coast Guard aircraft and the patrol boat "Point Noel". Finally, after having been shooting at his pursuers, Stansbury delivered himself peacefully, and the crew regained control of the ship. The second incident lasted longer, and involved several of the crew members, constituting a true mutiny.

The tanker "Ypapanti", flying the Liberian flag, was denied entry to the Philadelphia harbour due to pollution and safety issues, and set anchor in international water close to the Delaware Bay, while the ship owners were negotiating its admission.

On the 23rd of May, while negotiations were on their way, the crew, headed by the Boatswain and the First Officer, mutinied demanding their pay and complaining about the ship's dreadful condition. The Coast Guard decided not to intervene for the time being, since there was no threat to navigation; the United States government contacted the Liberian government in order to request its participation in the negotiations with the crew. However, after some days of conversations between the ship owners' lawyers, the Liberian government and the mutineers' representatives, no possibility of reaching an agreement could be envisaged.

On the 25th of May, the Captain of the "Ypapanti" warned the Coast Guard that the mutineers were holding hostages and threatened to flood the engine room with fuel and set the ship on fire; this information was confirmed by a crew member who managed to escape the ship swimming until he reached the Coast Guard patrol boat "Alert", which arrived at the scene on the 29th of May and remained in contact with the ship until the conclusion of the mutiny.

On the following days, the Liberian government requested formally the intervention of the United States; a plan was drafted by the FBI. After an ultimate negotiating effort, and having reached no agreement, the "Ypapanti" was finally assaulted on the 22nd of June by a team composed of Coast Guard and FBI forces, which joined their efforts in order to achieve the first significant maritime hostage rescue in modern history.

5.10 Immigration related violence

Attempts against people who intend to enter a country illegally from the sea are frequent, even before they reach their target; although this is an illegal act, violence occurs aboard ships of larger or smaller deadweights, ships nonetheless, and therefore it is due to mention them. At times, determining subsequently whether the act was committed in international waters or in territorial waters becomes difficult; therefore, jurisdictional issues are raised; other times there are no witnesses present, and in most cases, witnesses refuse to talk for fear of their illegal status being discovered or of retaliation.

Nevertheless, even though it may not be possible to prove the authors' guiltiness, facts are fully recognised by authorities, such as those that occurred back in August, 1979, when the skipper of a fast motor boat that was introducing illegal Haitian immigrants into Florida forced 18 passengers at gunpoint to throw themselves overboard; a mother and her five children were drowned.

In July, 1980, the crew of the "Dieu Qui Donne Y" threw overboard another refugee, because they thought that he was possessed by evil spirits.

The "Jesula" left Haiti in July, 1981 with about 200 to 250 people aboard. Its skipper requested money in exchange of food and water, and those unable to pay suffered hunger and thirst; those objecting the manner in which the voyage was being conducted were hacked to death with machetes, killed by stabbing or strangled. According to witnesses, 16 died because of complaining, while dozens were thrown overboard as they died of starvation or thirst; however, the FBI could not prove anything because the vessel, the crew and the passengers were Haitian, and because of the scant collaboration of the country's authorities.

5.11 Ecoterrorism

Acts of violence based on environmental issues go astride between political activism and the hindering of the legal development of some activity that, under the environmentalists' point of view, may damage the environment. Nevertheless, there are some good arguments to define such activities as a disguised form of terrorism, since some environmentalist organisations have not completely followed the nonviolent resistance model that in many cases unifies environmentalists and pacifists.

A clear example is found in the campaign against whaling; while the Greenpeace association began already back in 1975 with its nonviolent interposition methods between whaling ships and their victims, others employed much more drastic and violent methods.

Thus, on the 15th of July, 1976, FBI agents entered the home of an American diver and confiscated C-4 explosives, blasting caps, detonator cord, diving equipment and a two place submarine for use in attacks against Russian and Japanese whalers. Whalers "Sierra", "Ibsa Uno" and "Ibsa Dos" were the targets of attempts with explosives by the Sea Shepherd Conservation Society, presided by Paul Watson, to whom a previous attack to the whaler "Sierra", occurred on the 16th of July, 1979, was already attributed. The American citizen Rodney Coronado was tried in court for the destruction of the Hvalur Whaling Company whale oil processing plant and for the sinking of the "Hvalur 6" and "Hvalur 7" in Reykjavik harbour on the 8th of November, 1986.

While most environmental campaigns focus on demonstrations seeking global public opinion support, it should not be discarded that their actions could shift from mere hindrances to an actual ecoterrorism.

5.12 Conclusion

These are diverse forms of violence, maybe not very frequent, and occasionally affecting only very specific types of ships, but nonetheless they are violent acts that occur at sea. The fact that one or more persons, either driven by their convictions or by a wish for quick gains, may commit crimes against property and endanger the lives of many innocent people is as reprehensible on land as it is at sea.

6 Ship security application case

6.1 Work scheme

The following sections address IMO's requirements, as well as the recommendations from the IMO and the various organisations, in the following manner:

a) Recommendations and requirements will be addressed first.
b) Subsequently, two applications to the ship "Sedna" will be studied (Sections 6.7 and 6.8 in this Chapter).

6.2 Passenger ship security

In the face of all the currently existing regulations, there are processes that should be carried out in order to prevent unlawful acts and piracy aboard ships.

First action to be taken (irrespectively of threats being present or not) is being comprehensively acquainted with the ship herself. In this manner, if a day should come when a threat would occur, much work would have been accomplished in advance.

An information plan should be prepared in two parts, aimed respectively at the inside and at the outside of the ship, of which everything down to the smallest details should be known in order to protect, comprehend and analyse the following:

- Ship and her access or location.
- Which areas have free, surveilled, controlled, restricted or forbidden access.
- How many and which people should be protected, and what security level is required.

A) Plan for the inside of the ship

The following should be known and analysed:

a) Access ways:

- Doors and internal or external closures (number and strength).
- Portholes (number, layout, and existing security systems).

- Characteristics of corridors and stairways (lengths, drops, slopes).
- Lifts or goods lifts, if existing (location and operation).
- Access to sensitive internal areas, such as engine room, command bridge, control and communications rooms.
- Trapdoors, ventilation ducts and other orifices the dimensions of which may provide access to a person.

b) Distribution networks:

- Lighting: electrical panels, main switches, fuse boxes, emergency equipment.
- HVAC equipment, if existing.
- Water: location of tanks, valves, auxiliary pumps, etc.
- Fuel and gas circuits: valves, identification (labelling).
- Alarms: systems, triggering and disconnection modes, scope and effectiveness.

c) Weather decks:

- Layout
- Lighting
- Ventilation outlets
- Access ways to the inside of the ship

d) Utilities:

- Internal communications layout
- Engine room
- 002 room
- Archive, drawings and reserved documentation room
- Fire extinguishers
- Total ship crew

B) Plan for the outside of the ship

The following elements should be also observed, known and analysed:

a) Access ways to the ship, any kind of entrances to the ship, and access ways from the shore.

b) Surroundings, considering particularly:

- Distance to ships or closest dock (usual berthings depending on the port)
- Maritime transit of the area (smaller vessels, fishing boats, etc.)
- Are nautical events usual, such as yacht races
- Vulnerability while berthed (various communications, isolation)
- Buildings, maritime stations and nature of nearby ships

d) Auxiliary surveillance means:

- Autonomous ship lighting
- Other means (check performance): port patrols, terminal or station access control, closed circuit TV in the port facilities.

This is the information plan to consider in the face of any suspicion, thus being able to determine what target to protect in a more effective manner.

6.3 Security

Once the information plan is ready, it will be possible to know which areas of the ship are more or less unprotected, and which are in need of more or less protection. Two types of protection may be identified:

1. Fixed protection.

It involves the existence of an enclosure, with different devices as several types of sensors (optical, acoustic, infrared, photoelectric, CCTV, etc.). In emergency cases, specially trained personnel should be stationed in elevated ship areas, in a manner that they may communicate between themselves and with the person in charge of the watch, verbally or by telephone.

2. Mobile protection.

In the case of security based on patrols and surveillance rounds, this should be carried out by one or two people on watch, considering the possibility of being accompanied by suitably trained dogs when possible.

Permanent rounds should be made, without a fixed periodicity and with changing routes. Patrollers should carry a good communications system with them, enabling them to keep in contact with the whole security group. Bearing in mind that several areas aboard are not covered (due to the Faraday effect), a drawing or foreknowledge of communication barriers should be available, in order to have alternative solutions to solve the issue.

6.3.1 Protecting the outside

This large outside area should be protected with a combination of personnel and systems, thus preventing or controlling access of persons to forbidden areas.

Personnel available to control:

1. Guards stationed in areas that allow watching the outside of the ship.
2. Patrols in smaller vessels or vehicles, if the port surroundings in the berthing area allow it.

Control systems:

- Television cameras scanning ship sides
- Photoelectric cells

6.3.2 Identification

Once aboard, the basic objective of access control is to identify people that intend to access an area, by preventing, controlling or allowing access, depending on the case, based on previously established criteria.

6.4 Means of division

Classification of division physical means depends on the kind of pirate or chance agent. According to the division needs of a passenger ship, three main application groups of passive means may be identified:

- Protection against undue access: bulkheads, transit locks, locks and closing devices.
- Protection against coactions and aggression: counters, cabins, armouring.
- Protection against tampering: cabinets, showcases, safes.

6.5 Accreditation card

In order to control internal circulation on the ship, one of the most usual and easily applicable systems available is *accreditation cards*. Due to the existence of several internal departments on the ship, and the eventual rotation of crew personnel manning them, displaying an accreditation card provides for the following security conditions:

- **Physical identification:** In areas with a "posted" division criterion, an accreditation card is the only element representing the access level of each person to the regular users.

- **Prevention:** Regular users of a restricted access area, when faced with one or more persons not holding the due accreditation, have the right and the obligation to take the preventative measures deemed suitable under each circumstance.

- **Dissuasion:** The mere existence of an accreditation card creates an image of organisation and internal control, which may dissuade a third party from trespassing authorised limits when not holding the appropriate identification.

- **Electronic identification:** the accreditation card may be the base support for electronic identification elements, according to IMO's proposal on the personal identification card (IC).

In order to ensure the accreditation card functions, it should satisfy certain quality and design requirements. The minimum characteristics that should be considered as required are:

1 - Structure:

- Size similar to that of a credit card
- Security transparent laminated coating, preventing its removal without damaging existing data.
- Electronic identification element

2. Electronic identification element

3. Personal data

- Name, position, photograph

Current technological development and regular use of information technologies allow the quick issue of the required accreditation cards with every guarantee, by using the following items:

- Physical support with basic data
- Computer with digitalised card
- TV camera
- Printer

6.6 Structure of a control system

The basic structure of a control system comprises the following:

a) Data collection unit. This is the capturing or reading equipment of the identifier element, the most common being:

- Keyboards
- Card readers (magnetic strip, chip...)

b) Control unit. This equipment analyses the collected information, compares it with the preestablished database and decides in every occasion the due action.

c) Response unit. These are electrical mechanical devices that physically block access; they are capable of opening automatically if the control unit sends the appropriate command signal.

This basic set is used for controlling an access point in one or both circulation directions; the programming of the preestablished data is done locally and directly at the control unit, known as *Autonomous Access Control System*.

It is possible to connect several control units to a "central management" system, which will program, update and customise the preestablished databases for each unit; communications will be through a dedicated data network. This system is known as *Central Access Control System*.

The *Central Access Control System* provides greater flexibility in processing new registrations and cancellations and allows collecting at a single station actions or incident histories; therefore, it provides higher operating performance, although the requirement for a communications network involves a higher cost.

6.6.1 Means of control

Amongst the technological means available for personnel, correspondence and vehicle control, the following may be mentioned:

- Walk through archway metal detectors
- Handheld metal detectors, for individual checks
- X-ray scanners for hand baggage and parcels
- Metal detectors, for correspondence check
- Gas sniffer explosive detectors

Security personnel manning control points should carry out the set of necessary actions in order to verify that persons are authorised to enter and that their entry complies with the relevant regulations in force; they should prevent entry of unauthorised persons, therefore they are to identify everyone attempting to access the ship. So, access control should take place in a physical place or location where people or objects are identified and accredited to allow them entering the ship that is being protected; therefore, the best location is on shore, prior to the boarding (waiting) halls, and before accessing directly the ship.

6.6.2 Procedure for acting

Different kinds of people access passenger ships:

- Personnel whose fixed workplace and residence are on the ship.
- Persons occasionally boarding the ship (visitors, passengers, consignors, cadets, authorities, etc.).
- Under the ship operativity criterion, personnel may be, for both cases:

    a. In the payroll of the company or owner
    b. In the payroll of an external company providing services (cleaning, maintenance, etc.).

Control should be carried out by verifying their identity with the security accreditation or another type of company document. If no document is available, it is due to prevent access until verification has been completed by enquiring from the supervisor about personnel on the payroll. For every crew member, the following should be taken into account:

- authorised access level
- authorised time window.

6 Ship security application case 137

6.7 Security aboard the "Sedna"

This first application is made under less official (more realistic) criteria on a fictional ship, highly valid for any unit in the worldwide fleet.

The first action to be taken in order to be prepared in front of any kind of threat, unlawful act or any type of piracy, is having an information plan.

Documents available on board that may be identified as information plans are:

a) Ship drawings:

- firefighting control drawings
- engine room drawings
- fuel tanks drawings
- CO_2 room drawings
- drawings by decks
- cabin layout drawings
- aerial layout drawings
- ventilation drawings
- alarms, lighting drawings, etc.

b) Documentation for every device on board (instructions manual)

c) Required books aboard (almanacs, STCW, COLREGS...)

d) Security Management System (SMS). A file specifically created for the "Sedna", which addresses all security related subjects, from mandatory checklists (security rounds, newly recruited crew members...) to sea pollution.

6.7.1 Information plan for the "SEDNA"

Inside of the ship

    a) Access ways
    a.1) Doors or internal closures
    Number, drawing information, strength, (nonexistent or difficult to obtain data)

    a.2) Stairways
    Length: from drawing
    Drop: from drawing

    a.3) Lifts or goods lifts
    Location: car deck
    Operation: manual. Location from where pumps should be operated (engine room) and pumps for stern ramp and shelter ramp drives.

a.4) Access ways to internal areas

- Engine room: number of entrances (afore the car deck's central bulkhead, and astern the bulkhead. No restricted access).
- Bridge: three entrances (two from the wings and one from the inside).
- Control panels: number (one single panel in the navigation bridge, which allows monitoring safety doors when opening and closing). Detected deficiencies (the panel does not operate properly, as some fuses are out of order, and therefore they do not provide the required information).
- Trapdoors/ventilation ducts/orifices of manhole size.

b) Distribution networks

b.1) HVAC equipment

Heating and air conditioning are available in all dwelling areas on the ship (cabins, chambers, navigation bridge, engine control room), but not in corridors, holds, tanks, engine room or storerooms.

Heating is electrical; radiators may be individually set; air conditioning is general for the whole ship (i.e., where air outlets are fitted).

b.2) Alarms

- System: by sections and general
- Triggering modes: manual and automatic
- Scope: total.

b.3) Weather deck

- layout: 5 decks
- lighting: each deck is lit with fluorescent tubes or powerful floodlights
- ventilation outlet on each deck
- access way to the inside of the ship.

b.4) Utilities

- external communications layout: every utility has a telephone for communicating with the rest of the ship;
- engine room: communications by telephone on the ship's network; two personnel entrances;
- CO_2 room: located astern, in the manoeuvring deck; no communications available;
- fire extinguishers: located at each utility, easily accessible.
- total ship crew: basic (17), current (21).

Outside of the ship

a) Ship access

- Ship entrances
- Stern ramp access and pilot gangways on starboard and port sides
- Access from shore: stern ramp.

b) Surroundings

- Distance to ships or closest dock:
    - Port "X": Closest ship: 40 m from the bow
    - Closest dock: 15 m from the bow
    - Port "Y": Closest ship: 60 m from the bow
    - Closest dock: 30 m from the bow
- Yacht races held in the port:
    - Not affecting the ship's situation
- Communications from the dock: dock-ship by radiotransmitters
- Buildings, maritime stations, closest buildings to the dock are the shipping company's offices, as well as cargo warehouses of other companies.

c) Auxiliary surveillance means

    c.1) Own lighting
Ship's own lighting in car decks, shelter and upper decks
    c.2) Other means
- port patrols: within a 4 month period, only once has a police car been seen in port "X", never in port "Y";
- access control to terminal or station: port access control booths (two access ways);
- closed circuit television in port premises: no data available.

6.7.2 Protecting the outside of the "SEDNA"

Guards

Surveillance responsibilities for the outside of the ship falls on the dock access control booths, which are in charge of allowing or preventing people attempting to enter; with this, surveillance is nil. For this reason, any vehicle or pedestrian may enter the premises untroubled.

Barriers allowing access are at a height of 3 metres, therefore a car, a motorbike, a four wheel drive, a people carrier, etc., all fit perfectly underneath the barrier, so that it becomes unnecessary to provide any information to the personnel on watch.

If the guard is inside the booth, or has left, or is doing paperwork or in any other situation, access is free. This poses a great threat to ships, and in this study case, to passenger ships, as there is great freedom for introducing in the dock, the cargo or the ship herself any kind of substance, whether explosives, drugs, smuggled or illegal goods, etc.

Once the barrier has been crossed that provides direct access to the dock and the ship herself, there is freedom of movements within the whole are, as there are not guards either in the ship's surroundings, except for the officers on watch at the ship's ramp (since, as this ship also takes Ro-Ro cargo, there must be an officer at the boarding ramp).

Television cameras scanning the sides

Nonexistent. There is only one surveillance camera aboard the ship, on the starboard side of the stern ramp; its display screen is in the navigation bridge, where there is normally nobody for controlling entries and exits.

Access control

As detailed in the recommendations and requirements to be implemented aboard, in order to have a comprehensive control of persons entering and exiting the premises of the ship herself, all personnel should hold an accreditation card.

Such accreditation card does not exist for the "Sedna", so anyone could access any ship area without having to give any explanations. The only identification that might be considered as such is that of personnel in uniform:

- Bridge personnel: blue trousers, white shirt, blue jumper and epaulettes
- Engine room personnel: same uniform to go about the ship; blue overalls to access the engine
- Stewards and purser: black trousers and vest, white shirt
- Sailors and boatswain: blue overalls.

Even though the whole crew on board may be identified, there will always be people entering and exiting the ship not belonging to her, for example, Mafi drivers, cleaning personnel at each port, those carrying cargo drawings, agents, those accompanying passengers to the ship, clerks handling documentation, couriers.

Magnetic strip

The electronic identification card (other types could be also used) saves much work, since it allows real time control of personnel on board and the functions they may be carrying out.

The problem with passenger ships (not cruise ships) is that, since they make a regular daily crossing, always to the same port, same dock and with equal situations, a false visual confidence builds up. People approaching the ship are trusted, as "they are always the same ones" and they are well known; in this way, threats, smuggling and any other kind of unlawful acts are made easier. If a new person is hired by the company, the procedure the company adopts is the following one:

- The person is hired at the offices.
- A fax is sent to the ship, reporting that a new person has been hired to do the cleaning when arriving at port. The fax provides only the name of that person that should show up (not always), therefore there is no control; anyone could access.
- The person comes to the ship, boards her and carries out the task.

Entering the ship is as easy as climbing up the stern ramp and entering through any stairway without going through any security check, whether outside or inside the ship. Once on board, there is freedom to act, since crew members on watch have to stay in the car deck (officers, sailors, boatswain and cadets).

If the ship had this kind of cards, officers on watch would have another task, i.e., controlling people who access the ship, but in this manner any unwelcome surprise would be prevented.

6.7.3 External personnel control

In order to access the ship, the card's magnetic strip should have to be swept through a reader, which would display on a screen (monitored by the officer) access time, personal identity and task to be carried out on board. Assuming it was cleaning personnel, the time that has been contracted by the company for their task should be known, i.e., their work schedule. Once their time would be over, the personnel would have to exit the ship, sweeping again the magnetic card through the reader; in this manner, a total control would be achieved.

Once the authorised time of a person for being on board would be over, an alert would appear on the access control screen, warning that some unauthorised person is still on board. From then on, appropriate measures would be taken.

Throughout the process, visual controls should be in place, such as TV cameras, in order to follow everything going on aboard.

Prior to boarding, vehicles should be inspected on shore.

6.7.4 Antiterrorist/antipiracy security in passenger ships

Against external aggressions at the port

It is difficult to define police missions at ports without bearing in mind the responsibilities of the various maritime and port operators. Port authorities, maritime authorities, consignors, companies holding port public domain concessions, etc., should assume responsibilities within an overall security concept inasmuch security is nowadays a global enterprise; to a larger extent, responsibility fragmentation in the maritime and port environment demand a complex coordination.

Port authorities should take into account that it is at the port where highest risk hypothesis and highest probabilities for aggression hit their maximum levels.

By using their own dock security guard service, they should carry out a diligent and effective control on port access ways. A second access control should be established for the enclosure around the ship; this enclosure, if not fixed, i.e., not of a permanent nature, should be adapted on every occasion with other passive measures that may act as a barrier.

Any anomaly or suspicion raised on these controls should be reported to the State Security Forces for assessment.

Missions and responsibilities of the port security guard service, in security matters, should be defined in each port's security plan. With respect to the type of risks herein analysed, the security plan should be submitted for approval both to the Port Master and to the Government Subdelegate, who will be counselled by those responsible for both maritime and civil security.

Berthing areas for ships susceptible of being targeted for aggression should be, inasmuch as possible, always the same ones; they should be fenced and isolated, fitted with access control stations, sufficiently lit, and under direct surveillance of the dock security guard patrols, assisted on specific occasions, depending on the various threat and risk circumstances, by the State Security Forces.

If closed circuit television and monitored surveillance system is available at the port, it will be useful to implement at the control room perimetric surveillance with mobile cameras and zoom lenses. The head of the control room should thus be enabled to decide on sending a patrol in front of any anomaly detected. This person should also act as the liaison with the security forces. In case of reasonable suspicion, one or two hours prior to the ship's scheduled arrival, dock and berthing areas should be searched, following the instructions of, and working together with, the specialised teams of the security forces, including bomb experts and trained dogs whenever they be deemed necessary.

During port stay, the ship should be guarded both by on shore patrols and from the sea, so that the whole ship surroundings, including mooring lines, are safe. Such measures may be replaced or enforced by a direct watch on the ship perimeter from arrival to departure from the port.

The possibility could exist, independently of the naval means that the State Security Forces may have available, that port authorities, particularly those receiving at their ports a significant transit of cruise ships, should form teams of dock security guards that, in coordination with the existing security system, may answer to the need of counting on maritime guard on the water, within the port's service area.

Port authorities should coordinate with those in charge of the ship's internal security, normally through the consignor, before and after the ship arrival at port, or directly if necessary.

Port authorities should provide for security measures at the dock and in the water:

- Effective port and boarding area access control.
- Selection of berthing area; inasmuch as possible, always the same one, this allowing to permanently adapt facilities and passive security measures to the objectives.
- Closure and control with physical barriers of an area 50 metres ahead of the bow, behind the stern and across the docked side.
- Inasmuch as possible (due to the inherent difficulty), closure and control of an equivalent area to the above on the water side, by floating barriers.
- External lighting of ship perimeter.
- Check point for cargo and weighing.
- Port premises security, in collaboration with the security forces.
- Designating a security head (CSO), to be in permanent liaison with the State Security Forces.

A dock security guard patrol, capable of assisting and communicating with the security forces, should be established in the boarding and loading areas. Such dock security guards maybe have been charged, in fact and by right, in the last times, with an excessive margin of demands on civil security, which cannot and should not be separated from port security.

On their side, 1st category Maritime Authorities, those reporting to the Merchant Marine Directorate General, in the measure in which their territorial deployment coincides with general interest ports, deal with ship owners and consignors and are in special and privileged positions in order to obtain and provide information and assistance to police forces when necessary. To that end they should integrate any planning organisation addressing security matters, since often the organisation and planning of maritime security under their competence exhibit certain significant areas of overlap with port security and civil security.

Furthermore, local and area centres of the State Society for Maritime Rescue and Safety are in the position to provide useful information, both about ships and routes and ship owner companies.

The consignor should deliver to police and maritime authorities at least 96 hours in advance a passenger and crew roll, in order to cross check identities with a database and carry out a risk analysis and threat detection.

State Security Forces should provide assistance, inasmuch as possible and depending on risks and threats associated with her nationality or other factors, for the ship to be escorted by a patrol boat from the vicinity of the port entrance to her berthing. In the face of higher danger hypotheses that would appear to be more evident, the possibility of escorting potentially targeted ship in territorial waters should be considered.

In exceptional cases, on ship arrival at the port, a meeting should be held between representatives of the State Security Forces (Spanish Guardia Civil and National Police), the persons in charge of ship internal security (usually private security) and those in charge of maritime security (Maritime Authority personnel) and port security (Dock Security Guard).

By coming to an agreement on the liaisons to be established, on persons in charge and on specific preventative measures at the port and the ship, services should be assigned depending on threats and risks; this meeting should reveal which measures have been implemented and which not, so that eventual shortcomings maybe covered inasmuch as possible by port, ship or private security, if deemed appropriate. In any case, tasks to be carried out and agents should be defined, this being significant for both ship and port security plans.

All this should be defined for every port facility (Port Facility Security Plan) in a security protocol that may be designed with various response levels, based on a specific case history.

Regarding people aboard, identity checks should always be carried out, as well as a background check in case of reasonable suspicions, both for crew members and for passengers. Certain terrorist elements, under the pressure from their training or action quarters, may be compelled to use a ship, particularly a merchant ship, in order to avoid border controls and move to a haven where they may count on an infrastructure for hiding and obtaining support from similar groups. They may appear aboard hidden as stowaways, if they count on some help.

A feeling of security and control is always a most essential preventative tactic, a security on control of persons that should not be below that seen in country border and airport control. On this respect, sometimes maritime controls have become too flexible, merchandise control having become more liberalised, while it is the main reason for ports existing.

Intelligence services of the State Security Forces should draft lists of ships that, according to a risk analysis including nationality, capital, cargos, crews, routes, ship owners and main sailing areas, may be used by terrorist groups for their purposes, or may be actually controlled through ship owners acting as middle companies and are flying flags of convenience or are substandardised. These updated lists should be made available to customs, tax and police bodies that are in charge of security in the marine environment and ports.

In case of a cruise ship with high risk due to passenger nationality or other factors, with a scheduled disembarkment and stay in a city for a certain period of time, local authorities should be involved in the security system so that security may be reinforced as much as possible, depending on personnel availability, in port surroundings and the commercial area. Shipping companies know how important on shore passenger security is when making port calls.

Ship bottom inspections, when required, should be carried out if possible by state security force divers, whenever risk of strike is evident.

From a more current perspective and for routine cases, there is no problem in having the inspection carried out by divers from a private company, such as a highly specialised port security service, if it is a preventative activity. In any case, any doubt, incident or suspicious parcel should trigger the intervention of the State Security Forces.

Shipping companies and private companies, such as dock and facility concession holders

When such organisations use a dock concession in maritime and port public domain areas, thus using intensively or exclusively a determined part of the port, they should assume the responsibility for its security, under the demand of port and police authorities; they should carry it out at their expense, complying with some minimum requirements that include the obligation of controlling:

- private vehicle access to boarding areas
- passengers
- cargo
- boarding services, in particular supplier personnel identity

Concession holders should draft lists of all vehicles and people with authorised periodic access to cargo warehouses and port services, and submit them to port, police and customs authorities (Spanish Guardia Civil, Customs...).

The above should allow a verification of personnel data and significant circumstances. A parking lot should be arranged for all vehicles, far away from active boarding and loading areas, by at least 50 metres.

Private security personnel should be in charge of these obligations; in Spain, it is amongst their duties to assist the State Security Forces. Such missions are not incompatible with the defence of goods, interests and personal protection, which is their main duty.

Being a matter of general security, concession holders and/or shipping companies should report to the police forces any suspicious discovery of parcels or unjustified cargo aboard the ship. Such packages or parcels should be kept under surveillance while reporting them. The area around the object should be cleared and cordoned off in order to avoid injuries in case of an unexpected explosion.

The shipping company should provide the police authorities with information about the stowage companies that service ships at the ports, as well as about companies supplying other services.

Regarding personnel, the shipping company should allow only authorised and identified employees to access information related with embarkment or loading operations of the ship.

All those with responsibilities on ship security matters, both aboard and on shore, are essential to the performance of an appropriate security system, whether specifically dedicated to it or not. These personnel should have a head to act as the liaison with the State Security Forces.

Seriousness and rigour in the adopted measures inside the ships and for access ways, as well as for those other services supplied on shore, have a significant impact on security; therefore these personnel should be aware of their role and of the implications of the threats. Preventative surveillance provides useful information, hinders access to the ship to a large extent and dissuades those attempting an aggression.

Establishing restricted areas on shore assists in controlling and channelling access to holds and on shore cargo handling areas, thus enabling the shipping company to generally prevent the use of the ship to unlawful ends and avoid acts of sabotage and terrorism.

Passenger baggage should be checked systematically, particularly in cruise ships. In these pleasure trips, passengers have always available all their voluminous baggage, which is not the case in aeroplanes, where the baggage stays in the hold. This will force measures to be maximised, particularly at the boarding port. Furthermore, ship perimeter inspections should be carried out by the State Security Forces, either in case of threats or when it is deemed necessary, whenever relevant information on risks or threats is obtained, when the presence of terrorist elements is detected, and when existence of explosives or other potentially deleterious substances is suspected.

Controlling ship access

A ship hull constitutes a clear, easily defined boundary. Protecting this boundary creates a physical and psychological dissuasion for people intending unauthorised entry or attempting to cause material or personal damage. Measures adopted for protecting it hinder intrusion, allowing crew members and security guards to detect such and, if necessary, to seize intruders and prevent aggression.
All doors, scuttles and access ways to holds and storerooms not in use while at port should be kept locked, under the supervision of the personnel on watch.

Overnight, appropriate lighting should be provided over deck and alongside the hull.

Ship areas on water side should have appropriate security means, in order to avoid smaller vessels lieing alongside or approaching the ship closer than 50 metres. Floating barriers on water side of the ship are useful.

On the hull itself, double armoured doors should be fitted in order to provide an in between tight space, both in the access to the cabin where the command post and navigation instruments are located and in the access to the engine room. This would increase the chances of preserving both ship command and operation from terrorist actions; however, in actual extreme situations, this measure places the Captain in front of a terrible dilemma, since those seizing the ship will be holding the remainder of the crew and the passengers, and will exert grave coactions in order to force the Captain to accept their demands.

Measures strictly affecting immediate ship security will be handled by her security personnel, particularly:

- Access control
- Close ship perimeter control on dead works
- Passenger control
- Crew control
- Sensitive area bounding and passenger use restriction
- Ship side close lighting
- Deck lighting
- Closed circuit television
- Specific identity cards for crew and passengers, which increases security aboard, particularly when controlling ship access during port calls.
- Communications according to security requirements, both with port authorities and the Merchant Marine Directorate, and in particular with the State Security Forces.
- Liaison with those in charge of port, maritime and civil security.

The ship may be also accessed from her submerged part (ship bottom). Systematic inspections should be carried out on the submerged hull of certain ships when entering the port, in order to dissuade potential strikers and verify non existence of attached explosives.

Preventative measures aboard

The object is establishing permanent or routine procedures that may reduce the probability for a new critical event.

Prevention occupies the wide base of a pyramid, followed by evacuation, when this constitutes the most feasible solution for protecting passenger and crew lives; up on the vertex lies intervention, always with a doubtful, unpredictable outcome.

Action planning will be driven by previous knowledge of the ship and of the port's maritime surroundings, as well as of the typology of passengers depending on transit and population areas. Therefore, such knowledge should be acquired by:

- Preparing a risk area map, first for the ship, and then for the port area, according to their higher risk characteristics.
- Identifying those operations in the ship that may be considered routine activities. It is then very easy to identify which are strange, unusual, troublesome, and that in general will require crew response.

- It is very important that each crew member should wear a badge showing name, position and location in the ship. Wearing a uniform, an image is given of order, seriousness, leadership, when necessary, and of acquired or bestowed authority. Nevertheless, it is not recommended that a photograph should be included because, in case of negotiating, it prevents exchanging people.
- Passengers, on their side, should be identified with name and surname in their boarding pass, which should coincide with those in their official identification document (card, passport, etc.). On shore personnel should provide passenger lists, having fulfilled the first verification requirement.
- Defining access control, taking care of performance at each access. Suitability of locally installed or remotely located (control room) protections should be assessed, in order to ensure proper control at all times and conditions. Entrances and exits, as well as their use, should be appropriately signposted.
- Verifying effectiveness, messages, posting, pictograms, colours and suitability of the signposting on the ship, paying special attention to those depicting directions, bearing in mind that fixed signposts are always showing the same mandatory paths, whereas, in reality and under certain circumstances, it may be necessary to transit in the opposite direction to that pointed by the signpost.
- Physically bounding, with the appropriate procedures, public, private or restricted access areas. The confusion caused by people in non authorised areas or passengers in crew areas or control centres (navigation bridge and engine room) not accompanied by crew members, must not be permitted.
- Signposting in critical locations of the facilities representing a risk if special care is not paid, such as pipes for liquids and fuel gases, electrical conduits and panels, etc.

6.7.5 Antiterrorist/antipiracy security in the "SEDNA"

Against external aggressions at port

To access the ship dock, several security systems have to be crossed.

In port "X", first access is through the Guardia Civil or port police booths. At any of the entrances, there is no problem for accessing; entry is normally by vehicle –including taxi cabs or any other public transport, like buses. Having examined the system, the following conclusions are drawn:

Out of a large number of entries and exits, people were stopped only twice, and documentation was requested once for entering the port. Therefore, not only it is easy to enter the port carrying any kind of materials, whether explosives, drugs or people, but furthermore, if access is denied at one entrance, it only takes trying at the other one, since control levels are very low.

Once this barrier is crossed, the dock may be reached, going first through the dock security booth; however, as previously discussed, this is not a problem. Therefore, there is freedom to act.

This situation would be for the specific case with the "Sedna", the dock where it is berthed and the features offered both by the ship and the dock. There are other stations in the same "X" port that show more rigorous security levels.

The shipping company, as the concession holder for the dock and facilities, and the company, i.e., its contracted personnel, should take over the control of:

Private vehicle access to boarding area

Boarding vehicles and passengers approach the closest part of the ship (boarding area) through a different location than the booth. At the access point there is a security guard from a private company, and some clerk requesting documentation.

Passengers

"Sedna" passengers board with their vehicle. The boarding area is an open space, some 60 metres away from the ship. Passengers do not board using an accommodation ladder, but through the car deck, boarding passes being collected in that area, so that when they reach the boat, the crew is trusting the check in previously done by on shore personnel. Therefore, it becomes difficult when it gets dark to observe passengers and their vehicles in the ship, and know exactly who is boarding.

Loading

Unloading begins the moment the ship berths, and loading follows. The most usual for this ship is a cargo of vehicles, platforms and lorries.

Everything that should board is stored nearby the passenger boarding area, in a specific area for platforms; they are normally there for a day, two as a maximum.

Documentation aboard, once the ship is loaded, is the following:

- List of registration plates of every lorry and platform
- List of passenger vehicles with number and names of occupants

For security reasons in a passenger ship, suspect parcels and cargo on vehicles aboard, whether in the car when boarding or as hand baggage, should be controlled. These measures are difficult to take, and in fact there is not much emphasis placed in checking passenger baggage.

The fact that the voyage may take few hours justifies passengers leaving all their baggage in the cars, taking only the necessary for spending those few travelling hours, most of which will be spent sleeping. This means a difficulty in checking any suspect package, parcel or person, and therefore a great risk for navigation and the ship crew.

The ISM Code establishes that security rounds should be carried out in order to verify that all ship spaces are threat free, safe and performing appropriately.

Patrols and security rounds

a) Objective

To establish an organisation and development system for patrols and security rounds in order to guarantee safety of human life at sea and environmental protection.

b) Procedure

- Patrols and security rounds should follow a surveillance route through corridors, chambers, weather decks, car decks, etc.
- Checking that:
    - watertight doors and scuttles are closed and secured
    - lighting is as expected for the ship
    - no water seepage is present
    - no oil or fuel stains are found on the car deck
    - firefighting and abandoning facilities are appropriately in place, with no hindrances
    - no unidentified objects or packages are found

They should check temperatures and scents. In the face of any anomaly or doubt, they should check with the Officer of the Watch.

Following is a proposed checklist for condition follow up:

SHIP: CODE: DATE: TIME;		CHECKED	
		OFFICER	SAILOR
01	VHF, Channel 67 communications with the bridge		
02	Watertight doors, scuttles, closed and secured		
03	Ventilation / Air conditioning rooms		
04	Special rooms: emergency engine, paint lockers, CO_2, electrical boxes and other storerooms		
05	Water seepage in cargo decks		
06	Life rings and associated lights		
07	Lifejacket boxes		
08	Lashing and objects on the deck		
09	Stack (eventual production of sparks)		
10	Eventual oil or fuel stains in holds		
11	Hold temperatures		
12	Cargo lashing		
13	Vehicle securing		
14	Fumes, scents, temperatures		
15	Ashtrays, paper bins, galley, offices, electrical appliances		
16	Passengers in non authorised areas or with dangerous attitudes		
17	Apparently abandoned objects or packages		
18	Overnight, drawn external curtains		

Stowaways/terrorists/pirates

a) Objective

To prevent the risk of stowaways/refugees, terrorists and pirates, which may gravely endanger the safety of people and goods, due to their ignorance of safety standards aboard or their aggressive attitude.

b) Definitions

- *Smuggling*: commerce, importation of goods that are forbidden by the Laws.
- *Stowaway*: a person embarking illegally, not knowing order and safety requirements on board, thus representing a serious danger; may be a smuggler.
- *Terrorist*: an individual attempting to control the situation by imposing terror.
- *Pirate*: a maritime offender or criminal.
- *Refugee*: a person who, due to war, revolution, persecution, political or economical crisis, becomes forced to seeking refuge in a foreign country.
- *Boat people*: a general name to identify vessels carrying refugees that flee their country for whatever reason; generally vessels are overcrowded, and do not count on sufficient means for extended survival. It is a Captain's duty to embark them to save their lives.

c) Procedures

  c.1) General

- On board access ways should be kept under watch in order to hinder boarding. Any crew member observing suspect people or packages should immediately report it to the Bridge Officer of the Watch for security verification.
- Should any incident occur, putting the ship to risk, the Captain should report it immediately, when possible, to the closest Maritime Authorities, to the designated person.
- Should an internal action occur, endangering people, goods or the ship in general, the company should report it immediately to the authorities and the P&I Club.
- When the Captain is informed about the risk, the crew should be informed and reminded of the importance of attitude, calmness, dialogue, priority being the protection of human life.

The whole crew should always keep in mind, in front of any kind of danger, that confidence in themselves, their professionalism and their experience, together with a collaborative, calm attitude, will increase probabilities of success. The following risks are categorised:

- stowaways
- refugees
- terrorists and pirates

Stowaways

Due surveillance should be exercised in all ports in order to prevent stowaways from embarking secretly. This surveillance should be more intensive in ports with a higher risk of stowaways.

At some ports, when the pilot comes on board for the exiting manoeuvres, he remains aboard until a last check for stowaways is carried out.

General precautions for preventing stowaways embarking:

- While at port or at anchor, keep scuttles and storeroom, pantry and galley doors locked when not in use. The crew should keep their cabins locked.
- Only people authorised by their relationship with the ship (authorities, consignor, cargo, suppliers) should be admitted on board.
- No unused ladders, scaffolds, ropes, etc. should be left hanging over the sides.
- Overnight, bow and stern should be well lit, these being preferred access point.
- While at anchor, install operating pressurised water hoses through the hawsepipe of the mooring anchor and on the stern.

Stowaways may board using mooring lines, gangways, ladders, inside bundles or large drums (seals and contents to be checked), may hide in lifeboats, among ropes or packages, etc.

Some countries punish stowaways heavily, and if the ship cannot prove that everything possible was done to prevent the act, she may be held and fined. For such cases, the Captain, in order to provide objective evidence of his special interest in preventing stowaways from embarking, will instruct before setting sail the Bridge Officer of the Watch and the Chief Engineer (this may be delegated to an Engine Room Officer) to carry out a visual inspection of all accessible spaces in the ship and to check locks, latches and padlocks of closed areas.

Security search or inspection rounds should cover all areas of the ship. When the Bridge Officer and the Chief Engineer report to the Captain that no suspect individual or package has been found, the Navigation Watch Officer should be instructed to enter the search in the navigation logbook, including the time of conclusion and the outcome.

If a stowaway or a suspect package were found, the Maritime Authority should be immediately notified.

Any non compliance or incident should be immediately reported to the designated person to inform the company high management.

Finding stowaways in high seas

The person finding the stowaway should report immediately to the Captain.

An officer, accompanied by two witnesses, should proceed as follows:

- The stowaway will be prompted to identify himself/herself: name, surname, nationality. The stowaway will be asked to empty the contents of his/her pockets and produce all belongings. The stowaway will be asked whether he/she boarded drugs or weapons.
- A record of the above will be taken (how was the stowaway found, what were his/her declarations, apparent physical state, documents, money, personal belongings, etc.); this will

be signed by the officer and the two witnesses; the stowaway will be prompted to sign (an "X" mark is sufficient if he/she cannot write). If not willing to, it will be stated in the record, and the officer and the two witnesses will sign it.
- Due to the possibility that the stowaway may be involved in drug or arm trafficking, an inspection will be carried out, with two witnesses, in the surrounding area to where the stowaway was discovered, or in possible access routes; this will be also included in the record.
- If drugs or weapons are found, a record will be taken, the officer and the two witnesses signing it.
- Found drug and weapons will be deposited in the Captain's safe, and they will be included in the customs manifest for the destination port.
- The Navigation Watch Officer will record this in the navigation logbook.

Regarding communications, the Captain should keep the designated person informed, who in turn should inform the P&I Club. The Captain should report the finding to the destination port consignee and to the destination port administration. The Captain should include a statement of the number of stowaways found aboard in the destination port arrival documentation.

The Captain is to bear in mind that the stowaway should be appropriately treated, given a bed, be under control and have restricted movements. The stowaway should be fed. Under no circumstance should the stowaway work on board.

The Captain should follow instructions issued by the authorities, if it were the case.

When the stowaway is about to disembark:

- The Captain should designate and officer who, in front of two witnesses, should take a record stating how the stowaway was found, with what belongings, that the stowaway was appropriately treated and fed, given a bed to sleep in, that personal belongings found on him/her were handed back, date and time of disembarkment, and to which authority was the stowaway delivered.
- The record should be signed by the officer with the two witnesses and the stowaway(s); if the stowaway(s) cannot write, an "X" mark should be sufficient; if not willing to sign, it should stated in the record, and then the officer with the two witnesses should sign again.

Refugees

The Captain faces a grave dilemma when finding a vessel full of people, requesting potable water or succour, in a coastal area with a marked risk; they could be disguised pirates.

The Captain should board them one by one, and they should be prompted to show everything they carry on them.

Records should be taken, and they should be treated as in the case above, i.e., as stowaways.

The Captain should report it immediately to the designated person, so that the P&I Club and the port authorities are notified if the ship is in a bay, at anchor, at port or near some coast.

If in high seas, the Captain should report it immediately to the designated person, to the consignee and to the destination port authorities.

The Navigation Watch Officer should make the relevant entries in the navigation logbook.

Terrorism and piracy

Distinguishing both concepts is not easy, since their aggressive behaviours are similar; they are all armed individuals putting the safety of people and goods at risk.

A merchant ship may be subject to an armed attack in any coast of the world, but those coasts that have little or no maritime surveillance are especially dangerous. Of particular concern are rugged coasts, shallow waters where the ship has to sail at a moderate speed, rivers, canals, anchorages; it is much more unusual that ships be attacked while berthed at port.

It is safer by day than by night; it is safer at higher speed than at moderate speed.

The most vulnerable parts of a ship are: the command bridge, the communications room and the engine control room.

When the ship is scheduled to sail in terrorism and piracy risk areas, the company should request from the shipper, loader, receiver, consignor, P&I Club, information on risks and the best manner to address them. This information is supplied to the Captain, who in turn passes it on to the crew.

When there is the opportunity, the designated person from the authorities of the nearby coast should be immediately warned.

It should always be kept in mind that human life protection is paramount, and that it is essential that both the Captain and the crew should make an effort to keep cool minded, calm, that they should negotiate some agreement, that they should accept their requests.

The Navigation Watch Officer should record any happenings in the navigation logbook when able to do so.

6.7.6 Suspects aboard

Acting on incidents aboard

Initially, they are controllable circumstances and conditions that, nevertheless, if not addressed in a logical and orderly manner by duly trained personnel, may go out of control and reach a higher level of seriousness, thus constituting an emergency. Emergency response should be as systematic as possible, answering to a process of identifying emergency situations, planning and training the intervening personnel. On a ship, more than anywhere else given its isolated condition, the emergency should technically be based on resorting to the ship's own resources, while waiting for the participation of external resources –rather far away in time and difficult.

Identification

Description consists in transmitting to other people observed facts, so that the most accurate possible knowledge about them may be gained. Description may be verbal (supported by graphs, drawings, etc.), written or mixed. Of the three types of communication, written is the most solid one, by means of a report. Description is based on observation, which is the first link of the observation-description-identification-communication chain.

What may be described:

- People: physical aspects, attitudes, etc.
- Objects: vehicles, weapons, places, etc.
- Facts: development, sequence, etc.

Person description report:

a) Personal data

NAME:	Full, including surnames
NICKNAMES:	All known
ADDRESS:	Current and former (if known)
ID:	Or passport, in case of a foreign person
NATIONALITY:	Original and acquired
OCCUPATION:	Name all
MARITAL STATUS:	If married, include spouse name

b) Physical features

Gender: male/female
Apparent ethnic type: white/black/Roma/mixed/Asian/etc.
Build: thin, normal, obese, etc.
Weight: approximate
Carriage: normal, upright, bent over, slumped shoulders, etc.
Marks: scars, freckles, warts, etc.
Disabilities: broken limb, badly healed injury, lack of some limb, deafness
Peculiarities: twitch, laughter, etc.
Voice: smooth, hoarse or harsh, sharp...
Manner of talking: slow, fast, clear, confused
Habits: clean, dirty, smoker (type and brand of tobacco), drinker

c) Morphological traits

Head: normal, large or small, round or semiround
Face: round, square, oblong, wide, long or thin
Complexion: white, dark, sanguine, sallow, pale
Ears: normal, square or round, triangular
Forehead: high, low, large, small

Eyes: normal, bulging or sunken, with bags
Eyebrows: small, large, thick
Nose: straight or greek, sunken, aquiline, wide or narrow
Lips: thin, large, tight, commissure upwards
Teeth: large or small, prominent or protruding, even
Chin: pointed, square, parted, dimpled
Hair: straight, wavy, curly, point insertion
Beard: short, pointed, rounded
Moustache: long or short, trimmed, drooping
Sideboards: none, large, gipsy-like, etc.
Neck: long or short, thick or thin, bulging, wrinkled...
Shoulders: broad, square, round
Hands: large, small, long or short fingers

d) Apparel

Clothes: looked after, working, business, expensive or cheap
Type, shape, colour: jacket, jumper, trousers, skirt, shoes, head wear: hat, beret, hair band, hood, helmet, etc.
Way of wearing: hand carried, on the head, tilted, pulled down...
Other elements: jewellery, watch, objects being carried.

This report, completely filled in, would provide an accurate portrait of somebody suspicious or identified as a suspect.

6.8 Yet another application of the Ship Security Plan to the same ship

In order to compare operating guidelines under different application criteria, another possible procedure is detailed for a Ship Security Plan, in this case managed under different specifications, but strictly complying with the ISPS (less operative, more official).

6.8.1 Captain and crew

The company issues an explicit declaration on the highest authority held by the Captain.

In case of conflict between the safety requirements and the security requirements applicable to the ship, the Captain should prioritise those necessary to maintain the ship's safety.

Since the Captain holds the highest authority on the ship, roles and responsibilities are not listed as they are clearly defined in this ship's Safety Management System (SMS) and are inherent to the position.

The Captain is the SSO (if required, the First Officer can hold this position, if in possession of accredited training).

Ship personnel with security tasks

Security related roles and responsibilities, in addition to any other stated in the plan, are:

- The Officer of the Watch should assist the Captain/SSO in security related matters as instructed.
- Deck and Engine Room Officers will be knowledgeable of their ship's security plan, for application on those aspects that may concern them.
- Subordinate personnel should carry out security tasks as instructed.

All ship personnel

- Should know at all times at which security level is the ship.
- In case of emergency, should act as planned, following instructions from the SSO.
- Should participate actively in exercise and drills as established in the plan.
- Should be attentive to any security related incident that may occur and report it immediately to the Officer of the Watch or their department head.
- Should participate with interest in, and take advantage of, training lectures and the training schedule as established for the ship.

6.8.2 Defining security levels

Ships are obliged to act in accordance to the security levels established by their Contracting Government or country of registration.

Level 1 is the normal security level under which the ship should sail.

When the authorities establish a security level of 2 or 3, the ship should acknowledge receipt of the instructions regarding the security level modification.

1. The ship must never be at a lower security level than the port facility she intends to enter, or at which she is berthed or moored.

If the ship intends to enter the port, or is already in it, where the level is higher than that of the ship, she will notify the PFSO at the port facility that steps have been initiated to match the port's security level.

The ship should be in close coordination with the PFSO, reporting any difficulty encountered in applying security, in order to take due measures.

2. The ship may be at a higher security level than the port facility.

In this case, it should be immediately reported to the competent authorities of the Contracting Country Government, in the territory of which is the port facility and the PFSO. The administration of the ship operating at a higher security level than the facility should notify the Contracting Government.

It will be required to fill in a maritime security declaration.

6.8.3 Security related communications and information

Bodies with which the ship communicates

In terms of security, the ship may communicate with:

- The company; direct contact with the CSO.
- Port facilities; direct contact with the respective PFSO.
- Other ships; direct contact with the respective SSO.
- Authorities:
    - Country of registration: normally, contact through the CSO
    - Other Contracting Governments: normally, through the CSO or the respective PFSO.

The person responsible for security related communications is the Captain/SSO.

If necessary, the Captain may communicate directly with the authorities.

Other communication systems, depending on circumstances

Ship / shore: GMDSS
                Mobile telephones

Within the ship: portable VHF kits (3)
                 radio intercoms (4)

Security level related communications

The applicable security levels should be defined by the Contracting Governments for ships flying their flag and for port facilities in their territories.

The ship should receive information on the security level at which she should operate from the authorities of its country of registration, or from the Contracting Government of the port facility at which she is or is going to enter.

Communication about the security level at which the ship should operate, established by the authorities of her country of registration, may be received aboard directly on a "Navtex" message or similar, or through the CSO, who will have been informed by the authorities.

Communication about the security level at which the respective port facility is operating may be received aboard directly from the PFSO, on a "Navtex" message or similar, or even through the CSO.

The Captain/SSO should contact the respective PFSO as soon as possible, in order to receive updated information on the security level applicable to the port facility at which the ship is or is going to enter, and to inform about the security level at which the ship is operating.

The ship should respond with no delay to any security level increase.

Acknowledging receipt

The ship should acknowledge receipt of any instructions received for increasing the security level to 2 or 3.

Acknowledgement of receipt should be sent in writing through the Inmarsat or other available means, from the Captain to the body issuing the instructions, with a copy for the CSO.

The acknowledgement of receipt should contain as a minimum:

- Ship identification, date and issuer
- Reference to the instructions received and their issuer
- Security level that the ship proceeds to implement aboard
- Confirmation that the associated security measures are being initiated
- Whether there are any difficulties in implementing the appropriate security measures.

Information that may be requested from the ship when entering a port of another Contracting Government

The Captain/SSO should have the following information available, in case it be required by the Contracting Government of the port in which entry is intended:

- International Ship Security Certificate
- Security level at which the ship is operating
- Security level at which the ship has operated in the last 10 port calls
- Confirmation of any special measure that the ship may have adopted in the last 10 port facilities she may have visited. These may include:
    - Records of adopted measures when visiting a port in a country not a Contracting Government.
    - DOSs signed with port facilities and other ships
    - If people or goods rescued at sea are on board: their known details, identity and the results of verifications carried out by the ship in order to define their situation from a security standpoint.
- Information as collected in the continuous synoptic record
- Ship location at the time of notification
- Scheduled ship arrival time at port
- Crew roll
- General description of cargo aboard

Contact locations of Contracting Governments

In accordance with the provisions of Rule 13, Chapter XI-2 of the 1974 SOLAS Convention (as amended), prior to the 1st of July, 2004, Contracting Governments should notify the IMO and make available to companies and ships contact names and data for:

- National authorities responsible for ship and port facility security.

- Organisations and officials designated as permanently available to receive and address ship security alerts.
- Organisations and officials designated as permanently available to act in case of receiving communications from other Contracting Governments that exert control and compliance measures according to Rule XI-2/9.3.1.
- Organisations and officials designated as permanently available to provide assistance or instructions to ships regarding security, or to whom ships may report incidents or other security related circumstances.

Furthermore, Contracting Governments should also notify the IMO, and make available to companies and ships, the information relevant to sites within their territories that are covered by approved port facility security plans.

Ship communications on security incidents

A security breach is any act that may threaten the ship's security.

All incidents or possible incidents should be reported, as well as the measures taken if applicable, in order to analyse them and prevent recurrence.

A security incident may originate, depending on its seriousness, a review of the assessment, a security plan amendment, or applicable security measures.

The method is similar to that described for the Safety Management System in order to report potentially dangerous non compliances, accidents and occurrences.

The ship should report to the CSO, and to the PFSO if at port. The CSO should report the incident to the authorities.

6.8.4 Applying security measures on the ship

The Code requires that specific security measures for the ship be specified, which may be adopted with respect to the following aspects:

1.- Ship access control
2.- Restricted areas
3.- Control of embarked cargo
4.- Control of ship provisions, consumables and spares
5.- Control of unattended baggage
6.- Control of ship security surveillance

Access to the ship

On board access control is based on ensuring the following sequence:

Step 1. Enabling a single boarding access.
Step 2. Watching and controlling after access aboard.

Step 3. Enabling a single access door to the Purser's Office.
Step 4. Limiting other access ways to the Purser's Office and restricted areas.

Means for accessing the ship

At port, all the personnel, both external and crew, should access the ship through a single way, enabled for this purpose. This access should be the accommodation ladder to the aft deck or, in order to compensate for the tidal height changes, the gangway on the lifeboat deck. A "no entry" sign should be posted at this single access.

Access point surveillance and control

A crew member should be designated, to be in permanent contact with the SSO or a delegate, who should check all access of persons by means of:

1. Identifying all persons entering and exiting the ship through that access.

- The person on watch should request name, company and purpose from every person external to the ship, attempting to board.
- The person on watch should inform the SSO on the VHF for the visitor's authorisation and escort if applicable.
- If access is to a restricted area, the visitor should be escorted.
- Access should be denied to anyone raising suspicions or not providing identification. The SSO should be warned, to contact and report in turn to the PFSO.
- Name and exit and entry times of crew members should be entered in the access logbook, in accordance with the form in Annex 9.

2. Visual surveillance of the ship pier side from the check point.

Purser's Office access doors

Only one door should be authorised for accessing the Purser's Office, and it will be known by all the crew. The remainder of the doors accessing the Purser's Office should be locked from the inside.

Other access ways

1. To the Purser's Office

All windows and portholes of the superstructure, as well as portholes on the hull dead works facing the dock, should be kept locked from the inside, unless the associated room is being used at the time.

The pantry access scuttle on the lifeboat deck should be padlocked, except when loading provisions.

The engine room access scuttle from the bow bilge is an emergency exit from the engine room in case of fire. Therefore, it should not be padlocked from the outside, but it should be locked from the inside so that it may not be opened from outside.

2. To restricted areas

Restricted areas with access to the outside should be locked, except when occupied by authorised persons.

Ship access security measures

a) Security Level 1

- Enabling one single access aboard
- Identifying all persons coming aboard
- Surveillance on pier side
- Enabling a single door to access the Purser's Office
- Restricting other access ways to the Purser's Office and restricted areas

b) Security Level 2

In addition to the above and to Security Level 1, the following measures should be taken:

- Informing the whole crew about the modification in security level.
- Allocating an additional crew member to security roles, particularly to carrying out surveillance rounds in restricted areas and ship sides.
- All visitors to be escorted by a crew member.
- All portholes on hull dead works, including those on water side, to be locked.
- All restricted areas should be considered as high risk.
- Depending on the kind of threat, a search of the ship might be considered.

- Contacting the PFSO again, if port facility assistance is required for applying any measure.
- All communication systems to be kept active.

c) Security Level 3

In addition to all the measures of Security Level 2, the following should be taken:

- Ship exit should be denied to crew members, except for authorised security tasks or for ship abandonment.
- As a minimum, three crew members should be allocated (one officer and two subordinates) to specific security tasks. The Captain/SSO may use more personnel if required.
- Access to the ship is to be generally denied, except for authorised or security related personnel (crew members, local authorities, police, firemen, etc.).
- A search of the ship should be carried out; and surveillance is to be increased with rounds and patrols.
- All communication equipment should be active; alert communications should be coordinated and maintained with the external security officers.
- Emergency and evacuation systems to be on alert.

Restricted areas

The following should be considered as restricted areas:

a) With outside access

- Navigation bridge. Located on the bridge deck. May be also accessed from the Purser's Office. Contains navigational, communications and steering systems, firefighting pump remote startup and outside lighting switches.
- Bow storeroom. It has two access ways, located at the forecastle and bow bilge. Inside are the emergency firefighting pump, the port engine and the paint locker.
- CO_2 room. Access on the under bridge deck.
- Cargo deck. Access ways to the hold are located at the forecastle and the stern bilge. Access to the hold during loading operations is authorised only to the relevant personnel. In case of valuable cargo, or that may be used for unlawful acts or activities (restricted area), additional measures should be taken.

b) With access through the Purser's Office

- Engine room. Access is from an internal corridor in the Purser's Office and *from the outside*, through a scuttle located in the stern bilge. The power supply equipment and the servomotor room are located in this area.
- Pantry. Access is from a corridor in the Purser's Office and *from the outside*, through a scuttle located on the lifeboat deck. The refrigerator chamber is also located in this area.

6.8.5 Signposting

All restricted areas should be signposted on the outside access, indicating restriction of unauthorised access.

6.8.6 Keys

The Captain/SSO has a record of key distribution and a copy of the keys for all security related locks and padlocks.

6.8.7 Authorised personnel

The crew and the company personnel should be authorised to access restricted areas.

External personnel to the ship should not be authorised to access restricted areas if not escorted by a crew member or company employee.

Measures

- At port and *at all security levels*, restricted areas with outside access should be padlocked, except when occupied by authorised personnel. The navigation bridge should be locked by key or inside latch. Access to the Purser's Office (through which access to certain restricted areas may be gained) should be limited to a single door, as designated by the Captain/SSO. The other doors should be locked from the inside.

- During navigation at *Level 1*, restricted areas need not be locked or padlocked. At *Levels 2 or 3*, the Captain should consider the convenience of locking the areas, particularly those at the forecastle.

- When at anchor and *at all security levels*, restricted areas with outside access should be padlocked, except when occupied by authorised personnel. The navigation bridge should be locked by key or inside latch. Overnight, Purser's Office doors should also be locked by inside latch.

6.8.8 Controlling the cargo

The Captain knows well in advance which cargo is to be carried, prior to arrival at port. The cargo comes on board backed by its own documentation, issued by the respective companies and bodies.

Types of cargos that are carried include:

- Bulk goods. This is the type of cargo most often carried aboard the "Sedna". Bulk goods are loaded by means of a loading bucket or a conveyor belt directly into the hold. Loading operations are carried out under the visual supervision of the First Officer, who may temporarily delegate to the Second Officer.
- Iron and steel goods. Due to issues inherent to the transportation of these goods (packaging inspection, package number verification, etc.), iron and steel goods are rigorously inspected on the dock by the First Officer prior to loading on board. Specific instructions are in place for this type of loadings.
- General goods. During loading operations, the officer in charge checks that the cargo being loaded coincides with what has been previously consigned. In case of observing damaged packaging, it should be checked that nothing has been introduced in the package.

Measures

In case that cargo to be carried would have a high value or might be used for unlawful acts or activities, the CSO or the SSO will coordinate with the PFSO prior to the arrival of the ship at the loading port, in order to agree upon additional security measures at the port facility during operations and port call.

At levels 1 and 2, no further supervision will be required.

At level 3, depending on circumstances and in coordination with the port facility, loading/unloading operations should be suspended.

Special case. Transportation of explosives

This kind of transportation is always done between Spanish ports. Goods are carried in containers, and in the inside, explosives are separate from detonators. Containers reach the port escorted by State Security Forces, and are loaded aboard immediately. Containers are lashed onto the ship with wire. The ship does not linger at port and sets sail once loaded. At the unloading port, once berthed unloading takes place, again under the supervision of the State Security Forces. The ship adopts greater security measures since these are considered as dangerous goods by the International Maritime Dangerous Goods Code (IMDG).

Since loading and unloading operations are watched by the State Security Forces, specific security measures should be taken by the ship while sailing or at anchor. These measures should include:

- During stowage, it should be ensured that the container door is facing the bridge (in order to facilitate surveillance) and that it is safely locked (padlock, seal, etc.).
- While sailing or at anchor, no lieing alongside or excessive approaching should be permitted, except for authorised vessels (pilots, Guardia Civil, etc.).
- In case of suspicious approaches, vessel identification should be requested. If suspicions persist, authorities should be notified.
- While at anchor by night, the container stowage area should be lit. The possibility of allocating a crew member to carry out rounds while keeping in contact with the Officer of the Watch should be considered.

6.8.9 Controlling provisions and services to the ship

Internal instructions should be applied for requesting, receiving and supervising supplies (consumables, kit, food) and services (workshops, Marpol) provided to the ship.

Provisions supply is according to the following process:

- The ship sends to the office an order list (pantry, spares, stationery, medicine chest, etc.) with an approximate monthly frequency.
- Once supervised, the office handles the orders with a ship chandler, generally a known one.
- The ship is informed about by whom, when and where are the orders going to be delivered, and also about eventual changes with respect to the initial order.
- Upon receipt, the ship checks on the delivery note whether the supplied goods coincide with those requested. Eventual deviations are rejected and reported to the office using the goods return form.
- Orders are immediately stowed aboard in the appropriate locations.
- Bunkering and oil supply are notified to the Captain sufficiently in advance. Control is ensured by the bunkering and oil loading procedures.

Regarding services provided to the ship, the process is similar.

The ship requests a service and the technical department confirms who will be assisting. Instructions specify that it is mandatory that the person carrying out the repair be escorted while working, and that the department head should fill in a report on the job at its conclusion, to be sent to the office.

Security Level 1

Procurement is as described above. Identity of ship chandler or service provider is verified.

Security Level 2

In addition to the application of Level 1, a random check of the products should be carried out, by opening the packaging.

Security Level 3

Reception of supplies should be suspended.

6.8.10 Unattended baggage

There is no unattended baggage on this ship, therefore this security item is deemed not applicable.

6.8.11 Controlling ship security surveillance

Surveillance from the ship on the ship herself and her surroundings should be possible at all times and under all circumstances. In order to keep this surveillance, the following should be in place:

- Lighting
- Security guards and/or watchmen and/or personnel on watch on the deck
- Automatic intrusion detection devices

6.8.12 Lighting

The ship has permanent inside lighting in all areas.

The ship has outside lighting covering bow and stern areas, as well as sides, both pier and water side, including access control areas and holds. Sufficient portable floodlights are available for backup if required.

While sailing, the ship will have the lighting authorised by law in order to sail within regulations.

The ship is fitted with an emergency sequential startup of diesel engine and generator that ensures lighting.

Surveillance personnel

Ship personnel to whom surveillance tasks are assigned (access ways, rounds, etc.) should be equipped with handheld VHF sets or radio intercoms, whistles and safety torches.

They should keep in permanent contact with the SSO or the designated person through the established means. They should report immediately any incident that may occur.

Regarding private security companies, the SSO should consider the need for contracting them should exceptional circumstances make it advisable.

6.8.13 Ship search

Should a ship search be required by circumstances or the security level, the following is to be taken into account:

- A person in charge of the search should be designated, normally the First Officer.
- A search plan should be set, identifying areas to be searched and sequence.
- Search teams (2 people) should be allocated to each area, fitted with communications equipment. Preferably, areas should be assigned to personnel normally working in them, particularly the engine areas.
- Mark areas already searched, physically and on the plan.
- When dealing with a bomb: restricted areas should be searched first, as they are more vulnerable; handheld VHF sets should not be used.
- When searching a given area: start at the lower part and progress upwards, and from bulkheads to the centre.
- When searching decks and outside areas, special attention should be paid to waste bins, lifeboats, limber holes and any container in which objects may be introduced.

6.8.14 Automatic intrusion detection devices

If automatic intrusion detection devices were to be used on board, they should activate a visual and/or acoustic alarm in an area permanently manned or surveilled.

Measures to be applied:

a) At Security Level 1

- **Lighting**

   While berthed or at anchor: usual inside and outside lighting.
   While sailing: regulatory outside lighting.

- **Personnel assigned to surveillance**

   While berthed: one crew member in charge of access control; from the control point, the whole ship side to the pier can be watched.
   While at anchor or sailing: personnel assigned to navigational watch.

b) At Security Level 2

- **Lighting**

While berthed or at anchor: outside lighting to be increased; additional dock lighting to be requested from the port facility if necessary.
While sailing: regulatory outside lighting; lighting to be increase if allowed by regulations.

- **Personnel assigned to surveillance**

While berthed: One crew member in charge of access control, watching the access permanently; the other crew member should carry out surveillance rounds every 3 hours.
While at anchor: personnel assigned to navigational watch; a round should be carried out every change of the watch, with special surveillance on restricted areas.
While sailing: personnel assigned to navigational watch; a round should be carried out every change of the watch, with special surveillance on restricted areas if the state of the sea allows it.

c) At Security Level 3

- **Lighting**

While berthed: as for Level 2; additional lighting should be requested from the port facility if necessary.
While at anchor: as for Level 2.
While sailing: regulatory outside lighting plus all outside lighting if circumstances allow it.

- **Personnel assigned to surveillance**

While berthed: all the necessary personnel, under the SSO's judgment, to be engaged in surveillance tasks.

Furthermore:

- they will coordinate with external personnel in charge of dealing with the threat;
- an underwater hull inspection should be considered;
- keeping the ship ready to depart should be considered.

While at anchor: in addition to the requirements for Level 2, a round should be carried out every 2 hours.

While sailing: personnel assigned to navigational watch; a round should be carried out every change of the watch, with special surveillance on restricted areas if the state of the sea allows it.

6.8.15 Contingency plans

This section addresses action plans in emergency cases and provides actuation patterns to tackle the event.

These patterns may serve for carrying out the exercises and drills mentioned in the previous section.

The following are included:

1. Bomb threat / suspicious parcel
2. Stowaways
3. Ship occupation or hijacking by armed strikers
4. Piracy
5. Castaway succour and rescue

6.8.16 Bomb threat

Every bomb threat should be taken into consideration, response being immediate and systematic.

Any crew member should report immediately to the Captain/SSO or the Officer of the Watch if a bomb warning is received.

The Captain should contact the CSO and notify the authorities, and the PFSO if at port.

The following situations may be encountered:

Bomb letters and bomb parcels

The outside aspect of a mailed letter or parcel bomb usually exhibits the following features, which may assist the crew in identifying a suspicious parcel or letter:

- Bomb letters often bear marks such as "Personal" or "Private". Inaccurate name, position and address of the addressee appear usually in distorted writing, homemade labels or cut and paste characters. Wires, aluminium foil or oil stains may be present, as well as a peculiar scent. They may be stiff, unequal or skewed. They may have excessive postage.
- Bomb parcels may be poorly wrapped and may show a note reading: "Fragile - Handle with care", or "Urgent - Do not delay". They may have an irregular shape and soft or bulgy areas. They may buzz, tick or sound as containing liquids.

Written bomb threat

- Everything received should be kept, including envelopes and wrappings.
- Once the message is recognised as a bomb threat, any unnecessary manipulation should be avoided.
- Care will be taken to preserve any clues, such as fingerprints, calligraphic or typed writing, paper and postage, since they could prove essential for identifying the sender.
- While written messages are usually associated with general threats or extortion attempts, never should any written threat, warning about the placement of some artefact, be underestimated.

Telephone bomb threat

There are two reasonable explanations for someone calling to warn about a bomb going to explode at a given time:

- The caller knows or suspects that a bomb has been or will be placed, and intends by calling to minimise personal and material damages.
- It may be the same person that placed the artefact, or someone who may have been informed about it, intending to create a panic atmosphere and disrupt normal activities.

The receiver of the call should:

- Remain calm; register every word.
- Listen to voices or peculiarities in the conversation, trying to distinguish background sounds that may assist in identifying or locating the call.
- Be alert to the recurrent use of certain words or sentences.
- Attempt to recognise a national or regional pronunciation.
- Register date and exact time of call reception.
- Not hang up for as long as possible.

- Attempt to have the caller answer as many questions as possible (writing down the answers):

    When will the bomb explode?
    In which area of the ship is the bomb?
    What type of bomb is it?
    What does the bomb look like?
    Where are you calling from?
    What is your name and the name of your organisation?
    Why have you placed the bomb?

Actins after receiving a bomb threat

If the ship is at sea, the Captain/SSO should consider from the onset the possibility of putting back to a nearby port, taking the ship to shallower waters and anchoring, or even abandoning ship.

In all cases, and with the assistance of the CSO inasmuch as possible, the Captain/SSO should assess eventual damages to the ship and persons. They should also analyse the required mitigation actions (ship division, cancellation of any running special operations, disconnection of fuel intakes, rescue equipment, firefighting, etc.), including total ship evacuation.

In any case, and depending on the situation, the following measures should be initiated:

a) Bomb situation I:

Telephone threat; no information about place or time of explosion.

- Carry out a swift search of ship areas.
- Close watertight doors and scuttles.
- If the bomb is found, take the precautions as detailed below, and wait for the bomb disposal experts.
- If not found, proceed with ship evacuation.

b) Bomb situation II:

Telephone threat; information about bomb location available, but not the explosion time.

- Evacuate the areas adjacent to the indicated area.
- Close watertight doors and scuttles.
- Carry out a detailed search of the indicated area.
- If the bomb is found, take the precautions as detailed below, and wait for the bomb disposal experts.
- If not found, proceed with ship evacuation.

c) Bomb situation III:

Telephone threat; information about exact bomb location and explosion time available.

- Evacuate the area adjacent to the indicated area.
- Carry out a detailed search of the indicated area.
- If the bomb is found, take the precautions as detailed below, and wait for the bomb disposal experts.
- If not found, cordon off the area and wait for external assistance in order to locate the bomb while there is time remaining
- Evacuate the ship if nearing explosion time without having neutralised the bomb.

If a bomb or a suspicious parcel appears or is discovered, the Captain should take the following actions, as required.

Actions when discovering a bomb or a suspicious parcel

Under no circumstance should anyone be touching or manipulating the parcel. When discovered, it should be immediately reported, providing a short description if possible; subsequently, the following guidelines should be applied:

- Report as indicated above.
- Do not touch, manipulate, shake or open.
- Do not get close.
- Do not use metallic tools, handheld VHF sets, water or open flame in the vicinity.
- Do not cover the object with metal plates; sand bags may be laid.
- Open doors, openings and ventilation hatches in the room where the bomb is, in order to diminish the effects of an eventual explosion.
- Cordon off the area where the artefact is found, and block it with an encompassing restricted area (including, if required, doors above and below).
- Do not allow entry of unauthorised personnel.
- Evacuate adjacent areas, including above and below.
- Wait for external assistance and bomb disposal personnel.

6.8.17 Stowaways

A specific procedure is in place within the company's Safety Management System that addresses the prevention of stowaways coming aboard, as well as the ship and company response in case of a prevention failure resulting in a stowaway boarding.

Guidelines as detailed in the procedure should be followed.

North Africa ports should be considered as special risk locations for stowaways boarding.

6.8.18 Ship occupation or hijacking by armed strikers

When such a situation occurs, the Captain/SSO should be immediately informed. The remainder of the crew should be warned through the available means.

The Captain/SSO should activate the ship Security Alert System (if implemented) and additionally should attempt to communicate directly with the office, the CSO and/or the corresponding authorities in order to report the attack.

Recommended actions

- Except for the Captain/SSO and the officers, who preferably should be the speakers to the strikers, attempts should be made if possible to flee or hide in order not to be held.
- No resistance should be offered to armed attackers, unless as a last self defence resource for life.
- Aggressions should not be answered, either physically or verbally: be passive, but not submissive.
- Stay as calm as possible, and advise other crew members in the same sense.
- Attempt to maintain ship safety.
- Keep in mind that attackers may not be acquainted in detail with ship operations, capabilities and limitations, and that routing actions may appear suspicious to them. Become indispensable ("only the crew knows how to handle the ship", etc.).
- Offer a "reasonable" (not unlimited) assistance. Attempt to enter a "grant/obtain" dynamics.
- Attempt to establish the nature of the strikers (pirates, terrorists, etc.).
- Gather information about their pretences and their lead times.
- If their pretences come down to robbery, facilitate their targets, without offering more than required.
- Collect as much information as possible about the attackers (number, gender, description, organisation, etc.).
- If the attackers wish to communicate with the authorities, provide the means, but do not act as mediators in eventual negotiations.

Particular case: hostage holding

Assault and capture

- Do not panic.

- Attempt fleeing amidst the confusion, before hijackers gain full control and gather hostages.
- If possible, isolate the perimeter of the risk area, in order to avoid other crew members entering it.
- Evacuate as much as possible from the area people that have not been seized.
- Keep calm and avoid tension to increase.

Negotiation and wait. Actions when assistance is not available to the ship

- Establish a single negotiator with the hijackers.
- Make it clear to them that the negotiator is not empowered to make concessions.
- Understand exactly their pretences and lead times.
- Never threaten or use violent language, neither give them orders. Attempt to decrease tension until external assistance is obtained.
- Inform them that their petitions may be fulfilled, and will be studied, but do not promise an immediate concession, under the pretext that the negotiator is not authorised for it.
- Do not overvalue hostages, as this gives the hijacker a sense of power.
- Let hijackers talk; do not interrupt them.
- Do not make concessions without getting something in return.
- Do not exchange hostages.
- If a commitment is made, it should be sincere and credible.
- The negotiator should attempt not to show any emotions or excitement, by using a calm, neutral speech.
- Attempt to create an impression of activity ("something is being done"), even when no actions may be taken.
- Attempt to create the impression that their reasons are understood.
- Keep in mind that it may be a long, patience demanding process. Time runs in the ship's favour.

Rescue and liberation

If hostage holding gives place to a rescue operation by the authorities, hostages should keep the following in mind:

- If rescuers surprise arrival is noticed, no reaction should take place in order to avoid hijackers noticing it.
- During the rescue assault, the rescue team may find it difficult to differentiate between hijackers and hostages; it is therefore advisable to keep still in order to facilitate identification.
- Do not panic and run; rescuers could shoot at people running.
- If called to halt, stay still and obey orders from rescuers for identification.
- Do not protect or hide hijackers.
- Do not take photographs during rescue.
- The best way to behave during rescue it to lie immediately on the floor, hands on head, ears covered and mouth open, staying like that until instructed otherwise.

6.8.19 Piracy

The "Sedna" develops its nautical activity essentially in European Community waters (except for some occasional port calls in Morocco and Tunisia). No pirate strikes are known in these areas, neither are they considered as risk areas internationally.

High risk areas

All studies on piracy agree in stating that the higher risk geographical areas are:

- South China Sea littoral, including Thailand, Vietnam and the Philippines.
- Singapore and Strait of Malacca areas.
- Central and South America, particularly Brazil's coastal waters and ports.
- Western Africa, particularly Nigeria.
- Gulf of Aden, Yemen
- Somalia
- Areas close to China, India, Sri Lanka and the Caribbean.

Recommendations

Should there be risk of piracy, the following should be adopted:

a) While berthed

- The best dissuasion is keeping a watch.
- Only authorised people may embark; personnel on watch should be very strict at the checkpoints.
- Non essential access ways should be locked; those that are required to be open should be kept under watch.
- Rounds should be carried out, keeping in communication with the Officer of the Watch. Such patrols should be visible (dissuasive effect).
- Lighting should cover all deck areas. Additional lighting should be in place for dark areas and water side.
- A handheld megaphone should be available, to put off any approach.
- Pressurise firefighting hoses for immediate availability.
- Fireman's axes, strategically placed, may be used for cutting ropes when used for climbing. However, axes may dangerously expose crew members.

b) While sailing

Precautions adopted for the above situation, in addition to the following:

- Increase visual and radar surveillance. Ensure that personnel on watch are equipped with binoculars.
- Increase speed and, if possible, sail in daytime.
- Make big course changes if a pirate approach is noticed.
- Request assistance from nearby ships and launch distress rockets.

Response to a mayday/distress call

Occasionally, attacks have taken place after the pirates have sent distress signal, causing the ship to approach to offer help. In other situations, distress messages have been used to rescue illegal immigrants as false castaways, in order to enter another country.

The following precautions should be adopted when receiving a distress signal or when confirming sight of lights or rockets:

- To begin with, do not respond.

- Gather all information possible on the issuer:
    - Situation/Call identifier/Flag
    - Problem details
    - Vessel description
    - People aboard
    - Any other data
- Report it to the maritime or coast guard authorities and to the CSO. Await instructions.
- If no reply is received from the competent authorities, the Captain should assess the situation and proceed as follows:
    - Move to an area from which the endangered ship may be seen

Situation assessment

- Ensure that all security means are operative. The Captain should then decide between rescuing and leaving the area.
- Report all actions made to the CSO.
- If passengers are taken aboard, they should be searched and placed in a secure area.

Strikes from smaller vessels

Attacks from smaller vessels may take place, manned by armed personnel or used as "weapons", while berthed, at anchor or sailing.

Depending on the threat, one or more of the following measures should be adopted:

- Have axes, shears, pressurised fire hoses, etc. available on the deck.
- Have distress rockets ready at the bridge.
- Ensure that ladders are appropriately stowed.
- Use any means (lights, whistles, steam whistle, etc.) to warn attackers that the ship is ready against their approach.
- Lock as many deck doors as possible for access control.
- Increase lighting.
- If possible, request assistance from the maritime authorities.
- If berthed, contact the local authorities to obtain information on whether additional measures should be taken.

Suspicious approach of another ship

Measures to be taken while sailing are:

- If possible, a minimum approach distance of 2 miles should be kept with all ships.
- When this is not possible, due to the transit or because of restricted areas, identification from all ships within de 2 miles should be requested over the VHF.
- Any smaller vessel approach should be dissuaded.
- If suspicious moves are observed, maritime authorities should be contacted.
- If endangered ships are seen, the ship should keep on hold unless there is full conviction of loss of life risk. Maritime authorities should be contacted for assistance.

Measures to be taken while at port:

- Any smaller vessel approach should be dissuaded.
- Identification of any smaller vessel approaching transit should be requested.
- If suspicious moves are observed, maritime authorities should be contacted.
- Patrols should be increased, particularly on the water side.
- Increase use of lighting at nighttime in port, in order to light the water side and stern.

Castaway succour and reception

From a security standpoint, when coming across a castaway or a group of castaways, procedures should be as follows:

- Finding of castaways should be immediately reported to coastal authorities, providing the following information:
    - Geographical position
    - Description of boat or raft (if it were the case) and the call identifier
    - Number of people aboard
    - Other details (apparent condition of the castaways, sea conditions, etc.).
- In case of castaways in the water, they should be boarded immediately. In case of a boat or a raft and depending on the circumstances (castaways condition, distance to the coast, sea conditions, etc.), instructions should be awaited from the coastal authorities, in case they come to the rescue.
- If circumstances force boarding them, castaways should be searched and then grouped as much as possible in the Purser's Office. Personal belongings that they may be carrying should be recorded and kept safely.
- Castaways should be identified, and as much information on the event as possible should be gathered (total crew in the wrecked ship, accident circumstances, whether they know of other rafts or boats, etc.). All the information should be passed on to the coastal authorities as soon as possible.
- Castaways should be prevented from accessing restricted areas aboard; they should be kept under permanent surveillance.

6.8.20 Other emergency situations

Those emergency situations (fire, abandonment, flooding, etc.) that may occur as a consequence of a criminal act should be addressed in accordance with the provisions of the emergency procedures included in the Safety Management System.

6.8.21 Ship evacuation and abandonment

Ship evacuation may occur as a consequence of an emergency situation as the ones mentioned above, or because Level 3 may have been activated aboard due to a threat.

If evacuation takes place while at sea or at anchor, it is "ship abandonment", therefore the corresponding emergency procedure included in the Safety Management System should be applied.

If evacuation takes place while berthed at port, the following should be kept in mind:

- All activities should be in accordance to the organisation chart for abandoning at port, designed for the ship (available on board).
- The Captain, or the First Officer if the former is absent, are the only authorised persons to order the ship's evacuation, taking into account, if applicable, the instructions from the external assistance.
- Once everybody has mustered at the dock, it should be checked that no one is missing. If anyone is missing, the Captain should decide what action to take.
- Information should be provided on the destination of the evacuated persons and on who is in charge of the group. The "safe area" should be located at least at 100 m from the risk area.
- No one should return to the ship until ordered by the Captain, based on the information provided by police or the bomb disposal personnel.

6.8.22 Security related equipment maintenance

The following are considered as security related equipment:

Lighting

Outside, inside and emergency lighting.

They are part of the ship security and operation equipment, and their use, test and maintenance are covered by the Safety Management System and its associated Programmed Maintenance System.

In case it is needed, portable backup lighting equipment is available. Maintenance of this equipment is limited to checking operation and storage, as well as having spare lamps available. This is integral to the verification described in the previous section.

Communications equipment

The ship may use for security related communications all available means, depending on circumstances and the communication addressee. This equipment includes:

- GMDSS equipment, including Inmarsat C and Radiotelex (world coverage). Preventative and corrective maintenance on this GMDSS equipment is guaranteed by the redundancy of some of them and by a maintenance contract with an external company. This contract is renewed yearly.
- Mobile telephones.
- Automatic Identification System (AIS)

Inspections carried aboard on GMDSS equipment are covered by the Safety Management System.

For ship internal communications, two radio intercoms are available (2 in operation + 2 spare sets) that are maintenance free; they are replaced when not working properly.

Furthermore, two way VHF sets are available (3), the maintenance of which is done by the external company.

Other equipment

- Crew members have a whistle and a torch.
- Rescue and firefighting means are part of the safety equipment and therefore are covered by the Safety Management System and the Programmed Maintenance System associated with it.

Any security related equipment implemented aboard subsequently should be maintained in accordance to the instructions of their associated manuals, and should be included in this chapter.

Ship security alert system

Rule 6 of Chapter XI in the 1974 SOLAS Convention (as amended) requires that this ship should have a Security Alert System in place.

Implementation aboard should be completed within the required date.

Once implemented, this chapter should include operation details, activation points and the procedures for testing, activating, deactivating and preventing false alarms.

Guidelines for the onboard operational use of shipborne automatic identification systems (AIS), Resolution A.917(22), approved on the 29th of November, 2001 (item 9 in the agenda).

The provisions of regulation V/19 of the International Convention for the Safety of Life at Sea (SOLAS), 1974, as amended, requiring all ships of 300 gross tonnage and upwards engaged on international voyages, cargo ships of 500 gross tonnage and upwards not engaged on international voyages and passenger ships irrespective of size to be fitted with an automatic identification system

(AIS), as specified in SOLAS regulation V/19, paragraph 2.4, taking into account the recommendations adopted by the Organization,

Objectives of AIS

AIS is intended to enhance: safety of life at sea; the safety and efficiency of navigation; and the protection of the marine environment. SOLAS regulation V/19 requires that AIS exchange data ship-to-ship and with shore-based facilities. Therefore, the purpose of AIS is to help identify vessels; assist in target tracking; simplify information exchange (e.g. reduce verbal mandatory ship reporting); and provide additional information to assist situation awareness. In general, data received via AIS will improve the quality of the information available to the OOW, whether at a shore surveillance station or on board a ship. AIS should become a useful source of supplementary information to that derived from navigational systems (including radar) and therefore an important 'tool' in enhancing situation awareness of traffic confronting users.

The AIS is able to detect ships within VHF/FM range around bends and behind islands, if the landmasses are not too high. A typical value to be expected at sea is 20 to 30 nautical miles depending on antenna height. With the help of repeater stations, the coverage for both ship and VTS stations can be improved.

The data is autonomously sent at different update rates:

- dynamic information dependent on speed and course alteration (see table 2),
- static and voyage-related data every 6 minutes or on request (AIS responds automatically without user action).

Table 6.1 Report rate of dynamic information

Type of ship	General reporting interval
Ship at anchor	3 minutes
Ship 0-14 knots	12 seconds
Ship 0-14 knots and changing course	4 seconds
Ship 14-23 knots	6 seconds
Ship 14-23 knots and changing course	2 seconds
Ship > 23 knot	3 seconds
Ship > 23 knots and changing course	2 seconds

7 Analysis of the interrelationships between plans

7.1 Analysis procedure

Previous chapters in this study provide a very accurate approach to the actual needs for addressing the main objective, namely the harmonisation of the emergencies of the ship.

To that end, it is necessary to identify, when possible, the dysfunctions that the implementation of the ISPS might create with other emergency and safety plans established and used for each ship.

Basic principles that direct safety and emergency or intervention plans should be considered, the actions or responses of which, aimed at controlling a situation resulting from an accident, may oppose those required in a security situation. Therefore, instructions that for a given safety situation may have an opposed direction to those that would be issued when entering a security situation should be identified, in order to find the most consistent, less contradictory procedure, so that all measures may be taken without mutual interference.

For a schematic presentation of the functional relationship between the Ship Security Plan and other safety and/or emergency plans, the diagram of figure 1.1 in Chapter 1 is still valid; according to it, once the perturbation has occurred, whatever the originating source or cause, security returns to a lower level once it has been trespassed, while other plans acquire each their corresponding significance depending on the situation.

Conversely, if a criminal act does not occur, safety plans should act at all times for maintaining safety and quality standards as required for the ship, and as committed to towards her effectiveness and image, in the various quality and operation management procedures.

For both cases, safety is that corresponding to the activity as a result of security; guard may never be lowered, either jointly or isolated regarding the rest of the principles, which from now on will have to share the same objective, focused on civil principles, handled by professional civilians and supported initially by civilians, although doubtlessly supported and assisted by, and with the close collaboration of, security experts, both civilian and from the State Security Forces.

This situation does not preclude that, depending on the security levels for each situation, emergency plan levels may be established and activated in parallel, which may make eventual responses to be more effective based on prior preparation of human and technical resources.

The development and application of emergency plan levels in consonance with those provided by the International Safety Management Code (ISM) and others involve states of alert and preparedness and even the adoption of specific measures that, should a criminal act occur, would make intervention team responses more effective by removing the surprise factor with which all emergencies initiate (circulating routes free for evacuation, less frights and improvisation, etc.).

In any other case, if the criminal terrorist action is detected by the manifestation of its consequences, the emergency plan should be activated in accordance to the provisions for any such emergency, as its text should envisage. Examples would be all cases included in the maritime accident category, irrespective of their originating source (Figure 1.2).

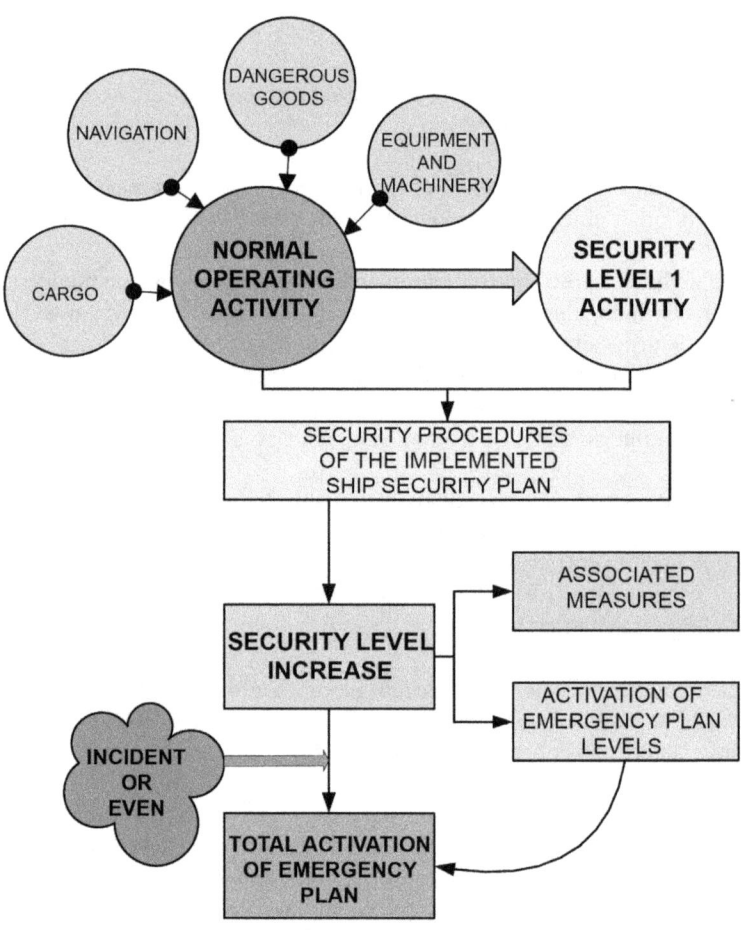

Figure 7.1

Nevertheless, the proposed criterion is to make use of a security level increase (from I to II) as if it were a prealert of something that might happen (a quantification exists on the degree of probability). Never before had maritime safety regarded in the maritime accident typology such security in advance to an event.

The interest, markedly significant, is in the capability of improving the effectiveness of an intervention by having human and material resources available in a more or less significant advance, applying the concept of prevention to the fight against an emergency.

This new situation allows to reduce, even to suppress, all type of improvisations, to improve the organisation of the resources available and to be and keep alert, knowing what the threat, the risk and the consequences are of that which is foreseen by the established security level.

The advantages, not limited to those already mentioned, open a wide horizon by enabling focusing and driving the final part of safety (intervention) to the widely desired levels, as they are expected and can be faced without surprises after they are manifested.

By admitting these principles, the need becomes evident for adapting, as much as possible, the contents of current emergency plans when addressed individually, in order to move on to an overall, concatenated approach to safety. It may be possible that many of them need no modification of any of the actions therein considered, whilst others may benefit from eventual modifications and updates, towards the final success of the intervention and the improvement of the human team quality in terms of safety.

It is therefore necessary, before entering a detailed analysis of emergency plans as considered in most ships, to interpret to its appropriate extent that eventual contributions will have an overall, but never universal, application, as this will always depend on the degree of updating and detail in the operating contents of the plans; it may be said that the proposed approach will be the more positive the lower the level of implementation of existing plans in a ship is, since contributions will be very positive and will represent a qualitative change for safety in such ships.

Finally, existing contradictions between the resolutions of security and maritime emergencies should be taken very much into account, since the actions required in each case may be totally opposed to each other, as the case may be with opening or shutting access ways, lighting or dimming areas of the ship, different communications and many more, depending on the emergency.

The working approach to determine to which extent plans, i.e., safety plans with respect to security plans, have mutual impact, and to which extent do they condition their development, will consist in analysing them from each other's standpoint, thus identifying their coincidences and differences, subsequently drawing conclusions, Therefore, it is not compliance relevant to the ISPS Code implementation that will be analysed, but rather the operating aspects of intervention, by which actions should be carried out with the participation of the available human teams.

7.2 Impact of security on the "safety" concept

Risks and threats as included in the "security" concept, which deserve consideration in order to find out possible relational implications with ship emergency plans, therefore representing problems that at times originate from the ship herself and her operation and at times from the port facility with which she is related due to maritime transportation operations, allow to proceed with their identification.

7.2.1 Risk classification

From antisocial activities:

- **Robbery:** Understood as defined in the Penal Code in force, i.e., including the factor of the exertion of force or intimidation on persons or force on objects, it is not deemed in its first meaning to constitute a typical risk for a port facility. In its second meaning, deriving from its typical activity involving the transit of passengers and merchandise, this type of risk has been traditionally one of the main problems for port facilities. Nowadays, the technical sophistication and the organisational complexity attained by some criminal groups, together with their international spread, has turned large scale robbery of merchandise and equipment goods into an actual threat for port facilities, having in many cases the connivance of carriers and even crews that seek in this way to improve their incomes. Therefore, a high level of risk is considered for port facilities.

- **Theft:** This kind of offence at a port facility, when not remaining a mere fault, originates from two kinds of sources. On the one hand, from personnel usually working there, who steal objects from their workplaces or from merchandises that transit through the facilities, normally being small in size since they are going to be "hand carried" by the thieve himself or sometimes in a private vehicle; the highest danger of this kind of offence, which occurs frequently, is that it may become continuous, causing a real problem in the long term, this besides the "mimic effect" that it usually causes, as well as the damage to the image of the port facility.

    The other kind of thief comes from outside the port facility. This is an action focused rather on passengers and their baggage than on merchandise, due to the difficulty in knowing the safety systems, storage, etc. It is deemed that a port facility has a medium level of risk in front of both kinds, but with a possibility for a noticeable increase if the number of passengers transiting through the port facility goes up.

- **Fraud:** Two varieties may be found of this criminal activity, one being the fiscal fraud against the State that owners or receivers of goods originating from a foreign country with a non compatible fiscal system may attempt; in this case, the State itself handles the control mechanisms it deems necessary, which obviously will integrate in the safety system.

    The other one is fraud or swindle using the port facility as a base for committing the offence between private subjects, mainly based on merchandise not complying with previously agreed conditions, this act being often allowed by the operating characteristics and structures of the port facility itself. Except for particular instances, risk for the port facility is deemed low.

- **Vandalism:** In some current developed societies there is a certain risk for damages on property done by rootless youths, who either wreck street furniture or paint graffiti on fences, walls or vehicles; it is considered that the port facility may suffer from this risk if such offences take place in its geographical area, damages caused being costly to remediate. Another more specific aspect are damages caused because of eventual labour conflicts at the port facility raised by some workers or external agitators, which in some cases may become acts of sabotage at the workplace. From the study, a low risk is derived for port facilities, except for the circumstances mentioned.

- **Kidnapping:** Economically driven kidnapping is not considered as a typical risk for port facilities.

- **Espionage:** In its industrial or economical versions, it may be that the activities developed at a port facility may be the object of this kind of risk, given the vital importance and value that information has in the current developed world; in any case, the diversity of information channels allow in many cases to access it from other places than where it originates; therefore, this is considered a low risk for port facilities.

- **Narcotic Trafficking:** The significance of this kind of risk in its form of large consignments and the high probability of it happening in a port facility cannot be missed, since these large quantities of substances use seaways for transportation from the production areas to the traffic or consumption areas; they are usually hidden in objects that are cleared as normal merchandise; in this regard, the State Security Forces, within the aforementioned fiscal control, carry out drug detection tasks.

  With respect to the smaller scale trafficking, it may be considered to be at a normal level within the country's framework; therefore, the risk may be considered as high for the first instance, and low for the second instance.

- **Aggression:** This type of event may occur anywhere where people come together; in the case of port facilities, they do not seem to be prone to such unless they are close to marginal housing, nightlife or prostitution areas. This may also change in case of labour conflicts that may occur between groups of workers or between them and the State Security Forces; in any case, this risk may be considered to be low under normal circumstances, unless the mentioned conditions occur.

Originating from terrorist actions

- **Firearm attempts:** This kind of action, always committed against people, is less and less used for indiscriminate strikes, due to its limited effectiveness in comparison to other means of aggression, being left only to selective actions, either with short firearms as they are easy to carry and conceal, thus allowing the aggressor to move about and approach the victim without raising any suspicions, their effectiveness being short ranged (less than 8 m for this kind of action), or with a long firearm with a telescopic sight, which allows distances ranging to 600 m. Neither case is considered as a typical risk for port facilities, except when a VIP visits the site or someone works at the facility who is under the threat of some terrorist organisation.

- **Aggression with an explosive device:** This action may be directed against people, goods, vessels, etc., given the great destructive power involved and the small size of the agent in comparison to other objects, so that it may be concealed in suitcases, bags, vehicles or any other object for transportation to the target. When the artefact is directed to people, it may contain shrapnel. This is the usual means for terrorist actions, as materials are easy to obtain due to their commercial or military use, or even making them. With respect to detonators, timers or radio controls are the most used, as they allow the executor to stay away. Another form of action is suicide bombing, by which the terrorist infiltrates in the target and actuates the device at the most suitable moment to cause the largest amount of victims or kill someone in particular. Port facilities have a high risk for these kind of strikes, due both to the increase in passenger transit and to safety measures that are mostly below those at airports.

- **Aggression with an incendiary device:** This type of artefact is aimed at destroying material goods rather than at acting against people; usually characteristics are low cost, simplicity and great destructive power, as long as weather conditions such as temperature, wind, humidity and those of the target, such as flammability, manner of storage, etc. are appropriate for an optimum result. Its use against facilities, goods, ships and cargoes at port facilities may be deemed as a medium risk.

  Another aspect to be considered is the use of smaller devices of the Molotov cocktail type in low intensity terrorist actions, if the port facility is in an area where such risks may exist, and within there may be some target; or that during riots due to labour conflicts or protests, such type of artefacts may be thrown against people and goods, the risk level depending also on the area history.

- **Aggression with chemical agents:** Amongst the risks being incorporated as action means of terrorist groups is the use of chemically loaded artefacts. Without going into further detail, such are directed against people, although they also affect animals. Based on their effects, they may be:

    - Dermotoxic, when acting on the skin
    - Hemotoxic, when acting on the blood
    - Pneumotoxic, when acting on the respiratory system
    - Neurotoxic, when acting on the nervous system.

  Ideal dissemination of these products is as a gas or aerosol, this requiring the associated equipment, either sited at the target or nearby, or on a land, water or airborne vehicle that may disperse on it the substances; however, the most effective use of these means is in confined spaces, as this avoids having to depend on weather conditions such as wind, temperature gradient, humidity, etc., which exert a great influence on the agent's effectiveness in open spaces.

  Another form this type of aggressive substances may take on are the so called binary weapons, in which two non lethal products become toxic when mixed, although this process requires a system or mechanism to do the mixing and dispersion.

  Regarding the risk of port facilities suffering this type of attack, wherever a large concentration of people is present within a confined space, like a cruise ship for example, such risk is present at a high level with respect to other special aggression means since, to this date, these are the means that have been used in several terrorist actions.

- **Aggression with biological agents:** Use of this means raises the great fear of human disease. These agents fall within two types:

    - Live beings: bacteria, viruses, etc.
    - Toxins: of animal or vegetal origin, etc.

    The latter are used in a very similar way to chemical agents, effects being also very close.

    Regarding the use of microbial beings, it is limited by UV rays, humidity and temperature conditions, which determine whether microbes may live and enter organisms in sufficient quantity to cause an infection. This involves an incubation period until the disease may be detected; once identified, it may be fought successfully by vaccination.

    Regarding dissemination means, aerosols, release by sabotage or use of vectors (infected animals) are the most usual. The easiest elements to use are air conditioning systems, which show ideal conditions for life and diffusion of living agents.

    From the above it may be derived that the risk of use at port facilities is limited to confined spaces, such as passenger terminals, public halls, ships, etc., where large numbers may gather; however, effects may take long to appear, so this could be deemed to be a medium risk, somewhat higher if used as part of a campaign to create a panic or health issues within a ship, mainly a passenger ship, when required by another type of action.

- **Aggression with a radiological agent:** This type of action consists in disseminating radioactive materials with the highest activity level possible in order to contaminate people or neutralise a facility, ship or area; this may be done by using an explosive or an incendiary explosive charge in order to increase the activity. As with biological and chemical agents, influence of weather conditions is significant in determining contaminated areas, its use being more dangerous to people in confined spaces. In any case, this may be considered a low risk at port facilities, due to the low usage to this date and to the difficulties for terrorist organisations in obtaining high activity radiological waste; furthermore, effects are on the long term, although it is yet another means for neutralising an area based on psychological impact.

- **Aggression with nuclear weapons:** At the present moment, excluding a war situation, it is not deemed probable that a nuclear weapon would be used, given the control exerted on them by the countries that have them. Indeed, their use would have terrible consequences for people and goods within their range, due to the combination of explosive, thermal luminous, radioactive and electromagnetic effects. As long as current estimates do not change, it may be therefore said that risk for a port facility is low.

- **Hostage holding:** This operation consists in a group of people holding another group of people by means of coercion, in order to achieve a political or economical goal, to have others freed, or to travel somewhere else. It is used both by terrorist organisations and during labour conflicts, although in the latter no firearms are used usually. When considering the two possibilities, i.e., that the act may be carried out on shore or in waters under the responsibility of the port facility, clearly the latter appears to be the most likely and the most difficult to solve, due to the problems associated with simultaneously boarding and controlling a ship in order to preserve the hostages' lives.

This type of terrorist action represents a medium risk for port facilities with passenger transit, due to the lower control exerted to the present date with respect to airport terminals. In any case, the risk analysis on each ship and line carried out by each company should be known.

- **Boarding:** Directing a hijacked ship against another ship or the port facility is an extremely grave action, since she may be carrying passengers, or may be carrying dangerous goods, either from an industrial origin or from a terrorist origin in order to increase the effect. It is deemed to be a low risk due to the low speed and manoeuvrability of vessels of a certain size, smaller vessels not being capable of causing significant damages.

- **Directed aeroplane crash:** Using an aeroplane as a missile against a building or facility, even a ship, involves prior hijacking.

From the standpoint of a risk study for a port facility, this may be considered as a low risk, as a port facility is not considered as a sufficiently interesting target due to the number of people it may concentrate. It is evaluated as too small to be hit by a passenger aeroplane, and if it is a smaller craft, effects would not be significant, as the Japanese *kamikaze* showed in World War II.

Originating from unlawful social activities

The following risks might be present on the ship and in any work related activity:

- o Risks when using machinery and tools.
- o Risks when handling loading, carrying and storage equipment.
- o Risks when handling power supply equipment.
- o Risks when handling tanks and containers used for product storage.
- o Risks when handling and using dangerous products and materials.
- o Risks deriving from circulation and carriage.
- o Risks caused by workplace environment and hygienic conditions.
- o Risks deriving from navigation.

And, with a higher incidence probability, risks related with crowds, masses and riots.

a) Crowds

A crowd needs not cause a riot. It is necessary to distinguish between the various kinds of crowd, since not all require an active intervention. It is essential to know when not to intervene and when to apply authority. The kind of crowd that may easily turn into an uncontrollable riot if appropriate measures are not taken is also important. A crowd is defined as a large number of people gathered in one body or group without any specific order. In general, a crowd is knowledgeable of the laws, and is willing to respect the principles of law and public order. This is due to the innate respect of a person for the law. It is more or less disorganised. For the time being, it does not have a leader or chief. It is hesitant and governed by reason.

There are different kinds of crowd. A *physical crowd* is a chance or temporary group of people that shows no group behaviour, just contact density. Such crowd has a common interest during certain moments, but still little organisation. There is no resolution unity, and members come and go. Such kind of groups will easily and directly obey an order. "Please move forward" or "Leave the area". Such group does not show a psychological unity, and therefore there is no further interest in addressing it.

There are however *psychological crowds*, crowds of people with a continued common interest, or responding emotionally to the same stimulus; examples would be a football match, a political meeting, an accident or similar situations.

A *conventional crowd* is that meeting for a specific reason, like a football match, or attending a stadium to see a show. Members of the crowd do not depend on each other, but they all have a common interest unit. In this kind of crowd, people's behaviour is controlled by very well established rules and laws for such occasions. Nevertheless, such crowd may become aggressive and uncontrolled. For example: when some spectators begin throwing bottles at the referee or the fights and disputes between people at football matches. Both examples show a tendency to developing aggressive behaviours. Such tendencies are restricted by a strict and rigorous application of regulations and laws.

An *expressive crowd* is so called because its members are involved in some kind of expressive behaviour: dancing, singing or watching a film. These groups express their feelings by releasing their energy through their motions. Such crowd is neither aggressive, nor does it use its energy to cause damage. It is much better that this crowd should carry on with their activity, letting them express themselves, as long as they do not breach the peace. If their expressive energy release is interrupted, underlying energies of such group might deviate towards more destructive and aggressive forms.

When a crowd builds up of people not coming from any specific place, but gathering to see an accident, a fight or a brawl, it is called a *curious crowd*; they are cooperative and intend to help. While such group gathers, the crew should attempt to disperse them, using at the same time their cooperation if required.

A disorganised group, willing to be driven to disorder, but hesitant until that moment because organisation, courage and unity of objectives are lacking, is a *hostile* or *aggressive crowd*. Such a group is made up of some determined leaders, some active participants and a number of spectators. They are rowdy and menacing, and mock and harass the crew. While under control, they will remain a crowd, but if control is lost, this group will cause a riot.

Crowd control is absolutely essential to keep it a crowd rather than letting it become a riot, thus neutralising the risk. It should therefore be kept in mind that controlling it is vital to prevent it turning into a riot.

To that end, the following steps should be followed:

- Gathering information on the nature and character of the crowd, and all information on the matter.
- Having a definitive action plan for any eventuality and keeping the bridge posted on the matter.
- Having an appropriate force available for controlling the crowd, apart from other negotiation lines for immediate use in case of emergency.
- Having all the public address equipment, systems of communication with the bridge, etc., ready, in good operating order, for eventual emergencies.
- Having the crew at their posts before the crew shows up, adequately informed and with precise instructions.
- Establishing a real time communications system so that the key persons may follow on the development of the event.
- Establishing ultimate boundaries for the crowd and keeping them. Halting a crowd is far easier than pushing them. A cordon barrier creates a beneficial psychological effect for restraining a crowd. People should not be permitted to cross over the established barrier, and prevented from tampering with it.
- There should be no contradictions between crew members, within the limits established by mandatory rules.
- Immediately removing from the crowd any sources of tension, such as hysterical, drunk or disorderly people, and trespassers of the rules or laws.
- Breaking up a teeming crowd before it becomes a hysterical, aggressive crowd.
- Means of precaution. The opportunities for throwing objects, such as bottles, may be limited by using paper glasses. In this manner the possibility is removed of some excited person beginning by throwing a bottle and the rest following the example.

One of the purposes of the crew when dealing with the public consists in clearing the way for the fire brigade during the crisis, should a fire start aboard. Swiftness is essential in order to unblock the way at intersections. Stepping on the hoses should be prevented.

Barriers should be used to avoid people getting close to the fire or accessing risk areas.

In case of brawls aboard, or even manslaughter, a crowd may gather that may become dangerous, restless or hostile. Such group is the kind of small crowd most difficult to keep under control. The first step is examining the area of the disturbance. If necessary, a task force should be organised to isolate supporters that may be harassing witnesses.

Should it be decided to remove someone from the group or even make a detention, remove the person from the area as soon as possible. Every crew member participating should take care of not becoming isolated amongst a hostile crowd.

It is essential to preserve the crime scene, and that procedures are followed as discussed in the chapter on investigation.

Place a cordon if it is an open space; if it is inside, allow no entry until the Security Forces take over the area when the ship arrives at port to initiate investigation.

b) Mass

When it is intended to shift the mass from passive to active and the multitude is organised, a collective spirit raises, conscientious individual personality vanishing in favour of a common feeling. Causes driving to this state are:

- Strong sense of power in the individual.
- The individual looses any restraint, being sheltered by the mass.
- Contagion, being within the multitude.
- Suggestion. The individual looses the conscientious personality and acquires a high level of excitement.
- The multitude is intellectually below the isolated individual.

Characteristics of masses are manageability, lack of restraint, suggestion and credulity. Multitude reasoning is based on very plain ideas by association with similar cases and generalisation of particular cases. A multitude lacks critical attitude. Imagination is representative, powerful and active. It all potentiates the possibility of a riot or even a mutiny.

c) Riots

A riot happens when the members of a crowd, under the stimulation of an intense excitation, lose their sense of reason and respect for laws, and follow leaders into unlawful acts. A riot is characterised by a clear organisation, having leaders that mark the direction to follow. Reasons for acting are common but, because of the high activity level, they are close to disaster, being governed by emotions.

The various kinds of riots show themselves aggressive, attacking, rebellious and terrorising. The action is unjust on one single side. Their goal is destroying people or property. There is also such things as *escape riots*.

Such are caused by groups full of fear, attempting to escape anywhere. A state of panic generates an escape riot. Power of reasoning is completely lost; rioters may come to the point of destroying one another if not controlled.

1. *Acquisition riot*, driven by the desire of acquiring something. Examples would be those seeking means of salvage in an emergency because there is no direction from the crew.

2. *Expressive riot*, expressing noisy fervour or joy, for example in a religious rite, a sports event, a New Year celebration. Such expressions may be destructive as a result of their high activity level, close to the disaster borderline.

When a riot builds up, there is some preparation first, i.e., a number of irritating events or vicious rumours that generate a tense atmosphere. This increases the activity level of each of the persons involved.

The first step in shifting from an already prepared, sensitive group into a riot is some circumstantial event. It may be an accident, an unanswered request for information, or some resentment against the shipping company for a badly rendered service. Maybe the expression will be more dramatic than previous ones. But by its nature it tends to call attention, mostly in an exciting way. The event causes a crowd to gather somewhere. Members begin to walk from one place to the other like a herd, attracting in turn curious onlookers.

As the event attracts more passengers, they come closer and closer to each other. Naturally, the crowd begins making contact one with another, and people begin to talk to strangers. They keep moving one with respect to the other without any reason, but they stay excited by the situation. This is how part of the atmosphere builds up. While moving about, the crowd gets more and more excited. Some people will leave the group to call their friends, to gain recruits, and to fuel rumours and hysterical excitement.

All this results in a spiral of stimuli. One excited person stimulates another, who in turn stimulates a third one. The third one may further stimulate the first causing an overexcitement beyond the original one. Thus, through stimulation, between one and the other, an atmosphere of tension and excitement may originate. As tension and excitement build up, people will act less by the stimulus received within the group.

This process creates an atmosphere of conformity within the crowd, as a collective hypnosis in which the individual loses control and responds solely to the crowd's collective reactions.

The individual loses his/her own conscientiousness. Any demonstration of brutality that may rise will be approved by the crowd. The whims and feelings of the crowd dictate the actions of the individuals. Then the crowd will vent, unleashing its wrath against a target chosen for violence.

	RISK SITUATIONS
Antisocial Activities:	
	Robbery, Theft, Fraud
	Vandalism, Aggression
	Narcotic Trafficking
	Hijacking, Espionage
Social:	
a)	Crowds, Masses, Riots
b)	Use of Equipment and Machinery
	Use of Power Supply Equipment
	Circulation and Carriage
Terrorism:	
a)	Explosive Devices
	Incendiary Devices
b)	Firearms
	Chemical Agents
	Biological Agents
	Radiological Agents
	Nuclear Weapons
c)	Hostage Holding
d)	Boarding
e)	Directed Aeroplane Crash

Figure 7.2

A riot that is not timely addressed during a crisis aboard may unleash a riot under panic. This originates from fear and ignorance. It is the terror inspired by an irresistible fear created by a very strong emotional state.

This irresistible fear may also create in an individual an irrational state or frenzied effort to attain safety. Panic riots are violent and difficult to control. This is due to the fact that people causing them are so excited that they act irrationally. Their actions increase personal and other's endangerment, rather than diminishing it.

From all this, a set of risks and threats may be summarised as in Figure 7.2, grouped in three main sections with highly differing manifestations of reasons and consequences, which establishes a degree of ship endangerment when affected by such.

c.1) Psychological characteristics of riots

Once the riot has been initiated, its members exhibit unique psychological characteristics. Knowing and comprehending them will be invaluable for controlling the crowd. Visible characteristics are homogeneity, emotion and irrationality.

Homogeneity of mind. Rioters hold the same attitudes, opinions, frustrations and common conflicts. Unity within the crowd is such that it does not seem to be composed of individuals, but by parts of a single mind.

Emotion. A riot consists in the high degree of tension and excitement maintained over the participants. Hostile emotions, hate, fear, prevail over mercy, love and other non aggressive emotions. While the crowd is acting, excitement keeps increasing.

This is sometimes known as *the spiral of stimuli*. Each rioter feels a total emotional excitement above his/her own, since each individual is surrounded by others, also excited. This causes each participant to get more excited.

When needs are not satisfied, tension within the individual increases. This condition or state is known as frustration. Release of tension is known as satisfied wishes. Emotions are always present in tension increase or decrease processes; i.e., frustrated wish or satisfied wish processes. Wrath may accompany frustrations or attainments; like when someone is not rewarded after carrying out an outstanding job.

Fear may accompany a frustrated effort for avoiding an injury threat. Direct handling of frustrations and conflicts of crowd members are the clearest manner of managing emotional excitement. This is indeed more difficult than what it may appear to be, due to the fact that unconscious frustrations of crowd members are usually concealed.

It could be that the wrath of rioters projected on a victim may be only an emotion accompanied by the discontentment of rioters, the violation of the victim's body or of property; however, current frustration may be an unconscious conflict between rioters, like the threat of loss by economical competition when the victim is involved in the matter, or unsatisfactory social experiences with the victim's social group (e.g., loss of reality). An individual's subconscious demands satisfaction, and this explains why violence in mutinies may last for several days.

Irrationality. There are two aspects of irrationality in a riot. The first one is the narrowing of understanding. A riot is panic, is the fire in a theatre, and collectively the crowd understands that there is only one step to follow. Such step is reaching the exit door. Since the exit that is sought is not the only available one, the riot will increase the danger rather than diminishing it. Irrationality in rioters does not consist in their stupidity, but in their lack of perception; i.e., the only thing they will be capable of is running towards the exit. This may be applied to all kind of riots. Rioters that want to lynch someone do not take time to consider other alternatives, they only think of hanging the victim. It is the same with those taking part in a mutiny; they have only one intention, and they do not stop to consider consequences or other alternatives; they will do everything possible to injure, destroy or damage anyone getting in their way.

Another aspect of irrationality in a riot is its impressive aggressive character. The same as with a child, they throw a tantrum and act violently to release their tension. When an adult, who should seek a more acceptable solution, acts in this way, his/her character is said to be regressive.

Mutiny. Rioters have lost the identity of their self consciousness to such an extent that such loss leads them to believe that they remain anonymous. They are generally right, due to the difficulties in identifying and arresting the authors of a disorder. The anonymity of an individual entails the loss of responsibility, which initiates a series of antisocial and illegal attitudes. Rioters forget completely their duties towards society and even their own families' welfare.

Universality. This refers to the impression that rioters get, that all the rest appear to approve of the actions of the crowd. The basic idea is that "everyone does it". This explains why rioters believe to be in the right.

c.2) Personalities in a riot

Even though rioters may have lost their individuality, certain basic features are still required, knowing the which should assist the crew in finding out how to control a riot.

The professional agitator. Such a person is experienced in taking part and promoting disturbances; does not allow being led by the stream of the riot and keeps his/her powers under full control. His/her actions are deliberate, calculated and directed towards attaining a goal.

Presence of some loathed person, or that belongs to an abhorred social class, may be enough for a crowd to initiate a violent action.

Certain psychological influences favour the agitator. If they are known and comprehended, forces designed to disperse the riot may be put into action.

- *Novelty*. That which is new or alien exerts a unique fascination over the average person. There is no doubt that an individual may subconsciously embrace with pleasure a change in the tedious routine of daily life, and may react enthusiastically to new circumstances.
    - In such a situation, habits that may have built will not perform completely. Specific stimuli usually governing actions will be absent and previous experience that was used for solving normal problems will not be able to be applied.
- *Investigation*. In a new or unknown situation, the inexperienced person will accept the suggestion from another who may appear to be experienced. Furthermore, rioters often do not know what the problem is or even that there is a problem. Because of not having a clear knowledge, they are ready to accept the ideas of the leaders. Ideas extend throughout the multitude, without it worrying about their consequences.

- *Contagion.* People become emotionally stimulated by the actions of others, even though they may not agree with the grievance that caused the annoyance. It is possible that they may participate of the emotion out of compassion; but sometimes it turns into wrath. People imagine that they have the same problem as the rest, and therefore get annoyed just by thinking about the abuse or damage.
- *Imitation.* A primitive desire to imitate others acts when an individual is amidst a riot. The individual fears that the fury of the multitude might turn against him/her if not agreeing with the others. It will take a very vigorous conviction in order to resist the desire to imitate.
- *Anonymity.* When a person is in a riot, self consciousness may be lost; the person may mix with the others thinking that he/she will not be recognised and therefore will not be blamed for any action.
- *Release of suppressed desires.* In a riot, the suppressed desires from a person that are normally restrained will be released. In this manner, the individual will feel without any hindrance and will participate actively in the actions of the riot. This will provide an opportunity to carry out things that formerly he/she did not dare to do.
- *Sense of power.* The size of a riot gives an individual a sense of power and the desire to use it. Most people like power, and they will use it when they feel they have it. This sense of power is increased by the lack of responsibility, and such combination may manifest itself in a dangerous manner.
- *Sense of right.* The common purpose of a riot makes the individual believe that his/her courage is just. Such rationale could be expressed in the following manner: *How could we be wrong in our wrath and doings, when our peers are also annoyed and do as we do?* This serves to convince all rioters that what they think and do is justifiable.

c.3) Riot violence and tactics

The activity of a riot is limited by the inventiveness and experience of the leaders, the weapons, the supplies, the equipment and other available materials. The level of violence in the activity depends on the people in the group, the place, the cause for the disorder, the weapons, the atmosphere and the ability and training of the leaders.

Kinds of violence that may be encountered are:

- *Verbal abuse*: insults, provocation, mockery and shouting are what may be expected in a riot. Use of the on board public address system by a false leader may increase the disorder.
- *Written abuse,* with posters, pamphlets and graffiti on the bulkheads against the commanders.
- *Noise,* caused by shouting and chanting and any other means. Chanting is very effective because it increases disorder, agitation and the aggressive attitude of the crowd.
    o Its rhythmic pattern, accompanied occasionally by small instruments (whistles), tends to increase the level of excitement and aggression. All this will serve to wear out and demoralise the crew.
- *Throwing* objects, anything that may be thrown by the crowd. These objects may be thrown from amongst the crowd or by rioters located outside of it.
- *Handheld weapons.* Rioters may be using several types of handheld weapons, for example, awls, clubs, knives or chains. The type of weapon may provide an indication of the spontaneity of the riot and the quality of the leaders.
- *Firearms*, which will probably be used spontaneously after being seized from the police force aboard. Another possibility would be that the organisers of the disturbance would intend to control the ship, to which end they would have introduced the weapons aboard.

- *Fire*, used by rioters as an attack instrument. They may light fires to protest. Prisoners carried aboard have in the past set fire to mattresses as a means of protesting.

- *Attacks on smaller groups*, on which rioters are capable of throwing themselves onto a person or a small group for hitting or killing.

- *Destruction of private property and looting*, on decorative furniture, tables, seats, etc., which may be tipped over, damaged or set on fire. Cabins and vehicles may be looted.

c.4) Tactics

Most used tactics in riots are:

A. Tactics of a riot are to extend over the ship in order to prevent free movement, especially of crew members.
B. An able leader will apply tactics for preventing the intervention of the crew and neutralise it if required. Such tactics may include arson, confusion, disorder and destruction of property.
C. Riot leaders may place women and children at the front of the crowd with the hope of achieving their goals.

c.5) Shifting from riot to mutiny

A mutiny is the use of force and violence to breach the piece, or the threat of using force and violence if such are used immediately. Of course, there have to be two or more people involved, for example a group of convicts who have managed to subdue their police escort.

A mutiny does not occur suddenly. It is the culmination of the tension developed in the community. It is necessary that the crew stay alert in order to recognise signals of such tension, so that preventative measures may be taken.

Such warning signals would be:

- An increase in the amount of rumours and protests, together with an increase in their sensationalist nature.
- Much more frequent incidents of resistance to the law, and an increase in the number of reports and complaints about the brutality (whether true or false) that the crew might have applied.
- An increase in the number of threats of violence, including fulfilled aggressions. One event is not significant, but when they occur simultaneously in several parts of the ship or along the voyage, they become a strong indication that more serious disturbances may occur.
- An increase in mistrust or resentment against the law and the conduct regulations established aboard the ship.
- Public booing and other reactions in front of the slightest provocation.
- Acts of vandalism by members of a minority, particularly in busy areas of the ship where their effect may reach higher levels.
- Appearance of menacing or insulting graffiti aboard, loose sheets, pamphlets and hate literature.

- Increasing antisocial activity by youths, including vandalism between bands or groups. This happens particularly when the minority's youths become involved.
- Progressive trend of demagogic groups and agitators to act openly and blatantly; to make propaganda against the group; to boast of a high degree of acceptance of their ideas.
- Meetings for protesting.

c.6) Controlling mutinies

In case of a very numerous riot, it should be dispersed, this resulting into a division into segments; segments should be separated, and then each segment dispersed. Only the necessary number of personnel should be used to carry out this procedure. When reducing groups, negotiation and communication of ideas become easier.

When there are smaller and disperse groups of passengers, it is much better grouping and addressing them. If they move about, close areas which they should not come back to, either because of navigational endangerment or to avoid contact with other passengers. A riot cannot be caught, but should rather be driven to an area in which it may pose the smallest hazard to the ship.

Leaders should be isolated as soon as possible, since a riot needs leaders to remain active. It is true that a riot without a leader is not a significant issue. Therefore, instigators should be separated from the group as soon as it may be possible. A professional instigator will normally operate behind the crowd, from a safe location.

Such an instigator uses one of the leaders within the crowd to do the dirty work. Instigators and leaders may usually be recognised by their activity within the crowd.

Any achievement of the rioters will make subsequent attempts to control them more difficult. Triumph of the authority aboard will demoralise riot leaders. As soon as they lose their leadership, they will usually fail in attempting to recover their positions, particularly if there has been a loss of internal authority.

7.3 Addressing antisocial acts

7.3.1 Relationship of antisocial acts with emergencies

Antisocial acts of the kinds that have been considered may require, in order to achieve their goals, certain acts of violence, such as the breakage of space and surface bounding elements. Doors, portholes and windows may be forced, and glass divisions between adjacent spaces may be broken; both damage eventual discrete needs for control actions during the exposition control phase, particularly in the confinement phase.

Under such conditions, visual controls should be considered in order to verify conformity of equipment and elements that have a higher impact, and therefore influence actively either the success or the disaster of a specialised intervention according to procedures.

It is evident that on those elements that may have been forced but without permanent damage, remaining in good condition for subsequent use, actions to be carried out by brigades will be limited to normalising alterations and returning them to the prior state, as long as it may be possible at that moment in time.

In those cases in which returning to normal conditions may not be feasible, situations arise that should be considered as uncontrolled propagation of variables.

Furthermore, individuals involved in and causing antisocial actions will be negative, harmful elements that should be controlled as soon as possible.

Narcotic trafficking falls also within this section; for such case, basically access control, both for people, baggage and parcels, as well as for provisions and spares, should be in place in all ports of call.

A critical situation may arise when the offensive substances are being withdrawn from the ship, at which moment traffickers may intervene using elements of force for which the ship may not be prepared.

Under such circumstances, and if there are signs that high risk situations may occur, the need for police forces participating with their own procedures becomes evident.

Finally, the hijacking of a ship should coincide with the assumption that hostages might be held, which is associated with actions included in the terrorism section, having a wider scope and related with a response typology of a wide range and variability.

Harmonisation criteria

In front of risks of antisocial actions, the update of emergency plans would consist of:

- Protecting safety and intervention equipment.
- Increasing the frequency of surveillance rounds, as well as the number of their components.
- Placing in alert and ready for use certain firefighting equipment, foreseeing small arsons sporadically provoked by vandalism actions.
- Sealing specific areas and spaces that might be used for concealing parcels and packages with offensive elements.
- Any other application of preventative actions that might be considered as the increase of the normal level prior to the appearance of an, in principle, minor significance emergency, that should in no case shift to a level of difficult intervention.

7.4 Deriving from social activities

7.4.1 Controlling multitudes in emergencies

This should be addressed similarly to antisocial actions, although an increase in damage is observed, since on the one hand it is specific and interest driven, to attain predetermined objectives in order to obtain the maximum demand pressure effect, and on the other hand, may possibly be carried out by a larger group, better led by charismatic leaders.

If with antisocial phenomena damage was indiscriminate, here well identified objectives are pursued; therefore, orientation may be towards hindering any type of intervention that may be attempted for emergency control.

Due to the specific construction features of a ship, which make her so different to on shore structures, the same groups causing the illegal action may find themselves involved in the consequences of the emergency, with which the responsibility of the brigades, which will be facing a larger risk, increases.

In whatever form a group of individuals manifest themselves, in most cases appearance will not be sudden or unexpected, as it will be the result and consequence of previous facts, thus known facts, and therefore the surprise factor should not be present.

Under such circumstances, the ship may adopt a safety posture that fits circumstances and the specific nature of the multitude, so consequences will be known or expected; therefore, it will be possible to choose the most appropriate alternative actions to each case.

The most acceptable ones should be applied to directing the multitude towards the safest, better controllable areas of the ship, least prone to having equipment or elements that are essential to maintaining safety aboard damaged. Naturally, anything susceptible of suffering any harm to its essential characteristics should be secured, either by enclosure or other protection means.

Harmonisation criteria

Besides those cited in Section 7.3.1.1 for antisocial actions, the following needs are mentioned for emergency plans harmonisation.

- ✓ Having alternative evacuation routes in order to reduce crowding.
- ✓ Preparing a hospital and a medicine chest in order to tend to people that are affected by high occupation density.
- ✓ Increase lighting in expected transit areas, particularly in access ways, in order to facilitate exit and reduce eventual accidents.
- ✓ Special attention, with increased control on persons carrying packages and hand parcels.
- ✓ While berthed, ship-shore communications for yard reception and risk reduction.

7.5 Terrorist actions

7.5.1 Related with explosives and fires

As is well known, the worst terrorism situation, due to the immediate manifestation of its effects and consequences, would be the activation of an explosive device aboard. It is therefore impossible to evaluate beforehand the extent and consequences of the subsequent damages.

In any circumstance, direct and indirect damages will affect a large number of firefighting elements and equipment, besides the injuries to members of the ship's firefighting and safety brigades, which in turn diminish effectiveness and possibilities prior to controlling the situation.

Nevertheless, the seriousness of the moment should not be considered as a final situation of complete passivity, but rather as a situation unleashing other alternative intervention lines that should have been considered previously. Actually, this does not differ much from consequences and situations raised from the actions considered within the safety concept, i.e., those deriving from accidental explosions in boilers, cargo tanks, flammable product pipes, etc.

Fire will always be a possibility associated with subsequent consequences of an explosion, whether due to the characteristics of the explosive device used or to the destructive effects caused on power, fuel or other circuits.

Harmonisation criteria

In the face of risk of suffering terrorist action, emergency plans update would consist in:

- Assessing and identifying prevailing and worse consequences.
- Considering eventual sacrificial areas.
- Alternatives to evolution phases.
- Application of techniques related to the previous items, consisting in evacuating certain more complicated areas, reducing presence of occupants in areas that are difficult to make safe, preventative closure of adjacent areas to hazardous spaces (i.e., fuel tanks, flammable product pipes, equipment without fixed protection, etc.).
- Alertness and preparedness of equipment for fast startup (particularly firefighting pumps and fire extinguishing equipment).
- Communication and information exchange with the members of the intervention brigades.
- Informing people apart from the crew, either personally or in small groups, in order to avoid panic, the highest the certainty is on the probability of the event becoming a reality.

7.5.2 Terrorist actions with weapons and NBC agents

Based on widely accepted principles, ships will hardly ever have an armed crew, although in certain types of ships and traffic, a variable number of public order forces or private security members may be available and used on the necessary occasions.

Under this principle it could not be possible, neither should it be expected, that any armed fight might initiate on board, except in very few extreme situations, since in the majority of occasions crew members would have few possibilities of success in opposing well trained criminals with a will to cause damage both to people and goods.

Even more so, when a terrorist action may involve weapons with NBC agents, possibilities of openly opposing them are nil, although there may always be a possibility that, when any way of negotiation may come to nothing, and when probabilities of not surviving become evident, actions may be initiated to recover control of the situation.

Nevertheless, come the worst, security measures may always be adopted that would be applied if the event would occur, which at this point in time are considered as preventative, anticipated to the emergency, providing higher levels of survival.

Harmonisation criteria

In front of the risk of suffering terrorist actions with NBC weapons and agents, updating emergency plans would involve:

- Assessing and identifying the predominating and worst consequences.
- Favourable alternatives related to both present and future weather agents.
- In relation to the previous item, considering the evacuation of certain more complicated areas, reducing presence of occupants in difficult to secure areas, preventatively closing areas subject to a highest impact and seriousness of the consequences.
- Alerting and preparing equipment for their fast startup.
- Communicating and exchanging information with the members of the intervention brigades.
- Informing people apart from the crew, either personally or in small groups, in order to avoid panic, the highest the certainty is on the probability of the event becoming a reality
- Setting up for immediate use safety showers, fixed systems sprinklers and manual hoses for spraying.

7.5.3 Terrorist actions with hostage holding

Again, this is a situation that is very difficult to solve, given the use of weapons and other elements of force. While this is carried out by people who are trained for such type of criminal actions, the dissuasive power of the crew to oppose them is scarce.

In such cases in which the use of force as the applicable response may only increase the level of endangerment of the lives of hostages, dependence on the negotiation process is well known, in order to recover the freedom of the hostages with full guarantee of their safety.

Any other alternative that may include use of force should be rejected, except when the admissible limits are exceeded. However, continuity of the negotiation process may derive to other alternatives and actions as required by each case, which may be initially unforeseeable.

In any case, such risk situations within the case of terrorism and the consequences of hostage holding have little relation with the typical emergencies considered for the ship's safety. Nevertheless, given the level of knowledge that presumably the crew may have with respect to terrorists, certain actions may be taken in order to reduce their freedom of movement, to produce some lack of security in their control of the situation and to increase the availability of favourable factors for negotiators, always avoiding limiting situations that may cause a dramatic outcome.

Harmonisation criteria

In front of the risk of suffering terrorist actions the consequence of which may be hostage holding, emergency plans would mostly not be affected, although certain strategies might be used together with the specific use of safety equipment and elements, such as:

- Intentionally causing small controlled failures, affecting the areas where terrorists are located.
- Preparing the ship for an eventual external intervention by specially dedicated forces.

- Such actions, like dimming, increasing lighting, closing access ways, opening them, etc., may affect the normal safety state of the ship, as well as the equipment available for typical emergency cases, aimed at different objectives than those during intervention.

7.5.4 Intended boarding in emergency preventative management

Besides the identification functions, the incorporation of AIS as risk situation identification equipment buys the ship some time prior to the boarding, which should be used even to its extreme and farfetched supply of information for decision making.

Although such risk situations occur usually in certain waters, the existence of waters exempt from such possibility may not be considered, although a lower probability may be considered.

Boarding is assumed to be done from smaller vessels, fast and fitted with assault equipment for accessing the ship by different means, depending on the type of ship, loading state, situation (at anchor, sailing, etc.).

In front of such situations, the ship should not suffer structural damage leading to an emergency situation due to the damages usually caused in a typical boarding; therefore, emergency plans would hardly need to be preventatively modified and adapted.

Nevertheless, such a possibility exists when boarding is intended to cause damage and a ship of sufficient size and tonnage is being used, with the intent of stopping the ship, assaulting her, kidnapping people aboard or robbing belongings, escaping later aboard boats or vessels ready for it. Sacrifice of the ship used for boarding is an aspect of minor significance with respect to the achievement of the terrorist objectives.

In these cases, the ship needs to be placed in the previous conditions to a boarding emergency, with the advantage that they are well known and applied in specific navigational circumstances, such as sailing in fog and high transit density, extreme bad weather conditions (at sea) and any other circumstances in which ship safety may be compromised due to the risk of collision, loss of structural integrity, water ingress, area flooding, etc.

Harmonisation criteria

Apart from the typical, accepted actions in order to prevent and bar access to the ship to assailants using water jets, strong dissuasive lighting, etc., application of all nautical safety measures that may increase ship safety may be considered, which from days of old constitute positive, preventative measures against an eventual boarding; it may be stated that, instinctively, they coincide with the needs imposed by the appearance of the security concept, which are:

- Closing openings that communicate and provide access to other floodable areas of the ship.
- Internal and external signals for alerting the crew and other ships that may be in the vicinity.
- Establishing specific security for people and goods that may be the targets of the assailants.

7.5.5 Directed impact of an aeroplane against the ship

This is a very unlikely situation, but not impossible, particularly when the ship is a passenger or a special transportation ship, or carries highly dangerous cargos due to their impact and consequences on its related environment (port facilities, towns, other ships, etc.).

The highest probability would involve the use of smaller aircrafts due to their manoeuvrability that would ensure impact. Seriousness of consequences would relate to the amount of explosives that the aircraft might carry and the impact point on the ship.

Unless the ship would be warned sufficiently in advance about the terrorist strike, preventative and anticipating actions would amount to nil or have little effectiveness; therefore, to include measures in emergency plans becomes virtually impossible; this situation, together with others in which rockets or remotely controlled elements may be used, with nonexistent warning and detection times, do not allow updating or improving intervention planning.

In these cases, assistance and succour will have to be external to the ship, like, for example, air interception of an artefact launched against the ship, and this is outside the response capability that may be expected from a ship.

7.6 Emergency determinants in security aspects

Risks and threats included in emergencies that are characteristic to the ship and her maritime operativity may in turn be related with the security concept, and should be therefore considered in order to find out possible interrelational implications, in correspondence with the type and activity of the ship, coinciding in any case with those of the emergency and contingency table, which have been previously defined overall in Figure 1.1 of Chapter 1 in the present study.

7.6.1 Action of possible anticipation, by typology

Main engine failure

- Related with a rigorous preventative maintenance
- Analysis of possible incidents caused on the main components, affecting the main engine
- Equipment part for which spares are required on board

Steering system failure

- Alternatives for steering (manual steering)
- Protected locations, far from each other
- Effective, permanent system of communications with the bridge
- Availability of sufficient steersmen

Electrical power plant failure

- Alternative power supplies, as required by SOLAS
- Secured against vandalism
- Maintenance to ensure permanent optimum state

Boarding

- All actions required for maintaining tightness, and to maintain it stable in floodable areas and spaces
- Closure of watertight doors
- Succour and rescue of injured or trapped people
- Emergency power supply for bailing pumps and lighting
- Application of possible techniques for underpinning bulkheads, decks and closure elements.

Area flooding

- Similar approaches to those for boarding

Fire

- Rescue and succour
- Division of fire zones
- Activation/Standby of pressurisation of firefighting pipes, pumps
- Brigade alert and preparedness
- Application of intervention plans

Man overboard

- Increase number of watchmen on the deck
- Preparedness of survival equipment
- Preparedness of the rescue boat and others

Medical urgencies

- Communications plan ready
- Preparedness of hospital, infirmary, medical materials
- Psychological preparedness in front of a known risk or threat

Search and rescue

- Review applicable techniques
- Internal interventions included (in structural wreckage, trapped people, etc.)
- Similar principles to those mentioned for Man Overboard

Request for assistance at sea

- Communications plan
- How, where, to whom
- Preparation of specific checklists

Helicopter operations

- Application of techniques in accordance with the IMO Manual
- Preparedness for execution
- Safety of the ship for operating with helicopters

Abandoning

- Analysis of affected people groups (by physical condition, age)
- As above, for expected areas
- Preparedness of crisis techniques

Spillage and pollution

- Preparedness of limbers
- Seek favourable balance of external agents

For each case in particular, contradictory actions should be found when considering those applicable as required by an emergency and those required by security. Thus, when applying the case of a fire aboard:

- Closure of certain access ways in order to isolate fire zones or areas for avoiding or delaying the propagation of the usual variables (flames, smoke).
- Controlled opening of access ways for the circulation, evacuation and mustering of people in safer locations; these same access ways and other additional ones will also be used by intervention brigades.

These two alternatives will be repeatedly occurring in most relations between safety and security, which may complicate, and for sure will, one of the two situations being analysed.

7.6.2 Emergencies related with antisocial acts

Emergency situations of which use is made to commit offences are not rare, these not stemming from a previously existing intention, but from the opportunity offered by the confusion and the initial moments until the situation is under control; likewise, such offences may not be related to a single, purely maritime emergency.

Nevertheless, they may produce an effect of a greater lack of safety than initially, which, depending of the type of ship, may create public concern together with a serious disorder and a loss of the necessary emotional stability of people present at the scene; these will need to be controlled and fought with actions parallel to those applied as demanded by the emergency.

In such cases, it is highly likely that the spontaneous occurrence of the emergency may be the factor activating a cessation of the hostile attitude, causing actions to be discontinued and shifting to a neutral or even a cooperative situation. At least, a discrepancy amongst the leaders will be produced, with a party intending to remain in a passive behaviour, awaiting the development of events.

The problem, however, shall remain to the extent and quantity of previous damages suffered by safety equipment and elements.

Harmonisation criteria

Ship security plans, even those for port facilities, should take into account determinants representing the situation when stemming from a previously initiated emergency situation.

It becomes evident when following diagram 1.1 in the introductory chapter that by security occupying the highest vertex as the directing item of all the partial aspects of safety, emergency plans include the necessary adaptations in order to comply with such objectives; however, from this standpoint it may be also necessary to take into account certain considerations that may modify the ship or port facility security plan itself, in order not to leave any weak points in the integrated safety system.

- Consider predominant factors and worst consequences.
- Consider perturbations and damages under the strict application of security measures procedures.
- Consider the evolution phases for the security case, to the extent that they may favour or damage those required by the emergency plans.
- Establish decision making criteria for those cases in which decisions might harm security measures to some extent when benefitting emergency plans.
- Establish sacrificial criteria for one of the two alternatives.

7.6.3 Emergencies as preceding terrorist acts

Certain emergency cases may coincide, or be made use of, to initiate acts of terrorism that were not initially planned by the terrorists (refer to the case of the "Aquille Lauro").

Such cases cause confusion and doubts when identifying causes, objectives and motives that lead to a terrorist act, whether because of an advance in time or because of a variation in the method.

Discrete intervention responses in certain locations on the ship, particularly those especially significant for safety, establish an immediate intervention dependence, as here it is a physical-chemical causal origin from equipment, structures and nature of the cargo in typical conditions.

Presence of criminals aboard will determine firefighting brigade interventions, but at the same time, since it is the crew who know better the structural and dimensional features of the ship, the situation will in turn create limitations to the actions of the intruders.

What in principle may be adequate for some, as time runs it will become negative, although tension and insecurity will increase for all, and in turn strain and the eventual occurrence of physical violence. In such cases, which could degenerate into hostage holding, actions initiated during negotiations could become distorted by intervention actions that might be carried out for safety; it is doubtful whether they would be well understood by the criminals, or whether they would consider them as distraction or even opposing actions.

Harmonisation criteria

Although originating from different actions and intentions to those addressed in the previous section, the measures to consider are very similar, since the common denominator is a criminal intruder tending to alter usual procedures in emergencies, now impacted by acts other than those related to intervention.

- Consider predominant factors and worst consequences.
- Consider perturbations and damages under the strict application of security measures procedures.
- Consider the evolution phases for the security case, to the extent that they may favour or damage those required by the emergency plans.
- Establish decision making criteria for those cases in which decisions might harm security measures to some extent when benefitting emergency plans.
- Establish sacrificial criteria for one of the two alternatives.

7.6.4 Emergencies related to unlawful social acts

Emergencies, when complicated by such type of acts, are directly related to the features of the social group, i.e., they depend on the objectives pursued by the group, very particularly by the nature and kind of leader or leaders directing the group

In many cases, the emergency itself will work against the intentions that the group would have developed, would the emergency not have gone in advance to their actions. Generally, emergencies produce a dissuading effect on those actions that can wait for a more adequate occasion later on in order to achieve its goals.

Furthermore, it is also frequent that the group would use the first moments in the emergency, during intervention preparation phases or even during intervention itself, to interfere or hinder it as much as possible, this producing sometimes a negotiated agreement that is quickly accepted by both parties.

When the hindering action of the involved social group tends to an inadequate use of equipment or machinery, or to placing obstacles to the normal flow of the emergency intervention, for the sake of simplicity it should be considered that intervention has a complicated evolution and actions will be negatively affected in time and effectiveness; therefore, they should not be stopped, and attempts should be made to keep the morale of the intervention brigade members high.

It is not rare to observe how a social group that are prepared for a criminal or forceful action depose, in front of an emergency, their belligerent attitude and side with the intervention, assisting and providing all their collaboration.

Harmonisation criteria

Again, measures to consider are very similar to the former, since human factor is the predominant and disturbing factor. Therefore, in addition to those considered so far, the following will also be necessary:

- Consider dividing intervention brigades to assign them to convince or control, depending on the case, the social group hindering the normal development of the necessary actions towards the emergency.
- The above will produce a limitation in the emergency control functions, but this will be the necessary sacrifice to integrate the situation.
- Consider the evolution of the case, whether in the improvement or worsening of the situation created by the actions of the social group, and correct them in one or the other sense, i.e., towards safety or security, as required.

8 Conclusions

Incorporation of the ISPS Code to the safety organisation in the maritime and port activity involves a significant, deep effort both in changing mentalities for introducing a subject previously only in the knowledge of the State Security Forces, and in the civil interpretation of all aspects composing the implementation of the Code.

Various regulatory sources that constituted the backbone and support for on board safety, such as the ISM, ISO standards on quality and other topics, become partly determined by the ISPS, since either the existing approaches require being reviewed, or at least they should include new references in order to complete the integral safety cycle, which, until the ISPS Code came into force, were not considered, at least with the level of compliance currently demanded.

In turn, the ISPS Code is not just a tool operating independently from other safety approaches, but it maintains particularly a strong link with port facility safety through the respective PFSPs, being related with such facilities due to the maritime business.

The close dependence between SSPs and PFSPs creates inseparable interactions within the overall consideration of the approaches to be followed in order not to interfere with the common safety maintenance system; therefore, both are forced into a harmonisation effort to reduce weak points in a complex organisation involving a large number of agents.

Now, based on the fact that the human factor is responsible for a large percentage of accident and emergency causes, the need is understood of potentiating due attention to the new positions created by the ISPS Code, namely the SSO, the FPSO and the CSO, so that they may fully carry out and be responsible for their duties, fulfilling them with the highest guarantees of effectiveness and success.

Ships always had available strict safety regulations, the SOLAS, construction and equipment codes, conventions of all sorts and covering all subjects, contributions from the classification bodies, training contents with the STWC, and many more, with the intent of increasing the safety of that which has become less and less of a maritime adventure and more a very technical, specialised activity.

The ISPS Code contributes many other considerations and a new safety concept, by which the ship will need not only to depend on her organisational schemes, but will require assistance from other spheres that are closely related with maritime transportation, starting with new ship designs based on the contribution of naval construction, which should allow building a technically safe ship, as well as incorporating security equipment.

Implementation of SSPs means introducing into the ships safety system a package of measures the contents of which equals to that considered in the whole safety environment, with all it means and represents for the responsibilities of security officers as referenced in the ISPS Code. The main difference is in the novelty of the subjects introduced, aspects which had never before been addressed under technical or professional criteria.

With all this, the study has allowed, having previously considered the various influence and determination blocks, to identify and resolve malfunctions or to propose improvement aspects for achieving the harmonisation of emergency organisational schemes.

Such approaches have been obtained in the two possible directions of the generated influences, whether in the relationship of security as a determinant of safety, or in the opposite direction, of safety considerations in its involvement with the appropriate development of security.

Under these circumstances, the study has allowed to achieve, besides the partial conclusions included in some of the chapters, the following peculiarities:

- A detailed analysis of aspects determining the operative handling of emergencies allows confirming, now under an objective justification, the need for harmonising the existing interrelationships between emergency plans and the ship security plan.
- Certain needs for updating and harmonising are also present between quality management schemes that the ship may have in compliance with ISO standards and those resulting from the ISM Code; planned objectives will not be attained with one or the other if relationship with new emergency requirements that stem from the incorporation of security does not exist. I.e., the operational organisation of the ship, in its commercial objectives, becomes determined by a demand to increase safety that goes beyond the ship's own structural boundaries, both becoming inseparable.
- The possibility of using risk assessment and quantification procedures as those used for on shore activities, since they allow a better perspective of the reality that the ship has to face and, at the same time, a higher effectiveness in the application of approaches and procedures.
- A level of judgement is reached for comprehending that the incorporation of security whilst maintaining crews to a minimum may represent impossibility for carrying out intervention tasks with the necessary level of quality that would ensure their effectiveness, whatever its type and character.
- Training level of the crew regarding aspects contemplated within security are scarce and insufficient when considering the amount of knowledge that has been incorporated to normal ship management; this is already so for routine level 1, even more when progressing to higher security levels.
- Integration of safety plans, although seemingly increasing the complexity of emergency management, avoids action overlaps and provides for a better overall comprehension, since it encompasses a larger number of variables that had not been so far considered; thus, no room is left for improvisation, and intervention as a whole becomes more technical and less random.
- The hitherto accepted emergency organisation in terms of allocating functions to each crew member based on the provisions of the organisational chart becomes very detached from, an afar off, the new demands stemming from the ISPS Code; therefore, they should be necessarily updated in accordance with the new parameters to be considered.

- While it is true that the Code has been implemented so recently that it may and should be updated as necessary, depending on the progressive detection of introduced processes that adequate better to reality (therefore, no pessimistic consideration should be assumed), it becomes evident that, in the face of the responsibilities assumed by security officers since the recent coming into force of the Code, the involved public administrations should make a great effort in favouring those actions that mean a realistic contribution to crew training requirements, so that they may fully assume the actions that, when required, will have to be carried out, which are expected from the outside to be of the highest effectiveness and efficiency.

Bibliography

Literature

MARÍ, R. *Situaciones de crisis en buques de pasaje [Crisis Situations in Passenger Ships]*. Barcelona. Ediciones UPC. I.S.B.N 847653 6852. 1998.

MARÍ, R., Librán A. *Seguridad pública en buques de pasaje [Public Safety in Passenger Ships]*. Barcelona. Ediciones UPC. I.S.B.N. 84-8301-692-3. 2003.

MARÍ, R. *IPEN Journal (Pan-American Institute of Naval Engineering)* "El PBIP y el reto para la construcción naval. [The ISPS Code and the Challenge for Naval Construction].", Issue no. 28, September, 2003. ISSN: 1011-5951. 2003.

MARÍ, R. *International Congress on Maritime Technological innovations and research.* "Influence of the Maritime Environment on the Casuistry of Organised Crime". 2nd. University of Cádiz. UCA Publishing Service, on CD. 2000.

Research Works

Identificación y análisis de la influencia de la vía marítima (puertos y buques) en la casuística de la delincuencia organizada [Identification and Analysis of the Influence of the Maritime Environment (Ports and Ships) on the Casuistry of Organised Crime]. European Commission. Task Force for Cooperation on Justice and Home Affairs. Police and Customs. October 1998/April 2000. Responsible and Main Researcher: Ricard Marí Sagarra. UPC.

Metodología y marco programático para el desarrollo de planes de protección de las instalaciones portuarias (PPIP) [Methodology and Pragmatic Framework for the Development of Port Facility Security Plans (PFSPs)]. Ports of the State Public Entity [Ente público Puertos del Estado]. November, 2003/March, 2004. Responsible and Main Researcher: Ricard Marí Sagarra. UPC.

Specialised Publications

ICHNIOWSKI, TOM. *ENR* "Domestic security defense covers multiple fronts: transit, seaports want bigger share of federal aid.", New York. 2004

HUGUES, DAVID. *Aviation Week & Space Technology*. "Still in deepwater: congress may boost funding further as USCG adjusts the program for counterterrorism." 2004

KERRY E. JULIAN. *Professional Safety* "Trucking Security.". 2003

CHO, AILEEN *ENR* "Containing container risks and connecting modes intermodal infrastructure planners take on security." 2003

WALL, ROBERT *Aviation Week & Space Technology*. "Coast guard nears decision on maritime patrol aircraft.". 2004

KIEFER, K. *Proceedings of the marine safety council*. "Establishing a port security committee." 2004

APPS, J. *Proceedings of the marine safety council*. "International port security program." 2004

MERRITT, M. *Proceedings of the marine safety*. "TSA administers grants for port security improvements." 2003

Links to Websites

Defence Security Service :	www.dss.mil
Federation of American Scientists:	www.fas.org
Global Defence:	www.global-defence.com
Global Security:	www.globalsecurity.org
Marine Corps Doctrine Division:	www.doctrine.usmc.mil
MI5:	www.mi5.gov.uk
Strategy Page: http:	www.strategypage.com
Navy Warfare Development Command:	www.nwdc.navy.mil
Revista Naval:	www.revistanaval.com
Special Operations:	www.specialoperations.com
Specwarnet:	www.specwarnet.net
US Coast Guard:	www.uscg.mil
The Free Dictionary:	http://encyclopedia.thefreedictionary.com
About.com:	http://usmilitary.about.com
Control Electronic Security:	www.controlelectronic.com
Insight Security:	http://www.insight-security.com
Security Worx:	www.securityworx.com
Autonomous Solutions:	www.autonomoussolutions.com
US Marine Corps Training and Education Command:	www.tecom.usmc.mil

www.ingramcontent.com/pod-product-compliance
Lightning Source LLC
Chambersburg PA
CBHW080432230426
43662CB00015B/2249